Best regards to Mark,
  Seattle, WA
    11 93
      Jim Drano

Family-of-Origin Therapy
An Intergenerational Approach

Family-of-Origin Therapy

An Intergenerational Approach

James L. Framo, Ph.D.

BRUNNER/MAZEL *Publishers* • NEW YORK

Library of Congress Cataloging-in-Publication Data
Framo, James L.
    Family-of-origin therapy : an intergenerational approach / James
L. Framo.
        p.   cm.
    Includes bibliographical references and index.
    ISBN 0-87630-590-7
    1. Family therapy.   2. Parent and adult child.   I. Title.
    [DNLM: 1. Family Therapy—methods.   2. Parent-Child
    Relations.
3. Sibling Relations.   WM 430.5.F2 F813f]
RC488.5.F72   1991
616.89'156—dc20
DNLMM/DLC
for Library of Congress   91-29310
                                                                CIP

Copyright © 1992 by James L. Framo

Published by
BRUNNER/MAZEL, INC.
19 Union Square West
New York, New York 10003

Manufactured in the United States of America

10 9 8 7 6 5 4 3 2

My family has always been there for me; they have given me much more than I have given them.

I dedicate this book to my parents, James and Madeline, who gave me life; to my sisters, Viola and Eleanor, and to my brother Michael—my friends as well as my siblings.

I dedicate this book to my daughters, Joan and Patty, both wonderful human beings, and to the memory of my sons, Jimmie and Michael, who will always be with me.

I dedicate this book to my wife, Felise, who has given me the gift of love, which in turn has changed my view of myself, has renewed my faith in myself, and has shown me how to love.

Contents

Preface

This book has truly been a labor of love and pain; its evolution has followed a tortuous course. Since my previous publications consisted of edited volumes, chapters in books, and journal articles, I wanted to write my very own book that would contain only my own thinking—one big book that was originally entitled, *A Dynamic Approach to Marital and Family Therapy*. Later the title was changed to the more ambitious one of, *An Intergenerational Approach to Marital and Family Therapy: Marriage, Divorce, and Family of Origin*. The book was to be my legacy to the field and was to contain the last word on the subjects at hand. This narcissistic grandiosity, of course, created such an impasse that I did not publish anything for years.

Eventually I followed the advice of my publisher, Bernie Mazel, and my wife, Dr. Felise Levine, to present my work in three separate volumes—one on divorce therapy, one on family-of-origin, and one on marital therapy. A piecemeal approach diminished my fear that when the large book was finished there would be nothing left to say. I decided that the first book to come out that was wholly mine should be on the work closest to my heart and basic to all my other work—my intergenerational approach to therapy. So in 1988 I began work on this book . . . .

Early in my career as a psychotherapist, it became apparent that the kinds of problems people had with themselves or in their intimate relationships had a lot to do with what they were still working out from their original family. Instead of having people talk *about* their families, as is customary in traditional psychotherapy, I took the unusual step of actually including the families of origin in the therapy of adults seen in family, marital, divorce, or individual therapy. There were no guidelines in the literature for doing this sort of work (e.g., Bowen rarely brought in the families of origin of his clients), so I had to learn the hard way. Having conducted over 500 family-of-origin sessions, I am now in a position to pass on my experience and to offer a kind of guidebook to therapists who would like to use this method.

I have attempted to present my work as honestly as possible, including even a chapter on the difficulties in doing intergenerational therapy as well as limitations of this method. Moreover, several times throughout the book I state the strong belief that therapists who do intergenerational work should work on their own family of origin issues. Trying to practice what I preach, I have not only had sessions with my own family of origin (siblings and other relatives since my parents were deceased when I started doing this work), but in the Author's Family Biography at the end of the book I lift the roof of the home in which I grew up and reveal some key events in my own family of origin, which shaped my life. No one will be surprised to find out that there is a relationship between my own personal family history and my conceptual approach to therapy.

The thesis in this book goes against the trendy movement in mental health in the U.S. toward the programs that advocate staying away from one's family for the sake of one's own survival. ACOA's (Adult Children of Alcoholics), AMAC's (Adults Molested as Children) and ACDF's (Adult Children of Dysfunctional Families) are advised to follow the 12 steps of these programs and to save themselves by going to various kinds of therapy. The exclusion of the family of origin by these movements is a mistake in my judgment. People who think they can give up on their parents and brothers and sisters are, for the most part, deceiving themselves.

A major conclusion of this book is that family-of-origin intervention is not a complete form of psychotherapy and will probably always be a specialized, brief procedure that, conducted in the appropriate way, can have powerful therapeutic effects in bringing about change—intrapsychically, in marital relationships, in the relationships between children and parents, and in the systems of the family of origin and extended family. These changes can carry over to succeeding generations. As the reader has probably surmised, I really believe in this work.

Although I have, on the basis of accumulated experience, added to and modified the procedure, and this present book represents the state of the art as of 1992, in truth I think the dimensions and potentials of this intergenerational approach have only begun to be explored. I anticipate that future theoreticians and clinicians will extend this work in terms of theory building, research, and clinical application.

Despite myself, the book is done. Later I will think of things I forgot to put in the book. But now that it's finished, the tension and guilt are gone, but a sadness has taken its place and that will last until I get to work on my next book.

JAMES L. FRAMO
San Diego, California

Acknowledgments

I wish to recognize, first, with deep appreciation, my wife, Dr. Felise B. Levine. She has not only been my friend, companion, mate, and cotherapist, but also has read the manuscript in detail and made many theoretical and clinical observations, only some of which are credited in the footnotes as having originated from her. Without her support, affirmation, and encouragement, this book would probably never have been completed.

Thanks go to Bernie Mazel of Brunner/Mazel, for his patience, for his confidence in me when my own flagged, and for not giving up on this project.

Natalie Gilman, the Executive Editor, who went over the raw manuscript and rearranged paragraphs and sentences, who corrected my confusion over "that's" and "whiches," is owed credit for shaping the book into its final form.

I want to express my gratitude to the couples, families, and individuals who allowed me access to their private pains and relationship struggles and who provided the basis for the observations made in all my writings. My ideas really came from them as they grappled with their personal demons and relational difficulties.

I am grateful to my students, who kept me on my toes, challenged me, and opened up their private lives in their family biographies.

There are many people in the family therapy field with whom I have shared ideas, friendships, and colleagueship. To list them all would fill many pages. They know who they are.

I have been heavily influenced by the theories of Murray Bowen and Ivan Boszormenyi-Nagy and the clinical artistry of Nat Ackerman and Carl Whitaker, all of whom I regard as my friends as well as colleagues.

I appreciate the warm receptions and hospitality that I have received from organizers and participants of workshops that I have given at various agencies and institutions around the U.S. and internationally.

Thanks and gratitude are owed the various typists who worked on the manuscript over the years: Janet Gibson, Debbie Kidd, and Angelina J. Gonzalo.

"Death ends a life, but it does not end a relationship,
which struggles on in the survivor's mind toward some resolution,
which it may never find."*

*From Anderson, R. (1970). *I Never Sang for My Father.* New York: Signet. (A play produced on Broadway in 1968 and made into a motion picture by Columbia Pictures, released in 1970.)

1

Introduction: An Overview

In this volume I will discuss what I consider to be the most important aspect of my work—involvement of the family of origin in the therapy I do with adults in marital, family, and individual therapy. My 35 years of experience in working with couples and families has led me in that direction, and since first publishing on this subject (Framo, 1976), I have conducted many more family-of-origin sessions. This family-of-origin procedure, which has been fine-tuned and has undergone important modifications over the years, will be described in such detail that others who wish to try this method will have adequate guidelines. In response to the many inquiries I have received about my intergenerational method, I will present as clearly as possible, with clinical examples, what I usually do in working with adults and their families of origin.

Repeated experience with this family-of-origin method has convinced me of the power of the approach in producing change, although I have a more sober appreciation of the limitations of the method, the precautions that must be taken, and the formidable technical difficulties involved. It is not an easy kind of procedure to do and it certainly does not always work. On the other hand, I believe that one session of an adult with his/her parents and brothers and sisters, conducted in this special kind of way, can have more beneficial therapeutic effects than the benefits derived from the entire length of a course of psychotherapy. Aside from the clinical validity of this intergenerational approach, a systematic research study on a follow-up of partners and their families of origin whom I had seen in the past presented data-based evidence of the effectiveness of this method (Baker, 1982). The method is considered a general one, not just applicable to people in marital and family therapy, but to those in individual therapy as well—indeed to all adults who need to sort out mixed feelings about parents and siblings.

This family-of-origin method is foundational and basic to all other therapies I do—individual, family (Framo, 1965a), marital (Framo 1978b, 1980, 1981), couples groups (Framo, 1973), and divorce therapy (Framo, 1978a). My book of collected papers contains the foregoing papers (Framo, 1982).

Even though I have the reputation for doing long-term therapy, family-of-origin therapy could be regarded as the ultimate *brief* therapy, in that the method involves approximately four clinical hours with the family. Ideally, the family-of-origin sessions are most generative when integrated with ongoing psychotherapy, but the family-of-origin work can stand on its own as a meaningful therapeutic experience.

Utilizing family of origin as a resource in marital, family, and individual therapy is the logical outcome and clinical application of the conceptual formulation that hidden transgenerational forces exercise critical influence on present-day intimate relationships (Framo, 1970). That is, current marital, parenting, and personal difficulties are viewed, basically, as reparative efforts to correct, master, defend against, live through, or cancel out old, disturbing relationship paradigms from the original family. In their choices of intimate relationships people attempt to make interpersonal resolutions of intrapsychic conflicts.

Most people do not *see* their spouses, children, or intimate partners as they really are since old ghosts stand in the way; the current significant others are shadowy representatives of past figures and are responded to as if they were split-off aspects of the self. When clients are prepared to deal face-to-face with the critical, heretofore avoided issues with parents and brothers and sisters, taking the problems back to where they began, they can clear away some of the filters and cobwebs that exist between them and their intimate others. Most people, for years, have been telling friends, therapists, spouses, and Dear Abby all the things they should have been telling their parents and siblings, the people most concerned. Furthermore, in family-of-origin sessions past bitterness toward parents and siblings can be dissipated, and mothers and fathers can be perceived as real people. By having the opportunity to come to terms with parents before they die, these clients do not have to spend their lives expiating guilt.

CATEGORIES OF CLIENTS WHO HAVE FAMILY-OF-ORIGIN SESSIONS

There are two general categories of clients for whom I conduct family-of-origin sessions: those clients who are engaged in ongoing therapy with me, and those who are not regular clients. Those clients who are engaged in ongoing therapy with me fall into one of four therapy contexts: (1) family therapy; (2) marital or divorce therapy; (3) couples group therapy; and (4) individual therapy. Although it is only *individuals* who have sessions with their families of origin, the therapy contract in this first general category begins as marital, family, or individual therapy.

Clients in Ongoing Therapy with Me

The family therapy context. When the family presents a child as the problem, I work with the whole family, or subgroups of the family, until the symptomatic child has been defocused and the symptoms have either disappeared or have been alleviated. Then, if the parents are motivated, I will work with their marital relationship, since I view most children's symptoms as a metaphor for the parent's marriage (Framo, 1975). Some of these parents, who originally came to therapy out of concern for a child, become interested in working out some of their own internal issues with their family of origin, especially when they recognize that they are repeating with their own children their parents' templates of parenting.

The marital or divorce therapy context. The couples that I see who request help for marital problems either do not have children or do not present their children as the problem.* I almost always treat part-

---

*Not all the couples I see are married; some couples are living together and are coming

ners together, and only under rare circumstances will I work with one person who has marital problems (for example, when one partner absolutely refuses to come to therapy and the motivated partner wants help in dealing with the marital situation). Consistent with my conceptual view that internalized conflicts from past family relationships are being lived through the present marital relationship (Framo, 1970), the large majority of my clients who have family-of-origin sessions arise out of initial work with the partners seen conjointly. That is, most family-of-origin sessions originate from the marital therapy context.

Some partners who originally present for marital therapy come to recognize that they are emotionally allergic to each other, and at that point, the therapy goals shift to that of divorce therapy—ending the relationship constructively so that the destructive consequences and pain of divorce are minimized and fairness for all is maximized.* Family-of-origin sessions with this population can help the partners discover, among other things, whether their divorce represents the completion of an old, incomplete divorce from the parents. These meetings also give the family of origin the opportunity to attend to the fallout from the divorce (e.g., concern of grandparents that they might be cut off from their grandchildren).

Couples group therapy. Perhaps the best context for motivating clients to bring in their parents and siblings for sessions is a couples group. The group process and sharing that occur in these groups eases the dread most people have about having family-of-origin sessions. (The family-of-origin sessions are held separately from the group, of course.) Couples group therapy is a powerful form of treatment in its own right for couples' relationship problems, but it is especially productive as a means of preparing clients for the family-of-origin sessions. The particular method I use for conducting couples groups is described in more detail in the chapter on Early Stages of Family-of-Origin Therapy and in a prior publication (Framo, 1973).

---

to therapy to either make their relationship better or to get help to end the relationship. I refer to these as "marital" problems because the mechanisms are similar. On the other hand, I think there *is* a difference in commitment between living together and being married.

*The author is preparing a book on Divorce Therapy.

Individual therapy. Although early in my career as a psychotherapist I did a lot of individual therapy (and group therapy), after I became a family therapist I stopped seeing individuals and only dealt with relationships in vivo. In recent years I have begun again to see individuals; having had experience treating couples and families, however, I work with individuals differently than I did before the family therapy experience—that is, I do family-oriented individual therapy. Some individuals, usually single adults, start therapy because they have insoluble intrapsychic conflicts and are symptomatic (suffering from depression, anxiety attacks, psychosomatic disorders, addictions, etc). Others begin individual therapy for a variety of relationship problems and are unable or unwilling to involve their intimates in treatment. I convert most individual cases into family cases, orienting the therapy toward exploration of their family-of-origin experiences, which usually leads to actually having sessions with the original family.

Clients Not in Ongoing Therapy with Me

The second general category of clients for whom family-of-origin consultations are indicated are those who are not in ongoing therapy with me. These clients come from three sources: (1) consultations done at the behest of out-of-town individuals; (2) parents who request sessions with their adult children; and (3) clients referred for consultations by other therapists.

Consultations done at the behest of out-of-town individuals. After my family-of-origin work became known, I began to get requests from individuals all around the country, mostly family therapists, for family-of-origin consultations. These individuals are strongly motivated to work on the important issues with their original family; they go to great lengths to gather family members together and bring them in, sometimes from long distances. They usually have overt and secret agendas, often having to do with saving themselves or others.

Parents who request sessions with their adult children. Although most requests by individuals for family-of-origin consultations are initiated

by adult children who want to resolve conflicts with parents and siblings (or wish to get closer or more distant), occasionally a request
comes from the older generation. Sometimes mothers or fathers, or
even both parents, have gotten to a stage in their lives where they
want to settle important matters with their adult children before they
(the parents) die.

Clients referred for consultation by other therapists. There are numerous
instances where psychotherapists, working with a particular client,
think, "This client really has to work something out directly with his/
her mother (father, brother, sister) if there's going to be any progress
in this case." Some of these therapists, being familiar with my spe-
cialization in this modality, have referred such clients to me for a one-
shot family-of-origin consultation. Most of these clients are in
individual therapy, but some are in other forms of therapy. These clients are seen for a preparation session (getting a family history, coming up with an agenda), are seen with their family of origin for two
2-hour sessions, are seen for a follow-up session, and are then
returned to the referring therapist. These consultations usually help
overcome impasses and move forward their ongoing therapy. Some
of these clients, with the family's permission, play the tapes of the
family-of-origin sessions for their therapists.

IS THIS INTERGENERATIONAL PROCEDURE THERAPY?

Throughout this book I use the expression "family-of-origin *therapy,*"
but I do not consider the intergenerational method described herein
as a form of psychotherapy in the usual sense of the word, although
the procedure certainly has therapeutic effects. Conventional psychotherapy implies that a client (couple, family) voluntarily enters into an
implicit contract in order to get help for a problem, whereas when a
family of origin agrees to a client's invitation to attend sessions, they
do not typically come in as patients consciously seeking help. There
are, to be sure, therapeutic consequences of family-of-origin work,
beginning when clients get past their inherent fear and ask their parents and siblings to come in for sessions, continuing throughout the

preparation process, proceeding through the two 2-hour family-of-origin sessions proper, and lasting long after the sessions are over.

Consider this aspect of the innate nature of family life: Families can provide the deepest satisfactions of living: unreserved and unconditional love; gratifying bonding; measureless sacrifice; enduring dependability; compassionate belonging; the joys and warmth of family holidays, dinners and vacations; the fun and play; the give and take; and knowing your family is always *there* when needed. Still, the hurts and damage that family members can inflict upon one another are infinite: scapegoating; humiliation and shaming; parentification; crazy-making; physical, sexual, and psychological abuse; cruel rejections; lies and deceit; and the manifold outrages against the human spirit.

During family-of-origin sessions, as the old family ways are reexperienced, as the family stories unfold (Stone, 1989), and as the positive and negative memories and feelings are stimulated, the family members start to deal with the foregoing life-and-death relationship issues, and they eventually tell each other what is in their hearts. The coming together of parents and adult children in this special context allows the truth to be told—often for the first time. The ensuing passionate exchanges, embarrassment, and intense anxiety is contained by the safe, holding environment of trust created by the cotherapists, which makes it all right to confront the people one needs. No matter how enraged people are at their parents and siblings, the deepest part of themselves yearns to love and to be loved by these irreplaceable figures. In this context positive feelings can emerge such that mothers, fathers, sons, daughters, brothers, and sisters can understand, reconnect, come to terms with and, finally, forgive each other. How to increase the chances of getting to these auspicious outcomes is what this book is all about. Although not "therapy" in the formal sense, these intergenerational encounters are usually unique healing experiences.

FAMILY OF ORIGIN AS HANDLED IN TRADITIONAL INDIVIDUAL PSYCHOTHERAPY

Most traditional psychotherapists, particularly those who treat individuals psychodynamically, subscribe to the philosophy that adult clients should work out past or current problems with parents and other relatives via the relationship with the therapist. In other words, the professional, utilizing his or her skills and personhood, should provide a corrective and therapeutic experience that will free the patient of crippling parental influences or, in cases of severely emotionally deprived people, should provide the caring and concern that the parents would not or could not give. Most traditional individual therapists regard the family of origin of their clients as the enemy, as noxious, and as undermining their therapeutic efforts. This attitude is epitomized by the book *Toxic Parents* (Forward, 1989). In the process of trying to help their clients become independent and free of their families, they see keeping the family at bay as part of their task. I have heard therapists speak of having to hang up on "destructive" parents who telephone; in this connection one of them said, "Never try to rescue a maiden who comes from a dragon ranch." These therapists believe they should undo the family madness and thereby save the client.

The usual therapeutic strategy for handling of the actual parents consists of encouraging clients to stand up to their parents (as in assertiveness training procedures), "working through" the conflicts with the therapist, or advising clients to avoid their crazy family and have minimal contact with parents who are considered to be "hopeless." One client I saw with her family of origin had been cut off from them for 15 years. She had taken the advice of a previous therapist to stay away from her family because they were "a bunch of cannibals." Sometimes the message is implicitly given that because the parents are "too old to change" and do not have much more time left, the patient should go along with the family myths for the sake of peace.

Typically, the communication is given that patients should stop trying to get from "bankrupt" parents that which can never be obtained. The therapist, never having seen the parents, has relied on the patient's description of what they are like—that they are "cold, rejecting, overwhelming, exploitative, double-binding, disappointing, too loving and possessive, undependable, irresponsible," and so on. Instead, the patient is led to the conclusion that the real satisfactions in life are available from other relationships, from one's mate and children, from friends, or from work. In short, most therapists write off the family of origin as a therapeutic resource.

Perhaps the primary reason for this state of affairs is that most individual therapists do not know what to do with the family of origin of adults they are treating. Until family transactional theory and therapy came on the scene, there was no conceptual basis or body of techniques for dealing with relatives. Indeed, the creative leap of family therapy was to take what was ordinarily regarded as an interference and to use it therapeutically.

To be sure, a rationale exists behind the decision of individual therapists to involve themselves as little as possible with family members of clients. While to some extent this policy, which was based largely on Freud's pronouncements regarding avoidance of family, was unrealistically rigid at times, it made sense, given the basic premises of individual therapy. The reasons given by psychoanalysts, for example, for keeping family out are well known: the transference field would be contaminated; the focus of interest is on the intrapsychic realities of the patient rather than the external realities of his family life. Even when it becomes apparent that the client is caught up in a web of "sick" relatives, the reasoning is that when the patient's ego grows stronger he or she will be better able to deal with the family pathology.

I do not mean to give the impression that individual therapy is rarely indicated. Whatever form psychotherapy takes in the future there will probably always be a place for individual treatment. The circumstances under which that special, confidential, one-to-one treatment situation may be the treatment of choice, however, or may be combined with family, marital, group, or other therapies, has not been sufficiently explored. I believe that even when a decision is made to do individual psychotherapy, a prior family diagnostic interview should be done, if at all possible, in order for the symptoms to be meaningfully interpreted in their intimate context (Framo, 1970).

But just because psychotherapists tend not to deal with families does not mean that families do not deal with them. Individual therapists often find themselves engaged in avoidance maneuvers in managing family members who try to intrude into the treatment process. How many therapists of children and adolescents have had to say after that fifth telephone call from a mother, "Mrs. So-and-So, if you want me to help your son will you please stay out of my hair?" or "No, I can't tell you how Suzie feels about you" (but with the private, unexpressed thought, "She'd be okay, you smothering bitch, if you'd stop driving her crazy"). How many therapists have had to say to mates, "It's hard to evaluate how much progress your wife is making" (with the private thought, "You ought to be seeing a psychiatrist yourself")? A not uncommon experience is watching two therapists at a cocktail party reproducing the argument of married partners that each is seeing separately.

The dynamics between therapist and family members are highly complex and have a life of their own even when the therapist does not permit any contact between himself/herself and the family. The fantasies and images of each about the other, with the client as the communicator between the two, can have a strong influence on the course of treatment. In those instances where the therapist allows an interview with the family, getting the patient's consent and usually seeing the family without the patient, a host of new problems arise. These complications run the gamut from open or suppressed angry feelings on both sides, to uncertainty about questions of confidentiality, conflicts about where the therapist's loyalties lie, competition for the patient, and even, at times, surreptitious coalitions between therapist and family members, both fancied and real.

With one couple I treated, the woman had been in therapy as a teenager with a therapist of the mother's choice; after every session the therapist telephoned the mother to tell her everything her daughter had said in the session. Another client had been sent by her mother for treatment to a well-known analyst—the patient's uncle, the mother's brother. Much more tragic is the story of James Wechsler, former editor of the *New York Post,* who wrote a personal account of the suicide of his son in the book *In a Darkness* (1972). In the Wechslers' efforts over many years to find help for their troubled son, they were systematically prevented from contact with the various therapists the boy saw. Only one therapist involved them in the treatment process, in multiple family therapy, but that effort came too late. Wechsler wrote, "We cannot avoid asking ourselves whether the course of events might not have been altered if, as at least some therapists now believe, we had not been excluded from participation in the treatment" (p. 222).

I have stressed numerous times that the family systems approach is not just a form of therapy or a technique but a radically different model for dealing with the human condition. One of the basic premises of family therapy is that people should be helped to fill their emotional needs, literally, through their intimates, through the people who matter the most, rather than through a therapist, a parental surrogate whose association with the patient is necessarily limited, professional and *as if*. This point can be illustrated by the film *Warrendale*, a worthwhile Canadian documentary about the institutionalized treatment of adolescents. In this film there is a scene where a teenager, beside herself with despair and hopelessness, is comforted by a psychiatric aide, and the girl says, "I really appreciate what you are trying to do, but how much more it would really mean to me if only my real mother hugged me." In his book, *The Theory of Psychoanalytic Technique* (1958), Menninger includes a chapter on regression where he lists all the things people yearn for in psychoanalysis that they are never going to get (e.g., unconditional love, forgiveness). The turning point in analysis presumably occurs when the patient renounces these infantile strivings in literal form and obtains gratification via the reality principle. But not all analytic patients can achieve this goal unless real needs are being met by the intimates.

Another limitation of individual therapy is that thousands of married people send their spouses to therapists in order to get them off their backs; every time there is an argument the mate says, "Don't tell me! Go tell your doctor." As a result, the client forms a more intimate relationship with the therapist than with the spouse; this is the reason why many married women cynically refer to their therapist as "my paid friend."

In our society the usual relationship between an adult male and his father is one of emotional distance; the distance is often one of light years. Men long to bond with their fathers and they cannot expect their mothers to help them with male bonding. At the end of a psychoanalysis a man can talk freely to his analyst about his relationship with his father, but he often still cannot talk directly to his dad. In contrast, family therapists bring son and father face to face to deal with their relationship, rather than have the son or father talk *about* their distant relationship to a therapist or make a father out of the therapist.

By warding off, negating, vilifying, or even neutralizing the significant figures in the lives of their clients, traditional therapists can get overburdened by the emotional demands of clients who should be helped to get their needs and expectations met by those who matter most to them. Subsequent chapters of this volume propose the thesis that by expanding their conceptual and operational range to include the family of origin in treatment, therapists can critically increase the power of their effectiveness in bringing about change.

BRIEF OUTLINE OF BOOK

First, I will describe the various stages of family-of-origin therapy: Chapter 2, *early stages* (introducing the idea of bringing in family of origin; relating current issues in therapy to family-of-origin issues; handling resistances); Chapter 3, *preparation phase* (strategies for bringing in family of origin; preparing the agenda); Chapter 4, *techniques used during family-of-origin sessions* (therapy procedures; description of how the sessions tend to go); Chapter 5, *postsession developments* (processing of family-of-origin sessions; feedback of findings of family-of-origin sessions to individual and marital problems). Following this, in Chapter 6, I will present the *difficulties, limitations, pitfalls, and contraindications* involved in the method. Because I consider this method to be a general one, clinically applicable to the wide range of emotional issues presented in individual, marital, and family conflicts, I will discuss in Chapter 7 *theoretical implications* (object relations theory tie-in; a proposed theory of therapeutic change), and in Chapter 8 *clinical implications* (evaluation of this method as a form of therapy; recommendations to therapists who conduct family-of-origin sessions; comparison of this method to those of other intergenerational family therapists; why people are so fearful of having family-of-origin sessions; and what the sessions can accomplish on the individual, marital, and original family system levels.)

Various methods of working with family of origin have been developed by other intergenerational family therapists (Bowen, 1978); Boszormenyi-Nagy & Krasner, 1986; Boszormenyi-Nagy & Spark, 1973; Haas, 1968; Headley, 1977; Kerr & Bowen, 1988; Kramer, 1985; Paul & Paul, 1975; Satir [Nerin, 1985]; Whitaker, 1976a,b, 1989; Williamson, 1981, 1982). Comparisons of the present author's method to other intergenerational family therapists will be made in Chapter 8.

The last chapter presents case examples. The first example details the integration of the family-of-origin consultation with a couple in long-term marital therapy. This is followed by three shorter vignettes that demonstrate the diversity of the family-of-origin consultation: a family-of-origin consultation with a client in individual therapy, a consultation with a self-referred out-of-town family that includes the divorced parents, and a consultation with a self-referred, out-of-town sibling subsystem who are trying to come to terms with their abusive parents now dead.

An Afterword follows where I present some thoughts about training in this method and relate some of my professional and personal associations to this work.

Several times throughout this book I state the strong belief that therapists who do intergenerational work should work on their own family-of-origin issues. In trying to practice what I preach, I have had sessions with my family of origin (siblings and other relatives since my parents are dead), and I decided to be self-disclosing about my family issues by including at the end of the book a brief history of my own family of origin.

2

Early Stages of Family-of-Origin Therapy

• relating current issues in therapy to family-of-origin issues; dealing with resistances

INTRODUCING THE IDEA OF BRINGING IN FAMILY OF ORIGIN

Early Resistances in Couples to Bringing in Family of Origin

In the earlier years I used to tell couples during the first interview of my intention to involve family of origin in the therapy. Further experience indicates that, with some exceptions, it is advisable to wait until a relationship is established with the couple. I found that too many couples were prematurely terminating therapy because the prospect of bringing in their original family was too threatening. I present the proposal as a routine procedure, along with the statement that the session will not be held until the timing is right and the clients are ready.

In previous publications I described the enormous opposition and intense fear expressed by the great majority of clients toward this proposal (Framo, 1976, 1981). In a recent book (Chasin, Grunebaum, & Herzog, 1990) where Peggy Papp, Norman Paul, Carlos Sluzki, and I demonstrated four different approaches to working with the same couple, there is a clear example of the intense anxiety and near panic manifested by a woman at the prospect of talking to her mother about important issues. Some clients feel that they have experienced such severe physical, sexual, or emotional abuse in their families of origin that the very suggestion of bringing in their family can precipitate violent outbursts, psychological disorganization, loss of faith in the therapist, and termination of therapy. With such clients (often called Borderline) the suggestion of a family-of-origin session cannot be made early in therapy.

Resistances are manifested despite the clients being in great pain and presumably willing to do anything to relieve their suffering. It is a matter of course for one or more of the following expressions to be stated when I suggest to couples that at some point each spouse bring in parents and brothers and sisters for a session: "What does that have to do with my problems with my spouse?"; "That's out of the question because they live too far away"; "I don't have any problems with my parents; my problem is my partner"; "I wouldn't do this to *them*" (perceiving the session as punishment); "My parents are too old and I don't want to upset them"; "I don't think they can take it; it would destroy them"; "I don't want to destroy my parents for my benefit"; "It wouldn't do any good because they'll never change"; "It could open up a can of worms"; "I don't have anything to do with my family; I don't feel I even belong in my family"; "After so many bad years things have settled down and I don't want to mess with that."

Occasionally, a client is receptive to the proposal or is intrigued by the idea; some even start contacting family members after the first therapy session. Sometimes one spouse is open-minded toward the idea, and the other is vigorously opposed. Some couples incorporate differences about this matter into the reservoir of their other disputes; for instance, one husband was furious that his wife rejected a family-of-origin session with her family out of hand, seeing her refusal as not wanting to invest in the marriage. In this case, I had to point out that these were two separate issues.

During the first few conjoint marital sessions, after the various dimensions of the couple's relationship and its breakdown have been explored, I collect a brief history of each partner's family of origin. The following inquiries are illustrative of the kinds of questions asked of clients in individual as well as marital therapy:

- How many were in your family?
- Your birth order?
- Are your parents still alive?
- Were there any deaths or losses in your family?
- What kind of work did your father do?
- Did your mother work outside the home?
- What sort of persons were your father and mother as you were growing up?
- Which parent were you closer to?
- What was your relationship like with each parent and with each of your brothers and sisters?
- What was your parent's marriage like?
- What was the family atmosphere?
- What kind of family was it?
- Were there any unusual events or traumas?
- Under what circumstances did you leave home?
- How did your parents feel about your spouse?
- What is your relationship like now with your parents and siblings—close, distant, superficial, cut-off?

Following each person's description of his or her family-of-origin history, I always ask the partner, in this case the wife,

- What is your reaction to your husband's account of his history?
- How do you see his mother, father, or siblings?
- How does your husband behave when he is with his family?

With some exceptions, as when the individual is caught up in in-law difficulties, spouses tend to be more objective observers of their partner's family. Often a partner will reveal some shameful or omitted fact the spouse left out in his/her account, such as a parent being an alcoholic or having committed suicide. A wife may disclose that her husband must telephone his mother every day; a husband may reveal that his wife never talks to her father.

Deaths and divorces in the family of origin are always noted as subjects to be explored more fully later on. Whenever I hear about a cut-off—that is, a client has terminated a relationship with a parent or sibling—my ears perk up and I may comment that that decision may be reconsidered following the work we do together. Reactions to this statement will range from incredulity to outrage to guarded interest. One client got up out of his chair and stood red-faced in the doorway, shouting, "I hate my parents with a deadly intensity you couldn't imagine. I'll give you a thousand dollars if you could ever persuade me to bring them here." After three months this client brought in his original family. In these early stages I make no effort to deal with the resistances; I merely state that their reactions to the idea of having a family-of-origin session are normal and typical.

Clients' resistances to involving their parents and brothers and sisters in their therapy occur naturally and inevitably in all therapy contexts (family, marital, divorce, couples groups, and individual therapy). Out-of-town clients who request family-of-origin sessions have overcome most of their reluctances although they, too, have their own resistances when they start making actual preparations for the sessions. Although hesitancy or downright refusal to bringing in family of origin occurs with practically all clients, the resistances are diminished and more easily managed in the couples group context. In the material that follows it should be kept in mind that most of the techniques for dealing with the resistances apply to all the therapy contexts even though the couples group context is discussed at length.

Couples Groups

Following several conjoint marital sessions, some couples are put into a couples group of three couples. The criteria I use for selection of couples for this group are age and stage of the life cycle: since each age group is dealing with different life-cycle issues, young couples are placed with young couples, and older couples enter an older couples group. Couples are not selected on the basis of such usual criteria as having similar problems. Scheduling problems prevent some couples from joining a couples group, and there are also couples who are unwilling, for various reasons, to come to a group.

My particular method of conducting a couples group is described more fully elsewhere (Framo, 1973), but in brief the procedure consists of the following: Sessions of two hours in length are conducted by a male-female cotherapy team; each couple is focused on separately by the therapists, and after engagement of a given couple, other group members are invited to give feedback to the couple. In essence, marital therapy is being done in the context of a couples group. This structured procedure, whereby each couple is worked with in turn, limits the size of the couples group to three couples. The emphasis is on the marital partners' transference distortions to each other, not to the distortions between individuals across couples. In other words, I do not attempt to make a family out of the group. In these early phases the families of origin are rarely mentioned, as the partners focus on their immediate marital difficulties.

From time to time during the course of discussing their marital problems, references may be made to difficulties with a mother or father or sibling or in the extended family or problems with in-laws, but usually those problems are considered by the couples as extrinsic to their marital difficulties.

In all the therapies I do I make it a practice to inquire from time to time about what is going on in the family of origin. For example, the wife's mother may be dying of cancer or a father and his brother are breaking up a business partnership with much bitterness. I have found that events such as these are not mentioned in the therapy sessions unless I specifically ask about the family of origin. Adults in marital or family therapy do not, ordinarily, volunteer information about their current relationship with parents or siblings; the therapist has to ask to get that information. When an issue with a mother, father, or sibling is mentioned, I am likely to state that that is a matter we will deal with when their family comes in; this assumption that there *will* be a family-of-origin session is pointedly made, even to those who had rejected the prospect of bringing in their family. In a sense, I am seeding the unconscious, normalizing the idea, and treating the subject as matter-of-factly as possible.

In this book only those aspects of marital dynamics will be discussed that are relevant to work with family of origin. Foremost among these concepts is the one having to do with the transference misrepresentations that all partners have toward each other. These perceptions, attitudes, and behaviors, based on anachronistic remnants of experiences with parents and siblings, are not always easy to detect. Marital difficulties, moreover, are compounded of a complex interchange of reality and subjective influences; some spouses' transference reactions are subtle because they are acted out during the course of the routine daily events of living.

Most of these kinds of distortions are not visible in the marital or couples group therapy sessions. Consequently, when members of the couples group give feedback to the couple in these early phases, they usually not only stick closely to reality factors, but also make fairly low-level observations: "I think you're a very nice couple" or "Maybe if you talked to your wife more, she might not crowd you so much." When group members get to know each other as the weeks go by, however, the feedback becomes more sophisticated. The transference manifestations, as the partners interact, gradually become more apparent to the other group members. The group quickly picks up on such obvious behavior as transference rages that are all out of proportion to the stimulus, or the way some people pursue so relentlessly a partner who clearly has nothing but contempt for them. Then these lay persons may give feedback on the order of: "I don't know where it's coming from, but it seems to me your wife doesn't deserve the punishment you're dishing out to her"; or "Why in hell do you keep running after somebody who obviously doesn't want you?"; or "Boy, you sure expect a lot from a husband."

Sometimes the feedback from group members forces people to question their exaggerated responses to spouses; other times I point out the irrationality. Occasionally the clients themselves become puzzled by the origin of an attitude or expectation which, by now, seems inappropriate even to them (e.g., a husband may say, "I wonder why I sometimes feel such rage toward my wife; she is really a good person and doesn't deserve it"; or a wife may say, "I guess I did expect my husband to make up for all the past pain in my life").

The therapists may elaborate on group feedback in order to accustom the group to think in terms of how the members slant, twist, and embellish their responses to their partners. I also encourage clients to examine the genesis and roots of their transference embroideries. (e.g., If a husband says his wife's put-downs make him feel humiliated, I may ask, "When, in the past did you feel humiliated?") When the timing is right, I make connections between *patterns* in the relationship with the parents and siblings with those in the marital inter-actions. For instance, one woman would give her husband the silent treatment when she was angry with him, a method her mother used with her father. Her husband found her silences intolerable, and he had decided early on that he would not use his father's tactic of with-drawal from conflict. He would consequently yell and scream at her and when he would get no response, he would slap her. She would then pack a bag and leave him, as her mother left her father. Then, like his mother, he would run after her and beg her forgiveness.

As I work toward getting group acceptance about bringing in fam-ily of origin, a number of techniques are utilized to make the inher-ently fearful prospect not only a palatable one, but one that will bring about benefits for all, including the family coming in. I have learned that the timing of reintroduction of the proposal is impor-tant. Although I have occasionally seen clients with their families of origin early in the therapy* in order to take advantage of the parents passing through town, generally speaking the sessions are more use-ful and generative when they are held toward the end of therapy. The reason for having the sessions later is that by that time the clients have made therapeutic progress, they trust the therapists more and they have come to recognize how past experiences are not working for them in the present and they have been prepared to deal with parents and siblings with the hard issues that exist among them.

The group process is also employed in the service of lessening the resistance. For instance, I will utilize the greater receptivity of some members of the group as examples to be emulated by the reluctant members. "Joe here is going to do it and I'm wondering when the rest of you will catch up to him." Gradually, the entire group comes to see that having the session with family of origin is a goal that most are working toward, and this aim becomes part of the group culture. Indeed, a kind of contest develops in the group as to who will be the first to bring in the family of origin. Those sessions come to be looked upon as the culmination of the therapy, almost as a kind of graduation ceremony. Furthermore, after individuals in the group

---

*Several therapists have told me that when they have a client who is an enigma, an early session with the client and his/her family of origin sometimes makes that person more real and understandable.

have had their family-of-origin sessions and report back to the group what the experience has done for them, others in the group get the courage to go through with the sessions.

There is, of course, considerable variation among the six individuals in the couples group in their readiness to consider bringing in their family of origin. Since the groups are open-ended, there may be some clients who have already had their family-of-origin session along with those for whom the possibility is still a frightening abstraction. Usually the ones who have had their sessions try to allay the fears of the uninitiated, in most cases telling them of the positive things they or their family members got out of the sessions. Even in groups where no one has had the session, some people are more ready than others to consider the idea seriously.

Those who are particularly anxious about the prospect renew their objections, saying such things as, "It would be a disaster"; or becoming more intransigent, "It's totally out of the question"; "I would be glad to tell you anything you want to know about how I feel about my mother, *but I will not tell her*. She is very defensive and paranoid and would go berserk or walk out of the room or go crazy if I were to tell her what I really think"; "I get along fine with my parents and brothers and sisters; I just can't get along with my wife." At this point it is not uncommon for clients to express fears of their parents dying if they were to come in. I am asked if it is possible to have an oxygen tank in the office, and inquiries are made about the location of the nearest hospital or physician. Clients who had been very bitter toward their parents suddenly become very protective and describe the frailty of parents.

Impasse in Marital Therapy

In addition to our interventions and the feedback of the group in dealing with the resistances, we also reintroduce the topic of bringing in the family of origin when the couple have hit an impasse in therapy. There are partners who cannot stop blaming each other, there are others who have bogged down or have hit a plateau, and there are still others whose relationship is so empty that I cannot get anything going between them. At a certain point I tell such couples that, for a while, instead of dealing with their relationship, I will have each person focus on self (in the context of the partner's presence or group) with the goal of eventually bringing in their family of origin. *The best way I know how to deal with impasses in marital therapy, whether as a single couple or in the couples group, is to move in the direction of bringing in the family of origin.* This move shifts the emotional intensity away from the marital relationship to the family of origin; just beginning to connect and deal with family-of-origin problems tends to defuse the marital tensions.

Special Resistances in Clients in Individual Therapy

Individual psychotherapy clients have always constituted a small proportion of my private practice caseload. I am able to convert many of my individual clients into wider system cases, particularly family therapy cases, but nonetheless I still occasionally see clients in extended individual psychotherapy.

In my early days of doing individual psychotherapy, and based on my psychodynamic orientation, I dealt directly with transference phenomena, which are ubiquitous in all therapy contexts. However, since I started working with families and couples in the late 1950s, and as the years have gone by, I have placed less and less emphasis on transference to the therapist as a therapeutic tool and have focused almost exclusively on the transference distortions between the intimates.

Many of the observations about resistances in couples to bringing in family of origin also apply to clients who come for individual therapy. There are, however, singular aspects to resistances of individual clients who struggle with having family-of-origin sessions. These unique resistances are grounded on the fact that individual clients develop more intense transference reactions to the therapist than do couples or families.

My wife and cotherapist, Dr. Felise B. Levine, collaborated with me in making the following observations about individual clients who are considering bringing in their family of origin. When there is an established relationship between a single client and the therapist, involving the family of origin is sometimes regarded by the client as an intrusion into the exclusivity of the one-to-one relationship. Other considerations, forebodings, hesitations, and skepticisms may be voiced by the clients when they feel safe enough to state their fears: "Will you like my family more than you like me?" "You may get other points of view from family members, which will invalidate my perceptions." "I will have to share you with my family and give up my special role with you." "I'm worried about how a family-of-origin session will affect my relationship with you." "What if you don't like my family?" "Somebody in the family may reveal a secret I would not reveal." "I'm afraid you'll believe my family about how messed up I am." In the process of dealing with each of these apprehensions, significant material is often revealed that will enhance the therapy.

Whether dealing with a single individual or with a couple, the early stages of involving extended family in the therapy process are a challenge to therapists' artistry in modulating clients' natural fears and concerns. Moreover, exploration of each of the client's fears usually makes more understandable the client's intrapsychic and interpersonal conflicts. As will be seen in the next chapter on the preparation phase, client apprehensions about having family-of-origin sessions persist until the sessions are over, and sometimes even afterwards (e.g., being reluctant to listen to the tapes of the sessions).

3

Preparation Phase

• strategies for bringing in family of origin; preparing the agenda

WORKING THROUGH THE MISGIVINGS

Resistances take on a different form in later phases of therapy as clients start thinking seriously about going through with the family-of-origin session. Most clients go through periods of painful indecision, weighing their dread against the intriguing possibility that there might be something in it for them. Even though those contemplating bringing in their family may be terrified, their spouses may find the prospect amusing: "Oh boy, can you *imagine* your family in here? I can just picture your mother and father; it would be hysterical!" Some clients who had seemed flat and vague in discussing their marital problems, suddenly come alive when talking about their original family. I have noticed that some clients, who had always been easygoing and cooperative during the therapy, undergo a personality change when discussing their family of origin. Some clients become tongue-tied, confused, suddenly struck mute, and some become obscurely loquacious. Some clients' IQs seem to drop to 50 when discussing their original family.

Others, previously mild-mannered and pleasant, abruptly turned hostile when I asked them to bring in their family. One man asked his father to come in and his father, he said, turned white, which frightened him, so he did not press the issue; nor did he follow through when his brother gave excuses as to why he could not come in. This man's inability to ask anything of his family-of-origin members tied in with his not being able to make any demands in his marriage, which drove his wife up a wall. Another client said, "Let sleeping dogs lie. I'm finished being angry with my parents, and I accept them now and don't want to tamper with that. I know I *should* bring them in, but I don't want to. I will do anything but this." She went on to ask, "Convince me. How will it do me any good?" Headley (1977) accepts clients' refusals to have family-of-origin sessions, whereas I prefer helping them work through their misgivings. Almost all of my clients initially refuse, but most follow through.

Here is a fairly typical exchange between me and the client during the preparation phase:

> *Client*: Okay. I'm ready to do it, but I know my family (mother, father, brother, sister) will refuse.
> *Framo*: Did you ask them?
> *Client*: No, but I know they won't come in.
> *Framo*: But will you ask?
> *Client*: It wouldn't do any good. Look, Doc, I know my family better than you do.

After a few such interchanges I will then get a telephone call from the client: "Guess what? I asked and they said yes. I can't believe it!" The great majority of family members who are approached the right way will come in; parents and siblings are usually much more interested in the client than we (the therapists) are led to believe. One of the most productive statements for clients to make to family members is "I need your help."

When clients tell their family "The doctor wants to see you," they are not taking the kind of personal responsibility that is required for a good outcome. Further, some present the invitation in a way that will elicit a rebuff. One man said to his father, "The shrink I'm seeing wants to see you to find out why you gave me so many beatings when I was a kid." This father, to be sure, refused to come in. Later, the client was able to get his father to come in by telling his father, "Dad, I need for you to come in for the family session because I want to get to know you better." Sometimes it is hard to tell how the client saw to it that the family did not get in. On the other hand, there are a few occasions where, despite the client's great efforts, the family refuses to come in; but the greatest resistance usually lies with the client. Generally, I know that a client is ready when he/she starts to deal with specific issues with family members before the session. One man met separately with each member of his family beforehand; he said, "When I go to that session, I don't want any surprises."

One of the messages I try to get across is that by bringing in their family and dealing with issues that have troubled them for a long time, they have an unparalleled opportunity to straighten out what were probably misunderstandings and misconceptions based on childhood comprehension. When the client says, "My parents will never change, it wouldn't do any good," I state something like, "Do not have this session to change your parents. You can't do that; you will be disappointed if you try. You should do this for yourself. You need to state your own perceptions and positions. You won't have to feel phoney anymore; you won't have to play the game of only telling your parents what you think they want to hear. You have the opportunity to be true to yourself and be more congruent."

I do caution, however, that parents should not be verbally assaulted or blamed, or that all truths need to be told; instead, the clients are encouraged to state their views without indictment or condemnation. However, there are people who express hatred toward a parent, who detail horror stories about what the parent had done to them. In this case, in order to help the person with the introject of that parent, I look for the positive in the parent, and I point out that when you hate a parent you hate part of yourself. To clients who see one parent as the angel and the other as the devil, I stress the positive in the devil parent and the negative in the angelic parent; such polarization has, of course, resulted in good-evil intrapsychic conflicts, which in their present-day lives are usually projected onto the spouse or a child.

One worthwhile question to ask clients who have mixed feelings about having the session is to ask, "What is the worst possible thing that could happen?" The most common fear expressed is that the session will tear the family asunder, that the members will end up alienated from each other. On the other hand, one client said his family members were distant from each other, and he was afraid that the session might lead to an old togetherness that was too threatening. But to those clients who are especially protective toward parents, I state that there may be some potential gains for their parents rather than harm.*

I inform them that some parents look forward to the session because it affords them a "second chance" to (1) clarify issues in a safe setting that *they* have with their adult children; (2) make up for the past, resolve their own feelings of having fallen short or even having failed their children; and (3) divulge secrets that they felt could not be communicated until the children became adults and/or parents and, therefore, could understand and not judge them too harshly (e.g., such secrets as a parent's previous marriage, or a parent having another child who is unknown to the children of the present family). Some parents prepare for the sessions on their own by collecting photographs, bringing family documents, and giving a great deal of advance thought to the session. Those parents who are assessing their own lives and reassessing their values are most able to see these sessions as a second chance for themselves. When the clients think that their parents need these sessions for the parents' benefit, their reluctance to having the session is often lessened. I instruct clients to tell their family members that they should think about the issues that *they* (the family members) want to deal with.

The Sibling's Influence

Sometimes it is the sibling(s) who looks forward to the session and prepares an agenda; a brother or sister can be influential in helping the client overcome his/her reluctance. On the other hand, sometimes the sibling is most resistant and manages to block the session from taking place. I have also noted that the spouses of siblings are frequently unwilling to have their partners attend; it is not quite clear to

---

*I am indebted to Helen Mandelbaum (1979) for these suggestions.

me why these spouses should be so threatened. Perhaps they feel that their mates are putting a higher priority on their family of origin than on them.

The Spouse's Influence

Usually one spouse is more ready to go ahead than the other; one partner's refusal to have the session is often perceived by the other partner as a lack of commitment to the marriage. However, even partners (and other group members) who reject a family-of-origin session, encourage the other(s) to go ahead, saying something like, "Of course it's not for me, but I really think you need to work out something with your Dad." Only once did I have a client who did not want her husband to meet with his family because she was threatened by her husband's closeness to his family. This case was written up in Peggy Papp's book (Papp, 1977) (Framo, 1978b). However, spouses usually want their partners to have the session because they sense that they will be less projected upon if the partner works out important issues with his/her family.

PREPARING THE AGENDA FOR FAMILY-OF-ORIGIN SESSIONS

When fears have been somewhat allayed and the individual has begun to see the possible benefits of the session, we are now ready to begin concrete preparations for the session. There are crises, impasses, and problems every step of the way; some crises, however, are serendipitous: Often much is revealed about the clients and their families as the preparation process unfolds. As a function of trying to get family members in, clients often discover things about their families and themselves that they never knew before. For instance, one client said she expected a refusal from her father, but that it was her mother who gave her such a hard time. Another client, who was the youngest of five sons and who had always seen himself as the weak baby of the family, began changing his self-perception when he found out his brothers were terrified of coming in.

Obtaining Detailed Family History

If the preparation occurs in the couples group or in marital therapy, I then start to deal with the most motivated person, and I elicit a detailed family history from that individual. Similar preparations, of course, are done with individual therapy clients.* This is the second time a family history is obtained from the client, the first one having been procured in the first or second therapy session; however, this history is much more comprehensive. Not only does this family history reveal more important facts about the family never disclosed before, but sometimes the shift to family-of-origin material smokes out hidden issues in the marriage. The agenda for the family-of-origin session is largely based on this history obtained from the client and is supplemented by the spouse's observations.

I instruct the clients to think about the important events that occurred in the family while they were growing up: what the family relationships were like; what were the mysteries, stories, myths, and secrets in their family that they wondered about; what questions are stuck in their heads that they always wanted to know but were afraid to ask; and, most important, what past and present issues exist with each member of the family?

During the recounting of the family history I may interrupt when I spot an issue: for instance, a client may say that he always felt he was a disappointment to his father. I will then ask, "Did you ever tell that to your father?" and he will reply, "Of course not; that's not the sort of thing a guy says to his father." I counter with, "Well, there's an item for your agenda." A client may comment that in her family all communication had to go through her "dishonest" mother, that they could never approach Dad directly; when I suggest dealing with that issue in the session she may look shocked. As one can see, the agenda items are made up of all the things clients have been concerned about through the years but have never dealt with. The agenda items,

---

*When gathering a family history in the preparation session for those who are not regular clients, I find it valuable to have a close relation participate: spouse, live-in partner, sibling, and so on. Richer, more detailed histories are obtained when someone in addition to the client gives perceptions, impressions, jogs the memory, points out discrepancies, reveals missing data, and provides support.

which are breaking the family rules essentially, are developed painstakingly because the client is being prepared to deal with the anxiety-laden concerns about their family members which they have been avoiding for years. As one client put it, "You are asking me to make the confrontation that I have spent a lifetime trying *not* to make!"

When the preparation is made in the context of couples group therapy, the group process is inevitably affected by the struggles of the participants over the family-of-origin encounter. When individuals relate their family histories, strong feelings are often stimulated in the other group members as they resonate to features in the history that relate to their own family experiences. The narrator of the history usually becomes more understandable to the rest of the group; when group members see what people had to contend with in their original family, the narrators are often viewed more sympathetically. Similarly, in marital therapy I prefer for the spouse to be present when collecting a family history. Characteristically, spouses develop more empathy when they hear the details of their partner's experiences with their original families. Furthermore, when the group members give feedback to the narrator, having heard the family history, they are able to make connections between events in the past, attitudes toward previous significant others, and the marriage relationship.

There can also be untoward effects of the relating of a family history: One man, after listening to various group members talk about how they had been cheated, overburdened, confused, double-bound, or exploited by their parents, burst into tears and said, "I've been listening to you all complain about the awful things your parents did to you, but you don't realize how much better off you were. At least you had parents! I never had a father!" Following this outburst, a woman in the group, who had always denied problems in her original family, also began to cry and related how her father had been in an accident some years ago and had withdrawn from her after that; she said she could empathize with the previous fellow's sense of loss of a father. Some clients, in the process of giving feedback to a member who has just related a family history, reveal facts or feelings about their own family which had been previously suppressed. This observation is one of the reasons I prefer to prepare clients for family-of-origin sessions in the couples group format.

Beck (1982) attempts to integrate family-of-origin work, based on the Bowen model, with the principles of dynamic group psychotherapy. Williamson (1982) sees clients alone or conjointly if married, and he then puts individuals in small groups of four and the couples in couples groups, where they engage in intergenerational exploration. The clients are prepared by writing autobiographies, by audiotaping letters and phone conversations with parents and presenting them to the group, and by finally having a three-day office consultation with their parents and the therapist. Williamson does not ordinarily include siblings in sessions with clients and parents. Headley (1977) uses the format of individual or marital therapy in preparing for sessions with parents. I prepare clients in several contexts: couples groups, marital therapy, ongoing individual therapy, and one-time consultations.

Who Should Attend the Family-of-Origin Sessions

Those who are familiar with my 1976 article on this subject know that the spouse is not present in the family-of-origin sessions. At my workshops most of the participants cannot understand why I do not have both partners in the session with each family of origin. A moment's reflection should make clear why spouses are not included: Many parents and siblings will simply not open up in the presence of their in-law. The in-law in most cases is still regarded as outside the family; as one mother said of her son-in-law, "He's not our blood." Furthermore, the presence of the spouse would invite the family to focus on the marital problems of their son or daughter, which diverts from the main purpose of having the client deal with his/her issues with family members. After all, clients may discuss matters from their early years, long before they met their spouse. But sometimes I have sessions that include both spouses with one partner's family of origin, either before or after a regular family-of-origin session, but goals typically have to do with handling the in-law relationships.

Decisions need to be made about which members of the family of origin should be invited to the session. Headley (1977) recommends analyzing the family situation carefully before deciding which family members to see together. She claims that there may be destructive combinations, and if a family member is described as emotionally explosive, it is better to see that person separately at first. Headley recommends that "sadomasochistic" parents should not be included and goes on to say, "The therapist . . . should avoid such a situation because the outcomes can be negative for all concerned. It is probably better to choose the parent who seems to be the most approachable and see what can be done with that person" (p. 130).

Headley's experience is not consistent with my own. First, as I have said previously, you cannot rely on clients' descriptions of what their parents are like; most adults in this situation view their parents through the curvature of childhood understanding and their perceptions (describing parents as monsters, cruel, fragile, selfish, helpless, etc.) are usually derived from distorted early images. Second, one cannot predict from an interview with a parent (or any individual) alone how that person will actually behave when interacting with their family members; the context is very different. My own preference, based on having conducted many family-of-origin sessions, is to include all the members of the original family, no matter how they are described. Some parents and siblings who come to the session could be described as borderline or clinically psychotic, but in the family of origin situation their interactional behavior, however strange, is viewed by me as an attempt to operate in the family milieu as best as they can. In the family-of-origin session, instead of being a "patient," they are mother, father, sister, or brother.

In determining who should attend the family-of-origin session, the first rule of thumb is to ask the client to bring in parents and brothers and sisters. When the parents are dead, we have a session with siblings and sometimes aunts and uncles. There are clients who are only children, who nonetheless want to do family-of-origin work in the sense of gaining some closure about their relationship to the dead parents. The lingering oppression of ambivalence about parents who are no longer living frequently results in symptoms of depression. I have used several approaches with such clients. One method is to have the client write a letter to each of the dead parents, expressing the mixture of feelings toward each. Another method involves the client setting up a tape recorder, sitting alone in a room, and speaking from the heart into the microphone as if talking directly to the parent. In my experience, few people can do the foregoing without crying. The clients then read the letters or play the tapes in therapy sessions. Paul and Grosser (1965) and Williamson (1978) have used similar methods, having the client speak into a tape recorder at the graveside of the parents. The sadness the client experiences in doing these exercises is compounded by the realization that one has irretrievably lost the opportunity to work things out with the live parent, that one can no longer have a give-and-take dialogue with Mom or Dad. Nevertheless, by expressing long-held suppressed feelings, negative and positive, and by finally saying good-bye to the parents, the process of mourning moves closer to healthy resolution.

When one parent is dead, I suggest the client bring a photograph of the deceased parent to the session. Then, I ask the clients who else was a part of the family as they were growing up—a grandparent, an aunt or uncle who lived with them, or anyone else who was significant to them during their formative years. In a few cases, a housekeeper or maid who was like part of the family was included in the list. One client, who said she rarely saw her parents because she was essentially raised by the maid, sent her maid flowers every Mother's Day—not her biological mother.

I have been impressed by the number of clients who state that the most important relationship of their lives is a grandparent. Many say something like, "The only person in my entire life who I felt really loved me was my grandmother (or grandfather)." They often relate how devastated and bereft they were when the loved grandparent died, sometimes mourning the loss more than the loss of a parent. (I am reminded of the fine Canadian film, "Lies My Father Told Me" about the relationship between a boy and his grandfather.) The significance of grandparents has been relatively ignored in the mental health literature (Bengtson & Robertson, 1985; Kornhaber, 1986; Robertson, 1979; Troll, 1983).

The necessity for including siblings. As far as I know, I am one of the few family therapists who insists that both parents *and* siblings be present in family-of-origin sessions. In my experience, the presence of siblings is critical to the outcome of the session. As a matter of fact, I usually will not hold a session unless all siblings are there. Sibling relationships, like grandparent relationships, have been understudied. For many years we did not have a decent concept about siblings other than sibling rivalry, and everybody knows that sibling relationships are far more complex than rivalrous. Only recently have professionals addressed sibling relationships in any serious way (Bank and Kahn, 1982; Kahn and Lewis, 1988; Scott, 1983).

I have seen great devotion, sacrifice, and love between siblings, but I have also observed unbelievable hatred. During one family-of-origin session the mother related that she loathed her twin sister, and then she turned to her husband and sons and said, "When I die, if you let her come to my funeral, I will haunt you from the grave." Some clients, who are quite willing to bring in parents, are adamant against bringing in a brother or sister. For these people the siblings are viewed as parents, whereas the actual parents are perceived as siblings.

Another interesting phenomenon about siblings that I have become aware of is that mental health professionals do not seem to recognize their importance in either the etiology or treatment of relationship disturbances. Compared to parents, siblings are considered an afterthought or viewed as peripheral. I can illustrate this point by describing a series of predictable events that occurred during many workshops that I have given. In my judgment, live family-of-origin interviews are the best means to illustrate this family-of-origin method at workshops. While preparing for a workshop I tell the conference organizers in advance to be sure to include siblings as well as parents in the interview. I write this in a letter, underline it, and state the request over the telephone. Nonetheless, about 80% of the time, the family of origin that shows up consists of only the parents. Finally, I confronted one conference organizer, reminded her of my request, and she replied, "You're right, you did ask for the siblings, and I wonder why I forgot?" In the process of examining her possible motives, she came up with the following possible explanations underlying the exclusion of siblings:

1. I want my parents all to myself.
2. My parents will die sooner and I will have to live with my siblings, so I prefer not to rock the boat.
3. My siblings could destroy my illusions about my parents; they could reveal secrets I know I would not reveal.
4. I might begin to view my siblings differently.

5. Siblings can more easily cut you off than can parents; parents tend to love more unconditionally.

Including divorced parents or stepparents. I am often asked what procedure to follow when the client's parents have been divorced or when the clients had been adopted. Guidelines are difficult to establish; who should attend the session is negotiated according to the unique circumstances of a given case. Usually I see clients with both divorced parents together, although occasionally clients have preferred to meet only with stepparents or with one divorced parent at a time. Bringing together divorced parents, even those still bitter many years later, can be very helpful to the adult children *and* can help the divorced parents to finally and emotionally let go of their former spouse. (Wallerstein & Blakeslee, 1989) Enormous anxiety often precedes these sessions, however.

Under some circumstances adoptees have been seen with both biological and adoptive parents, but usually they prefer to meet with the two sets of parents separately. These situations can be very sensitive and must be handled with delicacy, not to mention trepidation. For example, one client said she could not bring herself to meet with her biological mother until her adoptive mother died. Another client said that if he brought his mother and stepmother together in the same room it would result in murder.

Absent members. Some clients can get every family member to come but one person. One sister refused, saying, "I will *not* come in and do a hatchet job on Mom." (Actually, no one asked her to; she, of course, was angriest at Mom.) The clients, the group members, and the cotherapists will then put their heads together and offer suggestions as to how to approach that person. I will ask the client which person has the most influence on the reluctant one, and suggest working through that person. I say to clients "do whatever you have to do to get them in" in situations where having a family-of-origin session seems clinically necessary. One client took me literally: Despite the fact that his parent's divorce had occurred many years ago, his father was still extremely bitter toward his mother, and refused to come to the session, saying, "I will *not* sit in the same room with *that* woman" (the client's mother). The client approached him several more times and was still met with refusals. Finally, he said to his father, "If you don't come, you will never see me again." The father attended the session. This particular client had also gathered his family from around the world, going through enormous effort to bring them in. He said to me, "My family is very different from any you've ever had. We haven't been together in 14 years. In the past not even a death or earthquake would bring them together. I've gone through a lot, at great emotional and financial expense, to pull this off. I'm trusting my family with you. *You better be good.*" Such statements as these explain why therapist apprehension about family-of-origin sessions is part of the picture and why I need a co-therapist to conduct them.

Every now and then clients absolutely refuse to ask one particular family member to come to the session, although they are quite willing to bring in the rest of the family. It is obvious from the rise in tension and strong outburst from the client that this family member carries an intense emotional charge for the client. Statements such as the following are made: "If you want me to bring in my brother, the session is off"; "My sister and I haven't gotten along in years; I do not want her to know I've been having marital problems"; or "My father is crazy, impossible, and doesn't believe in therapy."

As one might guess, my stance in these situations is that whenever clients say they do not want someone in the session, that is the one person I must have at the session. When clients are unwilling to meet with all the family, I state that we will not have the session unless everyone is present. But there are times—such as when a family member is in the hospital or in a foreign country—that I do not stick rigidly to this rule. Carl Whitaker told me that he uses a speaker phone so absent family members can participate, a procedure which I have not yet tried.

Some clients are encouraged to write letters to their original family members, inviting them to the sessions, and to read them, before mailing, to the therapists or to the group if they are in a couples group. Certain principles underlie the composition of these letters. Clients are advised to send a letter to each family member separately, to avoid attacks or criticism, to state their positions openly, and to refrain from becoming defensive, thus averting an escalation of the emotional intensity. These are standard Bowen principles for reducing family anxiety.

Presession Anxieties and Sabotaging

As the date of the session approaches, however, the anxiety that was present in the client frequently spreads to the family outside. Sometimes members of the family will phone and ask for an explanation of the purpose of the session, but actually want reassurance. Some family members warn me to not touch certain topics, and I may also be advised not to include a particular family member in the session. One father called to say, "I have a bad heart and my doctor has forbidden me to come, but I am overruling him and coming anyway—even if it costs me my life—because I would do anything for my son." I should hasten to inform the reader that I have not yet lost a parent. Sometimes I can allay anxiety in the family members by having the client send each of them a copy of my original paper on the subject (Framo, 1976). The reading of this paper seems to alleviate fears about the session. The article has also prompted some family members to do advance preparation by sending me family biographies prior to the session.

I suggest to clients that when they request family members to attend these sessions they should not tell them that they are coming in for family *therapy*—a word that intimidates and frightens most people. Rather, it is proposed that the sessions be called family meetings, family conferences, or family reunions. One fairly frequent occurrence is that an outside person (e.g., family physician, clergyperson, friend, "leader of the clan" from the extended family) may advise a family member not to attend the session. A more sticky and frustrating situation arises when parents or siblings (of the client) are in individual therapy elsewhere and their therapist, implicitly or explicitly, discourages or prohibits their "patient" from coming to the session. Some therapists of individuals bad-mouth family therapy. A mother may call and say, "My husband's psychiatrist says it's too risky for him to come to the session; it could cause a psychotic break." The potential sabotage of an outside mental health professional can be a complicating factor in preparing for this kind of intergenerational work. Never is the difference in paradigms, between individual and systems orientations, more apparent than in this circumstance.

The cotherapists do not get involved in the mechanics of contacting the family of origin. The client is charged with the responsibility for inviting family members, working out the travel schedule and logistics, arranging for places for the family to stay when they come from out of town, and so on. Indeed, in the majority of cases, family members usually travel long distances to get to the session. We live in a highly mobile society (I have heard that only 18% of Americans die in the same place where they were born), and families tend to be scattered around the country. But in this age of jet travel, where no place in the country is more than five to seven hours away from any other place, geographical distance is not the obstacle; emotional resistance is the problem. Indeed, some motivated family members fly in from foreign countries. I also take advantage of family get-togethers on holidays and vacations.

Advantages of Having Two Sessions with a Hiatus in Between

One of the advantages that accrues from publishing is that other professionals read about your treatment method, begin to use it, and then introduce modifications that improve the method. At one of my workshops in St. Paul, Minnesota, I learned that a group there had been using my family-of-origin method, but modified the timing by breaking up the family-of-origin session into two parts, separated by an evening. I have since appropriated this modification and it has proven to be extremely useful.* The family-of-origin sessions are now held for two hours on a Friday evening (it's the end of the week and allows for travel time) and two hours on a Saturday morning, four hours in all. If the four-hour session is held on one day, we take a break in the middle for several hours. More recently I have been considering extending sessions to a third two-hour meeting, either for severely disturbed families or for those who wish to explore issues in greater depth. Breaking the session into two segments with a hiatus allows several valuable things to happen:

1. When the family knows there will be another session, they will sometimes risk more in the first session.

---

*I acknowledge this contribution by Merle Fossum and Rene Schwartz.

2. The family will have another opportunity to deal with matters that they couldn't bring out in the first session.
3. The second session can deal with emotional fallout from the first session.
4. The first session is a getting acquainted one; in the first session the therapists are strangers to the family. In the second session the therapists are more *in* the family, more trusted, and consequently the family usually opens up to a greater degree, goes deeper, and starts to deal with real issues involving one another.

Here are two illustrative examples that show the advantages of having the second session.

One woman asked her brother to come in, but he refused. After several more vetoes, he said he would come in under two conditions: his sister was not to disclose that he was getting a divorce and they were not to criticize Mom. In the Friday night session the client kept her part of the bargain. At the beginning of the Saturday session the brother turned to the mother and said, "Mom, I think you should know that I'm getting divorced, and get ready because I'm about to criticize you."

The second example is even more instructive. I had been seeing a couple whose primary problem was a breakdown in the relationship between the wife and her husband's family. The husband had four sisters, all of whom were Ivy League graduates who needed to display their erudition to the wife. The wife said she felt uncomfortable in the presence of these sisters since they always put her down intellectually. In the Friday night session with the husband's family, his sisters started doing their number on me, displaying a kind of academic superiority, questioning me about my research data, and making sarcastic remarks. I found myself getting increasingly angry and frustrated, and finally I just withdrew emotionally; my cotherapist ran the rest of the session.

That night I had trouble sleeping. I started off the Saturday morning session by saying, "Now I know how Suzie (husband's wife) feels when she is with you. You did the same thing to me last night with your cerebral derision. You all spent a lot of money to get here, as well as your valuable time and mine. Now you have two hours left.

You can either continue to put me down or you can get down to work and deal with each other." They then got down to work with each other. I do not think this could have happened if we had had only one session instead of two planned ones. (Parenthetically, a very embarrassing thing happened with the client of the latter example. Sessions are always audiotaped, and after the family left on Friday night, I was releasing my anger about the family to my cotherapist, without realizing that the tape recorder was still on. The tape was later lent to my client to copy, and after he heard my remarks, instead of being legitimately upset at me, he said, "You know, I heard your statements after the Friday night session, and I thought that was a very interesting technique you used.")

The break in between the two sessions also gives the co-therapists the opportunity to discuss the session, get some perspective on what happened the first two hours, and prepare strategy for the second half.

Preparing the Self-Referred

As my work became more known, I began to get calls from people around the country who were not my regular clients, requesting family-of-origin sessions. Most of these self-referrals were therapists who, having heard of this work through word-of-mouth and publications, wanted to work some things out with their original family. Since I was unable to prepare these people for sessions as I did my regular clients (since they were usually from out of town), I used to suggest that the individual develop the agenda in the first session, *with* their family. I have since learned that it is advisable to meet with the person for at least an hour, in advance, not only to get some family history and develop an agenda of issues, but also because it is necessary to have an idea of what kind of family it is and what I am going to be dealing with.

One striking experience convinced me of the advisability of having some knowledge about the family prior to the family-of-origin session. A university professor from a midwestern city requested a session with his family. During the Friday night session I learned that this man, very much opposed to the Vietnam War, had gone to

Canada rather than serve in the army. Since this was a Jewish family, I mistakenly assumed that they were liberal, so I said, "Good for you; if I had sons at that time I would have sent them to Canada too." Little did I know that that issue was of central concern to the family; namely, the family regarded him as a traitor for leaving his country to avoid serving in the army.

On Saturday morning the family remonstrated with me for making that statement and I agreed I had made a mistake. I not only decided thenceforth to have advance knowledge about a family, but also—and I should have known better—to keep my political and religious beliefs to myself. I should say, by the way, that these special, requested family-of-origin sessions have been most productive, as demonstrated by the follow-up study (Baker, 1982).

Audiotaping and Videotaping

Clients and families are informed in advance that audiotaping or videotaping of sessions is part of the procedure; rarely has any family objected. The families' listening to or watching the sessions afterwards is considered part of the whole process. Some clients bring their own cassette audiotape recorders to the sessions, as back-up in case my equipment fails: The tapes are loaned to the client to have duplicated.

I suggest that a copy of the tape be sent to any family member who could not be present. But what about the spouses of the adult children? I prefer that the spouses of the adult children listen to the tape. The spouses, not having been included in the session, often feel shut out; besides, spouses, after listening to the sessions, can contribute an important perspective to what happened. However, if I tell the family before the session that their sons-in-law or daughters-in-law were going to listen to the session, many families will simply not open up. As one woman put it, "I would never have said the things I did if I knew my daughter-in-law was going to hear this." On the other hand, if they are told at the end, some family members feel betrayed. This predicament was solved for me by a friend, Joe Steinberg, an attorney-family therapist, now a judge, who reminded me that privilege belongs to the client, not to the therapist. In other words, this choice was not mine to make. The client should negotiate with the family and decide who should listen to the tape.

Final Guidelines and Suggestions

Just prior to the session I recommend to clients final guidelines and suggestions. Clients are reminded again not to start off attacking or blaming their parents or siblings. I suggest that they tell parents and siblings what good things they got from them or to at least thank them for coming in. Some of these clients are very angry at their parents or a brother or sister, and I tell them that they will subvert their own agenda by making accusations; I suggest that they state their views without recrimination. The proposal is also made that clients begin the sessions with some self-disclosures. By telling the family things about themselves that the family may not know (e.g., that they are contemplating divorce or that they have been depressed for some time), they present themselves as models of openness for the rest of the family. I prompt the client again to tell their family members that they (the family) have a right to bring in their own issues for discussion. Furthermore, they are advised to inform the family that the relationships among *all* the family members will be discussed, not just the problems of the client. Families who have not been advised about this may feel tricked and get angry during the session because they thought they were being invited to discuss the problems of the client. The clients are reminded, moreover, that the purpose of the session is not for me to treat their parents or siblings; I am not conducting mental status examinations of their family members. I tell them that the sessions belong to the client and the family and that cotherapists *function as facilitators in helping family members to deal with each other.* Although clients are instructed to communicate these messages to their family, I know I will have to repeat some of them during the session itself.

Practitioners of this method should be prepared for occasional last-minute cancellations of family-of-origin sessions. I have seen such cancellations occur even with clients who were highly motivated. Some clients who cancelled just prior to the sessions had done a great deal of preparation, and I always find it interesting to speculate about the family dynamics that led to that decision. A few clients are just too terrified to go through with it, but some cancellations are based on a particular family member's last-minute refusal to attend, which is outside the control of the client. Later on, sometimes we hear about the confrontations, family fights, and behind-the-scenes strategies and maneuvers that took place around the issue of everyone participating in the family meeting. Intergenerational therapists have to learn how to handle the disappointments and frustrations of precipitous cancellations.

As a function of my increased experience with this method of involving family of origin in the treatment of adults, nearly all my clients now bring in their original family. I think that when therapists really believe in what they are doing, and there is trust, most clients will be open to their therapists' recommendation.* In my early paper on this method I stated, "Because of my convictions about what the process can do, I stick to the idea tenaciously, bringing it up at every opportunity as a goal that will contribute to growth more than any other thing they can do" (Framo, 1976, p. 199).

Since that time—now that I have a more sober appreciation of clients' fears, of the complexities and difficulties involved, of the potential pitfalls, of the hard realities of intergenerational work—I have toned down my enthusiasm. For instance, I now caution that the sessions are not likely to change people's lives drastically, and I moderate some clients' unrealistic expectations about what the sessions can accomplish. For example, clients need to be prepared for not being able to fulfill fantasies of what they can get from parents or siblings. Moreover, I inform clients of the risks involved (see chapter on Difficulties, Limitations, Pitfalls and Contraindications) and state that such sessions *usually* help. The issue of informed consent is involved here (Everstine, Everstine, Heymann, & True et al., 1980; Margolin, 1982).

I further remind clients that the family-of-origin sessions are not a magical panacea for all their problems. The experience is considered part of a process that requires ongoing work and follow-through. Cli-

---

*Some of the resistances to bringing in parents and siblings of clients may reside in the therapists themselves, who may be dealing with their own fantasies or apprehensions about confronting their own family members.

ents are also informed that their perception of the impact of the sessions is likely to change over time. For example, months after the session they may notice that Mom or Dad or a sibling or they themselves are behaving more considerately toward someone else in the family.

Some clients, for one reason or another, never have a family-of-origin session. However, I have noticed that my having made such an issue of its importance often brings about changes in the family-of-origin relationships. For instance, as a function of trying to get the family in, the client has usually broached the subject to the family member easiest to approach, usually a brother or sister. Then that person will contact another family member, who phones another, and the messages spread throughout the network. Subjects that have been avoided for years begin to be discussed, family members who have never done so before start to talk to each other about family perceptions or events, family cutoffs diminish, relationships get strengthened, and the system shifts—all of these changes occurring without the family having had a formal family-of-origin session.

For those who go through with the process, just before the family-of-origin session the anxiety level rises again in the client. There are repeated requests for reassurance that something awful is not about to happen. The client is braced by the therapists' declaration that they will be there to protect everyone in the family. If the individual is in a couples group, the group gives support, reminds the client to bring up certain scary items on the agenda, and looks forward to hearing how everything turned out in the session. Some clients feel primed, like a boxer before a match, and do not want to overtrain. Other clients enter an abnormal state of calm. But many continue to bite their fingernails nervously.

4

Techniques Used During Family-of-Origin Sessions

• procedures used for conducting sessions; descriptions of how the sessions tend to go

COTHERAPY

I prefer the cotherapy method when working with couples and families, although sometimes of necessity I have to work alone. Financial and logistical considerations prevent me from always working with a cotherapist. Although I have done cotherapy with other men, I think the male-female cotherapy team is the best therapeutic combination (Sonne & Lincoln, 1965). We live in a world of men and women, and I believe that this gender difference should be represented when doing psychotherapy. To be sure, cotherapy makes the therapy situation more complex and can even create difficulties, but a well-experienced cotherapy team that has the capacity to work through conflicts in their relationship, and who know each other well, can be a powerful therapeutic tool indeed. A cotherapy relationship can be like a marriage, and if the team cannot work out their differences they should, out of consideration for the families, separate.

The subject of cotherapy is a complex one, beyond the scope of this chapter (Rubinstein & Weiner, 1972); but suffice to say that the presence of a man and woman is especially beneficial and supportive for families in family-of-origin sessions. The therapists need each other in these sessions too. Although I can easily conduct other therapies alone, I find that I usually need a cotherapist to conduct a family-of-origin session; no other form of psychotherapy can rival the intense affect which such sessions produce.

DESCRIPTION OF EARLY PHASES: REDUCING ANXIETY AND GETTING TO KNOW EACH OTHER

The first tactical goal in a family-of-origin session is to reduce the family's anxiety level, which, by the time the session begins, has become severe and contagious. One objective measure of the acuteness of the apprehension is that, before the session starts, nearly all family members, in turn, have to go to the bathroom. So, in addition to Kleenex, it is necessary to have a nearby bathroom in order to conduct these sessions.

The first few minutes of the first session is usually awkward, even for the therapists. We* try to put the family at ease by introducing ourselves with our first names, by asking them if it is okay to call them by their first names (we were only refused once), and by making small talk about their trip to the session. We lead into the session by getting acquainted with each other. In the process of collecting identifying data, we note each member's appearance, manner of dress, who sits next to whom, their apparent attitudes, posture toward the session, nonverbal behaviors, and so on—things usually noted in a family session. They are, of course, sizing up the therapists as well.

It is important to treat the incoming family with respect, especially the parents. We ask the parents how old they are, what kind of work they do or did, how long they have been married, what part of the country they come from, and we ask every adult child in turn their marital status, whether or not they have children, where they live, and their occupation. Whenever we have something in common with a family member, we may comment on it in order to close the distance between us. If they would like to know something about us, we usually will answer these questions honestly. I think it helps to communicate in some form, without necessarily being explicit about it,

---

*I usually work with my wife, Dr. Felise B. Levine, as cotherapist, who is also a psychologist and family therapist.

that therapists are not immune to marital or family problems and that difficulties in these areas are well-nigh universal.

With some families one can josh and kid, whereas with others one has to be dead serious and "professional"; telling a joke to the latter kind of family would be like uttering an obscenity in church. In the old days this therapy behavior was called "establishing rapport"; now it is called "joining." It is helpful to let the family know that you appreciate how difficult it must have been for them to come in, and if you sense great reluctance at their being there (e.g., they have distasteful expressions or they don't take off their coats), it is useful to ask everyone how they feel about coming in. Another useful question is to ask each person what he/she would like to get out of the sessions. These questions will often reveal their fears, hopes, expectations, and understanding of the session. It may be the first time you discover what the family has been told about the session; you will find out that some families are well prepared and have their own agendas, whereas other families were told nothing and are bewildered as to what is expected of them. Families whose members have specific issues to deal with tend to have more productive sessions.

Early on it is appropriate to state the purposes of the session. The cotherapists state that they have been seeing the client in individual therapy or in marital therapy with his/her spouse; we tell them that the family may be aware of this. We say that since the kinds of problems people have with themselves or in their marriage are more understandable when viewed from the perspective of their experiences in their original family, we make it a practice to bring in the family of origin of the people we see. Another purpose of the meeting, we tell them, is to give all of them the opportunity to deal with issues they may have had with each other in the past or in the present. As strange as it may sound, we tell them, they may get to know each other even better. They are also told that sometimes, as issues come up, they may get upset or tearful or angry, but that these feelings are just a phase to go through. We indicate that our ultimate goal is to help them improve their family relationships, and the therapists' function is to assist them in achieving that aim.

The actual wording we use varies from family to family, but in our explanation of the session, we are trying to get across—albeit indirectly—several basic messages:

1. that the focus is not just on the client, but on everyone, the whole family;
2. that they are expected to deal with issues of consequence that have existed in the family;
3. that some rough times may lie ahead in the process of discussing the problems in the family;
4. that the therapists' role is not to treat them, but rather to function as facilitators in helping them deal with other;
5. that the bettering of relationships with each other is the guiding principle that makes the effort worth the pain; and
6. that our support provides the anesthesia for the anxiety that will be aroused.

Although we do not really expect that the families will fully comprehend these messages and will not understand until the latter part of the four hours, nonetheless the announcements do help set the tone of the meetings. These communications, at least, make the therapists feel better that they have put on record their own agenda and intentions. They also serve as a kind of informed consent for the family.

Despite the foregoing structure, most families initially believe that they are there to help the client or the person who requested the session. It is wise not to dispute this assumption, especially with resistant or "tight" families; the focus will gradually widen, as the session progresses, to include the interrelationships among all family members. Family-of-origin sessions, like most family therapy sessions, move in the direction of expanding awareness that the family members' problems are intertwined with each other. It rests on the skill and timing of the therapist to make palatable the transition from the "identified patient" to the family system. This process is advanced by the fact that everyone gets caught up in the emotional process as loaded topics are brought up and as the members interact with each other. In some families it becomes quickly apparent that some family members have to be handled with kid gloves; after we ask a few questions the extreme touchiness is obvious. A few parents or siblings announce at the outset that they have no intention of saying anything beyond their name and serial number. One sibling said, "If I hear any criticisms of my parents, I will walk right out." One father, who said, "I will not discuss anything from the past," said that if he brought up his acrimony about his children, there would be another cut-off. As expected, however, as the session progressed he could not deal with anything but the past. Very few family members are able to stonewall throughout the entire four hours. As a matter of fact, I saw this happen only once, with one family member.

The family-wide anxiety is manifested in a variety of ways in the early part of the first session. Some families are very guarded, responding with one-word answers to questions and looking as if they wished they were somewhere else, or were about to undergo root canal therapy without anesthesia. Some families talk with a forced rush of words, giving unsolicited protestations of their normality as a family, and saying such things as, "Doctor, we want you to know what a close, loving family we have." Other families speak in such abstract intellectualizations that I have to ask them not to talk like a textbook, that simple everyday language will help the session go better. A few families come in expecting a psychiatric interview, occasionally using DSM-III-R terminology to describe themselves or each other. The therapists indicate by their words and their manner that they are not there to "treat" the family, that they are not interested in diagnoses or how "sick" people may be; their role is explicitly defined as facilitators or consultants in helping the family members work through issues they may have with each other. It is not uncommon for some incoming family members to repeatedly proclaim that they view psychotherapy as "quackery"; usually, these are the ones who get the most out of the sessions.

On occasion, a family will come in combatively and start off with hostile and critical remarks aimed at the therapists. Great effort must be exerted by the therapists not to list their credentials, not to get defensive, and not to counterattack. The family will soon settle down, especially if you can get to the fear behind the anger or if you use well-timed humor to defuse their hostility. Incidentally, one *cannot* tell in advance, from the client's description, what the family will be like. I have heard clients describe their family as being like warm pussycats, and they come in attacking; I have also heard clients say their family is always angry and belligerent, and when they come in, we have a love-in. This kind of uncertainty is one of the reasons I do not like to conduct these sessions without a cotherapist. Family-of-origin sessions are unpredictable.

I am aware that the most anxiety-laden part of family-of-origin sessions is when the family members directly confront each other, face to face, often with truths that have been buried for so long and with dispelling of the family myths. Most of the resistances prior to the session had stemmed from these concerns. The clients, despite having been well prepared for the session, are sometimes fearful because they know what is coming. Because of these considerations, we try to postpone direct encounters of this nature until the second two hours, and if the confrontations threaten to come early on, and hint that they may be volcanic, we will attempt to soft-pedal, slow them down, or try to deflect from the heavy issues. Sometimes these events cannot be stopped, so we are forced to deal with and keep them under control.

CASE EXAMPLE

A young man had requested a family-of-origin session because he said his relationship with his father was too distant. He was not one of my regular clients, had come from out of town, and had not been prepared by us for the session. During the first few minutes of the session, he suddenly burst into tears and pleadingly said to his father, "I never felt you cared for me, and I want more closeness with you." The father crossed his arms on his chest and did not respond, so I knew my work was cut out for me. I acknowledged the young man's feelings and told him we would get back to them later, which we did when the father was more prepared to deal with his son.

There is a rule of thumb in family therapy that you are not supposed to discuss a family member who is not present. In family-of-origin sessions, I have found it helpful to discuss the absent member in the beginning of the session. This move is particularly useful if the missing person is a parent who is dead, usually the father. By focusing early on the deceased parent, the anxiety about the prospect of the family members who are present directly dealing with each other is eased, we learn more about the father and his meaning to the family, and, in addition, one can help the family work through some of their mourning (Paul & Grosser, 1965). The presence of a photograph of the deceased parent can help facilitate this process.

Sometimes, of course, the "absent-member maneuver" is operating—that is, the whole family has colluded to keep a significant member of the family away from the session (Sonne, Speck, & Jungreis, 1962). Whenever a family member who is expected to be there is not present, I explore the reasons for the absence. Usually I do not find out the real reasons for the absence until later in the session when the family feels more comfortable with us. Then I see how that individual's presence would have been threatening to the family's dynamic economy.

Some clients carry out our prior suggestions by telling parents and siblings the attributes they like and appreciate about them, acknowledging the good things they have received from their family, and thanking the family for coming in. Other clients tell me after the sessions that they "forgot" to tell their family those things. There are those clients, moreover, who do start the session by telling their family what had been going on in their own lives, often disclosing for the first time such news as their failing marriage, trouble with their kids, or deeper problems such as their inability to sustain an intimate relationship. Family members are frequently surprised to hear this news, saying they had no idea the client felt that way. These revelations usually get the family of origin off to a good start.

Not all clients are able to be this open in the early phases, even with the help of the therapists. Some of them become emotionally paralyzed in the early phases, like doctoral students taking the Ph.D. oral exam who cannot remember their own name. When the client is unable to talk, the therapists become more active by keeping the conversation going and by asking such general questions as, "What was it like growing up in this family?" Such a question usually stimulates discussion among the family members as different perceptions are put forth. We may inquire about the early years in the family, for example, by asking the parents what the client was like as a child. Another tactic to give the client time to get his/her thoughts together is to get a history of the family from the varied viewpoints. All of these maneuvers are considered as preparation for dealing with the prepared agenda, although there is value in the historical material.

Some clients, however, never do get to their agenda, or they deal with prepared issues obliquely because other family processes and issues take over. It is important for the therapists to be fairly active in the early phases; left to their own devices at this time, most families will become more anxious, angry, or detached. But the therapists' activity must be in a non threatening manner and tends to diminish as the family takes over.

In the beginning therapists should not behave too much like therapists—or, more accurately, in the way that people expect therapists to behave. Most clients (and families) expect therapists to take responsibility for the session, and for their lives, and it is tempting to meet these expectations. Although in some family therapy schools the therapist explicitly takes charge, is directive, and knows as the expert what is best for the family, in the family-of-origin sessions, at least by my particular method, such therapist behavior is contraindicated, especially later in the sessions. One level of dilemma for therapists conducting family-of-origin sessions is that while the therapists' obligation is to the whole family and not just to the client who initiated the session, *the visiting family members cannot be treated like patients.* They have not made a treatment contract and are not there for acknowledged help. We cannot ask "What are the problems?", so other methods of engagement are necessary.

Therefore, these sessions tend to be more social in the beginning. Certainly, you cannot intervene too quickly, or too deeply; you are in danger of losing the family if you do so. Premature interpretations are considered a sign of inexperience in all psychotherapies; in family-of-origin sessions they are definitely counterproductive. At the same time, one cannot stop being a therapist altogether. The compromise I have found to be most effective is to walk a fine line between being a consultant or facilitator and being a therapist, between guiding the session and yet having the family members be accountable for dealing with each other.

One aspect of the therapist's role is being like a traffic manager: redirecting questions, annotating, deciphering, and drawing attention to significant statements. Our activity usually consists of keeping the material flowing, using circular questioning, being supportive, asking people to respond to what another has said, and summarizing what they are saying (or perhaps going a step beyond what they are saying). Our metamessage, always, is that it is *their* session, *their* issues, and *not ours*. I may have to say, when they want to focus on the therapists, "Your problems having nothing to do with us; we occupy but a brief moment in your lives, whereas you all have a past history and will also have a long future together."

A striking example of the family wanting to deal with the therapists rather than with a family member, which occurs in nearly every family-of-origin session, is when a father wants to tell *me* how he views his son. I will usually have to repeat a number of times, "Don't tell me, tell your son." When he finally does talk directly to his son, he will do so in the third person ("he"). With one father I had to repeat 10 times the request that he address his son directly in the first person ("you"). Eventually, in most cases, family processes take over, and the family members will do what they are there to do; later on you do not have to remind them to address each other.

Sequences, Special Problems, and Caveats for Early Phases

After the family has settled down and has some idea of why they are there, issues begin to be dealt with, usually of neutral or moderate intensity. Those family members who plunge too quickly into heavy stuff (e.g., a parent's alcoholism) are slowed down, or the therapists divert to less risky or less intimidating material. Occasionally, in the first hour, when the therapists are still outside the family, the parents or siblings are mortified or outraged that the client is disclosing, in front of *strangers*, no less, the family's "dirty linen" or embarrassing family secrets. Some of these family members threaten to walk out of the session, perceiving that they were brought together to be humiliated. (Although a few family members have walked out, they always come back.) In these situations, the family may believe that the client's motive in organizing the session was of malicious intent, such as getting revenge on them for alleged maltreatment in the past or wanting to expose the family in all its private, naked ugliness. When this sort of event occurs and we inform the family that the ultimate goal of the client was and is to find a way to have a better relationship with parents and siblings, the anger diminishes and the atmosphere usually dramatically changes for the better. By the time the second two hours come around, and we are more in the family, they do not mind discussing intimate matters.

Family-of-origin sessions differ from each other considerably, even though there are certain predictable sequences. There are some dug-in families who never do let the therapists in and whose issues are probably too hot to handle. They perceive that disclosure of their secrets and myths would be too explosive and might have disastrous consequences. For example, one mother would not let her husband talk about *his* father, saying it could upset him and bring on a heart attack; she also refused to talk about her own mother. In some families there are hints of incest or sexual molestation, subjects which some families will not let us get near. There are some adult children who decide in advance that they are not going to deal with controversial issues or their anger toward parents. These kinds of families confine their discussions with each other to surface issues; sometimes they just share family stories about the "good old days." The latter types of sessions are not without value, however, because it is significant and salutary that the family got together at all.

Incidentally, the therapists can feel left out when families tell inside jokes or reminisce about past events, times, and places; this is *their* private family culture, access to which is closed to outsiders. When families relate their family stories, the therapists may feel excluded, so private associations about their own family stories may help attenuate feelings of isolation. Every therapist has personal associations to transactions that occur in family sessions. Along these lines I once wrote a paper on how the ghosts of the therapist's own family enter treatment sessions (Framo, 1968).

In addition to levels of candor and openness, other dimensions on which these sessions differ are readiness on the part of the client to bring up issues from the prepared agenda, perceptiveness of therapists in gauging the extent to which families are willing to go, the anxiety levels of both the families and the therapists, intensity of affect, content themes, and the degree of psychological-mindedness of the family. After about an hour or so most families begin to deal with issues of substance, usually prompted by an issue the client tentatively raises. It is always surprising to observe how different some clients behave with their original family, as contrasted with how they seemed when seen without the family. The clients who were forceful, articulate, verbal, insightful, and "together," in marital, individual, or couples group therapy sometimes, in the presence of their family, behave like children who don't know how to tie their own shoes. They will be silent, passive, stumble over their words, or utter inanities. Some clients need a push to get started, and the therapist has to gauge their readiness.

Other clients are well prepared and start bringing up sensitive topics, such as how they felt abused as children, or felt rejected, or thought the parents were too remote, cruel, uninterested in them, helpless, deceitful, always angry, selfish—all the complaints that people have about their parents. *The worst mistake a therapist can make in a family-of-origin session is to join the client in these criticisms and accusations.* Even the client who seems to be furious at the parent will ultimately resent it if the therapists are perceived as denigrating the parents. The therapists must tread a fine line between allowing the anger to come forth (but modulating its expression) and at the same time supporting the targets of the anger (usually the parents). The parents will need support at this time, which can be given in various ways.

I usually comment to clients that much of their recollection is based on childhood memories, which are subject to the normal magnification and distortion of small children, who can experience emotions only in gross categories. Another reassurance for the parents is to look for explanations for their own attitudes or behavior. Oftentimes, these adult children's resentments dissolve when they find out that at the time of the parent's harsh or neglectful behavior, the parents were going through difficulties that their children knew nothing about. Another parental behavior which almost always reduces bitterness, and which is interpreted by the aggrieved client (or sibling) as having a great significance, occurs when one or both parents apologizes for wrongs done to their child in the past. It is always interesting to observe the puzzlement and relief on the faces of the adult children as they try to reconcile this new information with the harsh memories of being wounded.

DESCRIPTION OF MIDDLE PHASES

Getting Past Anger and Negative Images

Unlike the psychotherapies where therapists try to get clients to get in touch with their anger toward their parents, I aim toward having clients get past their anger on the route toward compassionate understanding of parents. Consequently, we try to help the adult children to find out about and understand the extenuating circumstances that were present in their parents' lives, which help to explain any alleged mistreatment or indifference. We may, therefore, cast events in a different light and reframe apparently destructive or uncaring behaviors into good intentions.

CASE EXAMPLE

A client, joined by his sisters, castigated his parents for neglect, for being insensitive, for thinking only of themselves, and for only being interested in their mom and pop grocery store where they worked twelve hours a day, seven days a week. He also reproached his father for never taking him to a baseball game, or indeed for never having taken him anywhere. In response to this assault the parents were deeply hurt. During subsequent questioning, we learned that the parents, having lost all their money during the Depression, were terribly frightened of poverty and wanted to make sure that their children would at least have enough to eat. They honestly thought that they were fulfilling their obligations as parents by providing the necessities for their children. Besides, it was the way their parents had raised them. Furthermore, when the female cotherapist collected more information, she said to the mother, "You had four children in five years? That must have been awful, having three children in diapers! No wonder you couldn't pay enough attention to your kids." The adult children's resentments were no longer supportable in the light of these revelations, and they were forced to undergo that painful process of reappraisal that occurs when lifelong beliefs are found to be no longer tenable.

Some clients have an intense need to hold on to the negative image of the parents and need to nurse their hurts. It is only when the sessions are processed later that some of these "grudge-addicts" are able to let go of their vindictiveness. Some, unfortunately, despite all interventions, need to cling to their hatreds, are unable to exorcise their bad internal objects, and frequently project the badness onto their spouse. These are usually the clients who have multiple divorces. Oscar Wilde* once wrote, "Children begin by loving their parents. After a time they judge them. Rarely, if ever, do they forgive them." Forgiveness of parents is a central feature of family-of-origin sessions and usually happens during or following the sessions. This outcome is fortunate because when you forgive a parent you forgive yourself and do not have to suffer the manifold forms of self-hatred.

However, there are those adult children who cannot forgive. Their unconscious fantasy is that they will magically transform the hurtful past. They will savor the injustices to the end, citing such indictments as unfairness (that undeserved spanking that is never to be forgotten); negligence ("You were never there for me"); obliviousness ("You never really knew me, your own kid"); rejection, ("No matter what I did I never got your acceptance or admiration"); maliciousness ("You did some pretty rotten things to me"), and so on. These statements provoke pain, bewilderment, chagrin, guilt, and anger in the parents. One parent responded, "When are you going to stop blaming me? When is this over? Isn't there a statute of limitations for wrongs done by parents?" Such interchanges are a challenge to therapists who must be evenhanded about the conflicting interests; all of the therapist's deftness and artistry is summoned forth. And therapists are quite susceptible to countertransference reactions to these family transactions, based on incidents in their own family (Framo, 1968). It is intriguing to speculate whether another kind of transference reaction operates here: Do older therapists who have raised their children tend to be more sympathetic to the parents, and do younger therapists identify more with the adult children?

Except for those sessions where the family members walk on eggs to avoid controversy, anger and recriminations between family mem-

---

*From *A Woman of No Importance*, Act ii (1893).

bers are a near inevitable part of every family-of-origin session, a feature of this work that tends to frighten most people—therapists as well as clients. Some family therapists who work intergenerationally try to avoid having anger appear in these sessions by planning them in such a way that it does not happen. I view anger as an almost inescapable ingredient in the intergenerational encounter, stemming from the fact that all human beings require socialization in order to survive—a process bound to create some resentment toward parent figures, who, of necessity, must frustrate. As someone once put it, "No one has ever been loved the way everyone wants to be loved." The sense of outrage that we all feel about injustices done to us as children seems to be a deep and abiding one. Freud is presumed to have said (and if he didn't say it he should have) that what we love above all else is ourselves as children. Therefore, "How *could* they have done those awful things to that sweet, innocent child that was me?" The novel *Portnoy's Complaint* is a classic example of this anguished cry. I believe that since we are dealing with some of the deepest feelings in the human domain in family-of-origin sessions, with issues of psychic existence at stake, some passion is inescapable.

Carl Whitaker once put it differently: "The family is the place where there are life and death voltages" (1989). The anger in these sessions, as uncomfortable as it is at the time, is just a transition phase to be worked through, with positive feelings waiting on the other side. This process is analogous to the warm lovemaking that can occur between partners after the air has been cleared by a good fight. On the other hand, everlasting anger for anger's sake is out of bounds. *One worthwhile technique with alienated or embittered families is to have the mother and father tell each adult child what they like and appreciate about that person and, in addition, to have all their adult children tell each parent what good things they felt they got from that parent.* This intervention is particularly helpful in the later stages of sessions, which are characterized by implacable and mutual acrimony.

"Impossible" parents and justified anger. Thus far in this book you may have the impression that the client *should* absolve, understand, and be sympathetic to parents and siblings no matter what. Although most of these sessions usually have such outcomes, there

are those rare occasions where the attitudes or behaviors of some parents or siblings preclude *for the present* any kind of reconciliation or accommodation. Not all family members come in with good will or to make amends or work things out. Some are so obnoxious or difficult that the therapists' tolerance, skills, and countertransference reactions are challenged to the limit. Even though most of the abuses parents mete out to their children are found to be excusable or based on misunderstanding, some parents seem downright mean, rejecting, detached, unreachable, narcissistic, and so self-centered that they are oblivious to poignant entreaties from their children for acceptance or closeness. One can observe that these parents exercise the full range of guilt provocations, exploitation, tantalizing and never delivering (Fairbairn's [1952] "Exciting Object"), parentification, humiliations, teasing, accusations of treason, twisting their children's decent or autonomous motives into something evil or unhealthy, and having fixed views of their children that are impervious to reality.

In some families there is such massive deceit, dishonesty, doublebinding, and distortions of reality that I am reminded of the days, 30 years ago, when I saw schizophrenics and their families (Boszormenyi-Nagy & Framo, 1965). You know you are with this kind of family when you feel a little crazy yourself trying to make sense out of a situation where there is no meaning. In these kinds of families it is very difficult for clients to understand what is going on, much less to reconcile. For instance, most clients have a great need for parents to validate their memories, perceptions, and feelings about past events. When these validations occur, there is great relief and even an increase in self-worth in clients; they do not feel so crazy anymore. When clients do not get this confirmation—that what they remember did in fact occur—they vaguely distrust their own memory and senses and enter that perplexed state of mystification described so eloquently by Laing (1965). A family-of-origin session can provide the context for a long-term state of mystification to become transformed into a state of rage.

In the foregoing kinds of situations it is not easy, and even seems to be a travesty, for some clients to get past their anger and forgive. Clients who find their efforts to reach such parents to be futile, or are unable to help the parents take some responsibility for having inflicted emotional or physical injuries, will sometimes resent or feel betrayed by what they perceive as therapists' efforts to elicit premature forgiveness. As one client put it later in an individual session following the family-of-origin session, "You wanted me to forgive them too soon. Crimes were committed and you exonerated them while the jury was still out." How to balance the client's need for affirmation of past painful experiences with support of parents is a continuing critical test of therapist know-how.

What are adult children to do with the rage that fulminates inside of them when they see that one or both parents, or a sibling, is still crazy-making, double-binding, or rejecting? In these kinds of malignant situations, as well as the more benign ones where the parents are simply emotionally bankrupt and have nothing to give, follow-up individual therapy may be indicated. Although the sessions did not come up to their expectations, these clients are always glad they at least tried to work things out.

In later therapy sessions the clients may be able to abate or modulate their fury or their thwarted longing by recognizing that the parents did the best they could with what they had to work with. They will need to reconcile the wish with the reality; they will need help in accepting that their mother, father, or siblings are the way they are and that they will have to cut their losses and give up the dream. In these cases I emphasize that *just because the parents could not love, for reasons that may not be understood, does not mean that the client is unlovable.* Nor does it mean that clients should cut off from parents and give them up; the clients need coaching to become more of a differentiated self when with their parents (Bowen, 1978).

The titles of several popular books such as *Toxic Parents* (Forward, 1989) and *Divorcing a Parent* (Engle, 1990) suggest that some parents are so venomous that one should sever all contact with them. From my perspective, the knowledge that toxic parents had poison meted out to them should help one not take their behavior so personally. It is in one's own self-interest to understand and forgive even these kinds of parents without giving them up or sacrificing one's integrity of self (e.g., by taking "I" position stands, setting limits, commenting on double binds). Besides, I do not believe it is possible to divorce a parent; parents will always be in one's head.

Perhaps, having let go of the merger fantasy, clients may paradoxically get more from parents, or at least be able to get their needs filled elsewhere. Furthermore, at some time in the future some of the unconscious "seeding" that was done by the therapists during the family-of-origin sessions may germinate, and the parents or siblings may become less "impossible" or more available.

These worst circumstances that can occur during and after family-of-origin sessions, I repeat, are quite infrequent, and are more likely to occur with severely narcissistically wounded clients and families. In most of these consultations the various family members are genuinely trying to sort out their differences, their matters of substance, and find each other. During this process, although the exchanges can become pretty heated, there is an underlying sense of mutual caring. I suppose that when there is a complete absence of caring the family members would not have come in at all.

Sessions without anger. To be sure, not all adult children have negative feelings about their parents, not even residual anger. Indeed, some people who request family-of-origin sessions do so out of strong positive feelings toward parents and genuine concern for their welfare. The motive in these cases for having the family meeting is to give the parents a gift, much in the same way that adult children plan a celebration of the parents' 50th wedding anniversary. The family members may only be marginally aware that the kids are saying good-bye to their parents. During the sessions themselves, with these kinds of families, there is much sharing of family stories (Stone, 1989) and nostalgic resurrection of warm memories. When resentments and disappointments are mentioned, they are open and couched within the framework of deep understanding.

It should be remembered, however, that the natural state of feeling toward parents is one of ambivalence, and that even those clients who seem to have much bitterness toward parents usually yearn to vindicate them so that reconciliation would be possible. Only a small minority of clients have had revenge against their family as their overriding motive and are unable to let go of their acrimony.

Using humor. Humor, used judiciously, and appropriately timed, can sometimes defuse or detoxify the anger and apprehension that often permeate these sessions. The following interchange occurred in a family-of-origin session:

Mother:	"If you go ahead and marry that Jewish man, I will never allow your Jew kids in my house."
Daughter:	"Don't worry, you'll never see me."
Mother:	"Unless you can marry someone who comes from the right kind of family, I won't *want* to see you."
Daughter:	"You are a bigoted bitch."

Following this alliteration, mother stormed out of the office. After a bit the other daughter went after mother and brought her back. The tension in the room was unbearable, the daughters and mother were crying, and no one dared speak. At that point I said, "The one thing to keep in mind through all this . . . is whether Penn State is going to win the national football championship this year." Everyone cracked up and we went on from there. Subsequent to the anger phase in this case, mother and daughter made their peace with each other before the session was over.

The realization that parents are people. Another factor in these sessions that attenuates the anger is when the adult children hear some of the circumstances of their parents' backgrounds. When this information is not spontaneously proffered by the parents, we specifically ask each parent to give a brief history of their own family. Although the adult children may have heard some of the history before, there is something about this context that enables them to really hear the deprivations their parents may have been subject to, thereby helping them to view their parents more sympathetically. Sometimes the adult children, for the first time, are hearing some facts about a parent's family. One father, who had been abusive to his children when he was drunk, disclosed how he had lost his parents when he was six years old and how he had been shifted from one foster home to another, in some of which he had been severely beaten, not given food, and had been sexually molested. Following this disclosure his children, astonished at hearing this for the first time, clustered around the weeping father and hugged him.

Keeping the Discourse Going

During these middle phases, when the substantive issues are being dealt with, we intervene only enough to keep the discourse going. When meaningful dialogues or trialogues are going on, it is advisable for the therapists to stay out of the way. Usually, one person in the family, often a sibling, becomes the therapists' ally; this is the person who is most willing to risk and to open things up. This individual may make a comment like, "Haven't any of you wondered why so many of us are divorced?" Although siblings are usually helpful in opening up the system, occasionally they sabotage sessions or they act as spokespersons for the parents' resistance. In one session, whenever the client tried to bring up something important, his sister would make a remark like, "Why do you have to dredge that up?" Although the parents seemed to be cooperating, it soon became apparent that the sister's role in the family was to voice the parents' negativity.

Sibling relationships. There are times when the sibling relationships come to the fore. Often siblings review their past relationship with each other, when they were children; they explore past misunderstandings, family alliances, and impressions of each other, often finding out that each thought the other was the favorite. They get a chance to hear what the other siblings were experiencing during significant family events, and they check out each other's perceptions of the parents. In one family the siblings shared the view that one late consequence of their parents' venomous divorce had been that they were all damaged in their ability to sustain an intimate relationship. Sometimes a brother or sister is surprised to learn that their siblings felt the same way about something or somebody: "It's really a relief to find out I wasn't the only one who hated Aunt Emma, with her sloppy kisses and her mustache!" Instead of, as usually happens in families, only dyads sharing secrets, now the whole family is in on it. I have been impressed with how these sessions often increase the sibling bonds and caring; even prior cutoffs tend to get repaired.

There are also occasions when a sibling or parent monopolizes the session (or gets the most out of it). Some clients are not unhappy about that, saying they are glad that that person was able to use the session productively. Other clients, not able to admit that they felt some resentment, handle the matter by scheduling another family-of-origin session so they can deal with their own issues.

The cotherapists work together. During all this time the cotherapists are working in tandem, exchanging views in front of the family and sometimes splitting their functions. For instance, one therapist may shore up the parents while the other may confront the client. One therapist may tell clients that they were not just passive victims and that they must take some responsibility for their contribution to the family distress. The therapists, having already had a strong and trusting relationship with the client, can risk challenging the client or supporting the parents. Although some clients have resented this apparent side-taking at the time, later they are usually grateful for these therapist stances. The cotherapists can also help each other through difficult or embarrassing situations. For instance, when I feel especially frustrated or angry in a session with irksome people, and I am about to remove the velvet in my "velvet hammer" (as someone once characterized my approach), my cotherapist may joke and tease them out of their defensiveness. Sometimes one of the therapists is stuck and does not know where to go, and it is comforting to know that one's flank is protected and that the cotherapist will come up with something. When both therapists feel especially confused or lonely they may converse with each other about what is going on in the session, in the presence of the family.

The Marriage Relationship of the Parents

One of the most loaded topics in family-of-origin sessions is the marriage relationship of the parents, and one has to evaluate whether a given family will let you touch that topic. Although some parents talk freely of their marital difficulties, others regard their marriage as off-limits and greatly resent what they see as an invasion of their privacy. After all, they might say they came to the session to help their son or daughter, not to discuss a personal matter like their marriage. Nonetheless, there are occasions, in certain closed-off families, or when the client is too frightened to raise the issue, when I will state the forbidden and tell the parents, for instance, that I understand that they are about to separate. On these occasions, the disclosure leads to an opening up of the family. Some parents, at the end of family-of-origin sessions, ask for names of marriage therapists in their hometowns, a request I have always met.

All children wish their parents loved each other and when, over the years, there is much evidence to the contrary, children despair that they themselves can love or be loved. In the family-of-origin sessions there are occasions when the rancor and contempt between the parents becomes undisguised, much to the distress of the adult children. We have found it helpful in these situations to explore with the parents how they met and what their courtship was like. Children are always fascinated to hear the courtship stories, and sometimes they are amused and even embarrassed that their "old" parents once were romantic and did all the foolish things lovers do. However, I believe it necessary for these adult children to hear that these now-alienated parents once loved each other, for if they did not, then there is the belief that there is no love in this world or that the family unit is a fraud.

The Hiatus and the Second Session

As indicated previously, the family-of-origin sessions are divided into two two-hour sessions, with a break in between (a break of an evening when held over two days, and an interruption of several hours when held in one day). At the end of the first two hours we suggest to the family that they think about the things they want to deal with in the next segment. During the hiatus some families go out to dinner together, some go their separate ways; some family members continue the session on their own, whereas others avoid discussion altogether. Some people are unable to sleep that evening. It often happens that a dyad (two sisters, a brother and sister, a mother and daughter, etc.) will talk all night. Fathers usually do not say much in between sessions.

The great majority of families, when they return for the second segment, are primed to start dealing with the real stuff about their family—the dispelling of myths, the disclosure of secrets, the revealing of the covert alliances, the hidden loyalties, the collusive role assignments, and how the family members interpersonally resolve their inner conflicts. More honest talk occurs in the second two hours and a sibling may say, "Okay folks, it's time for the truth." The parents, since they are in the middle-age or late stocktaking stage, where they have been undergoing life review, are more prepared to re-evaluate their relationship with their adult children, are more open to reveal their own past traumas and unrealized hopes, their longings, and some can even approach the fearful subject of their approaching death. In the second two hours the therapists do not have to work so hard in getting the family to discuss important issues. It is the rare family who stonewalls in the second segment. When they really get down to work the insides of the family become exposed, and although it is scary, it is, at the same time, liberating.

Family Revelations and Their Effects on Therapists

The emotional transactions that occur in these sessions, especially at this time, can be very powerful indeed. The therapist(s) will, at various times, feel sad, mystified, anxious, entranced, crazy, joyful, surprised, confused, enraged, and moved to the core. It is painful to observe family members reach out to each other and not be able to touch. One remembers the fundamentalist father saying to his needy son, "I don't want you to love me. I want you to love Jesus." One is uncomfortable when a daughter, with great fear, tells her parents she is a lesbian. One is troubled when the adult children tell their therapist-parents that the parents gave greater priority to their clients than to their children. One is touched by the woman who related how, when her hated, immigrant mother was dying, she sang to her a Russian lullaby that her mother had always sung to her. One is touched by the fragile moment of a son asking a father, "Who are we to each other? . . . I need for you to let me give you something." One is embarrassed by seeing a renowned physician regress and cry and beg his mother not to say anymore that she doesn't have much time left. One is uneasy witnessing the son or daughter push aside the intrusive, hurt mother and try to reach the closed-off father. There is the pleasure in viewing alienated parents and adult children, or siblings, meet and embrace and "see" each other.

Some disclosures can be shocking and can raise the hairs on the back of one's neck: One woman, amidst convulsive sobs, told her father, a professional survivor through war and concentration camp, "When I was a child I had the eerie feeling that if there was nothing left to eat, *you would eat me.*" One can identify with the daughter who expresses regret that she was deprived of relationships with cousins because of the feuds the parents had with their siblings. I empathize with the adults who struggle against identification with parents and are terrified that they will become like them (Greenson, 1954). One can witness in these sessions what I have called the "gut" issues of family life—profound caring, rejection, dehumanization, shaming, hypocrisy, futility, compassionate sacrifice, disqualification, paralysis of feeling, devotion, disappointment, conspiracies of silence, deep satisfaction, persecution, safety, and the joy of belonging. The potential for countertransference reactions is great, although the concept of countertransference does not adequately describe the effects on therapists that family-of-origin sessions can have. That dead father they mourn can become your father, that mother's affectionate gesture can transport you back to your ninth birthday, the protectiveness and affection between two brothers or a brother and a sister can evoke a pleasant remembrance, and the argument between the parents may revive the memory of having heard *that* fight before (Framo, 1968).

New or First Behaviors

There are repeated "firsts" in these sessions, following the initial phases. For the first time a quiet, reticent father opens up or cries; for the first time a garrulous mother listens instead of talks; the first time the adult children hear about a secret half-sibling; the first time that arrogant brother apologizes; the first time an old misperception gets clarified; the first time Dad stands up to Mom or Mom defies Dad; and the first time, following years of alienation, the family members can "make up" and forgive each other. In quite a few of these families there has been a long history of cutoffs, sometimes extending back for generations. One family cutoff was iatrogenic in that a woman who went for individual therapy and told her therapist how terrible her parents were, was told by her therapist, "Your family is a bunch of cannibals! Stay away from them!" When this woman brought her family in for a family-of-origin session she had literally followed her therapist's edict and had not seen them for 12 years (in the intervening years she had been in and out of mental institutions). With families where there have been long-term estrangements it is not easy to bridge the gulf of time, distance, misunderstanding, and vendetta. Sometimes the chasm is light-years wide. But the fact that they agreed to come in, and for the first time in years they have all gotten together in one room, demonstrates the wish to patch the rift.

The Importance of Family Members' Peripheral Comments

Harry Stack Sullivan (1947) used to say that the "marginal thoughts" of clients in psychotherapy were more significant than what they were directly talking about. This dictum is especially valid for family therapy sessions where statements of great consequence, aimed at no one in particular, are spoken under the breath or said so softly one could hardly hear them. Some observations by family members, seemingly put forth as casual throwaways, often turn out to have much import. One must be attuned to "hearing" such remarks; sometimes the nonverbal behavior provides the clue. For example, one daughter said in a whisper something to the effect that her uncle (mother's brother) was too affectionate at times, a hint which prompted me to ask her whether she meant he had made sexual advances to her. This inquiry prompted significant glances between all the daughters, and then I knew I had stumbled onto an incest situation, confirmed later in the session. These peripheral comments are usually related to a shameful family secret, such as a history of child abuse. Occasionally, these veiled remarks are sarcasms or curses that the person would be too afraid to utter aloud.

Fostering Positive Interactions and Clarifying Misconceptions

In addition to being alert to the undercurrents of the interactions, we tend to reinforce the benign motives that are commonly behind apparent negative behaviors. We redefine perceived malicious intents and we relabel ostensible hostility as perhaps not being so purposeful. The systemic family therapy schools make frequent use of reframing and positive connotation, and these techniques certainly have their place in family-of-origin sessions, especially considering the extreme sensitivities in these unique situations.

We spend much time dealing with the unrealistic expectations that all people have about their parents (not unrelated to the unrealistic expectations everyone has of their marriage partners), and we explore the possible misconceptions that arise from the distorted memories of childhood. For instance, one woman had carried with her for many years the mistaken memory that she was hospitalized as a child because "my mother was too upset to take care of me." As it turned out, the mother said her daughter had been placed in the hospital under orders from her physician. There are those individuals who come to realize that it is possible for them to enjoy being with a parent; they may, during a session, come to see a pleasurable side to a parent that they had never noticed before. On the other hand, some clients have great difficulty accepting positive changes in their parents. One woman said, "They are more now what I wanted them to be, but it's too late. I still can't accept them." A useful technique to use with unforgiving clients is to have them reduce their expectations of their parents to zero, to absolute nothing, to make no demands, and to accept parents exactly as they are. Sometimes the parents under these circumstances can give more, and the clients can come to accept more.

FINAL PHASES: WEAVING TOGETHER THE THEMES AND MAKING HEALING INTERVENTIONS

During the final phases we attempt to weave together the apparently disparate themes from the preceding hours. We also encourage each dyad combination in the family, in turn, to face one another and dialogue about their relationship. As we approach the end of the four hours of sessions we start implementing a process of restoration and attempt to build in the mechanisms for future betterment of the family relationships. I like to introduce antibodies, so to speak, that will help prevent later tendencies for the family members to be either too disconnected from each other or, at the other extreme, too intertwined.

Occasionally, I will encounter a disengaged family whose members, having faced the extent of their uninvolvement with each other during the session, feel discouraged that they can ever become a family unit. Under these circumstances I tell them something like, "You *are* a family. This is a pretty rough world and everyone needs a family as a refuge. Everyone needs to belong to a family where people care for each other and come through for each other in emergencies. When someone in the family is born or gets married or dies, be there! These are the only blood relatives you will ever have." With enmeshed or fused families we work out issues of boundaries, autonomy, and distance regulation, and I indicate that families can achieve separateness without isolation. I tell them that only independent, autonomous people can truly love and that they pay a high price for all of them to be on the same central nervous system. When people feel each other's pain too much, they drag each other down. On the other hand, this kind of family is reassured that they will remain a caring family. With both the alienated and merged families, we have the family members face each other and attempt to negotiate what kinds of relationships they want from each other and what they can and cannot get from each other.

A recurring fear expressed by clients prior to their family-of-origin session is that at the end of the sessions the family will be left bleeding on the operating table. This eventuality never really happens when the therapist is experienced in this kind of work and provides the caring that is the anesthesia for the pain. One client wrote after her family-of-origin session, "I was grateful that you let my family go without any pieces left dangerously hanging out." A major therapeutic goal at the conclusion of the sessions is to have the family feel good about itself when they leave. When parents express the feeling that they must have failed as parents, we tell them, "You must have done something right. Your kids turned out pretty good." We stress the healthy features in the family, the depth of caring (even if they do not express it openly), and how we found them to be a really nice family. Once in a while we have to search hard for something to like, but this is rare. When you get to know people well enough and what they have had to struggle with, even the most offensive people become understandable and, therefore, more sympathetic as persons.

Just before the end of the session we stress that it would be desirable for everyone to listen to the tapes of the session and also to make copies to send to any member of the family who had to be absent. They are told that listening to the tapes will enable them to view themselves and the family with more objectivity; they will notice things that they overlooked at the time they were happening. We offer them future sessions, stating that our door is always open, and we indicate that we have simply started a process that they should continue on their own. Because of financial-geographical considerations, only about 10% follow through with subsequent sessions.

In the follow-up study on clients who had had family-of-origin sessions, a number indicated that they would have liked to have a session afterwards with one particular family member, even though they did not ask for one at the time (Baker, 1982). Consequently, I now offer the opportunity for any subsystem of the family to come in for a separate ensuing session (e.g., father and daughter, mother and son, sister and brother, etc.).

Families as a whole and individual family members have varied reactions in the closing moments of the last session. Some appear to be puzzled, some are in a state of euphoria, some are pensive and thoughtful, some look disappointed, and with others you really cannot tell how they feel. Whatever the reaction, we all know we have experienced together the powerful insides of the family and thus have become bound by our shared journey. Where there has been an emotional cutoff of long standing (say between father and son, two sisters, etc.) and they meet and connect and hug, these are very moving moments for everyone, including the therapists (who are sometimes included in the hugs). I have had some great scenes in my office, right out of an Arthur Miller play.

5

Postsession Developments and Results

• processing of family-of-origin sessions; feedback of family-of-origin findings to individual and marital problems

CLINICAL FINDINGS

It is necessary to keep in mind that most clients originally entered therapy for marital problems except for those out-of-town people who requested the family-of-origin sessions. Although most couples continue with either marital therapy or with the couples group following the family-of-origin session, some couples come only one or two more times. As stated previously, these couples regard the family-of-origin sessions as the culmination of treatment. Notwithstanding, it is necessary to debrief or process the family-of-origin sessions with the client. Of course debriefing is not possible with those clients who requested family-of-origin sessions and who came with their families from long distances. In those cases I suggest that they or another family member write to us in the future, giving follow-up information, but only rarely has anyone followed through. Some of these family members, who are already in therapy with another therapist in their hometowns, integrate the experience into their own therapy. I highly recommend that they listen to or watch the tape of the family-of-origin session with their regular therapist, provided the family gives permission.

At the therapy session after the family-of-origin session, I ask the client to give me his or her observations about the session, uninfluenced by my views. Some clients are elated, some are anxious, some are confused, and still others report being "stunned." I view the perplexity as a hopeful sign that lifelong beliefs may have been challenged by the session and some heretofore fixed views of a parent or sibling may no longer be tenable. One can detect in wistful statements that there is grieving over the loss of a pet hate or one's literal first loves.

If the individuals are in a couples therapy group, they tell the group what happened during the sessions, and give their impressions. The group is always intensely interested; other group members will say things like, "I thought about you all week and couldn't wait to find out how your session turned out." Some group members are engrossed in the client's account because they have already had their family-of-origin session and want to compare that one with their own. Others, who are considering whether or not to have a family-of-origin session, are eagerly waiting to hear whether the session was worth having. Since the majority of individuals give positive reports, most reluctant group members are swayed to go ahead with their own plans to have the session. This observation helps explain why the couples group format is perhaps the best for overcoming the inherent resistance. On occasion an individual will report that a family member had an adverse reaction to the sessions. Upon hearing that statement, a group member may become temporarily discouraged about having the session. In these circumstances I state that several months need to go by before the impact of the sessions can be evaluated. To be sure, there can be delayed negative as well as positive reactions, although I have only heard of two long-term negative reactions out of over 500 family-of-origin sessions I have conducted.

Most clients, when they relate how they experienced their family-of-origin sessions, first express relief, saying something like, "It wasn't nearly as bad as I thought it was going to be." Following their own reflections on the sessions, the clients are asked to communicate the responses of each of the family members after the last family-of-origin session is over. Then, we ask the spouse of the client to give his or her perceptions, since the spouse has observed the partner's and in-laws' behavior before and after the session, but also, on occasion, because the spouse has already listened to the session tapes. It has been my experience that the clients almost always listen to the tape recordings of their family-of-origin sessions, the spouses of the client usually do so, sometimes the siblings listen to them, but rarely do the parents want to listen to the recordings. When asked by their children why they did not listen to the tapes several replied, "And go through that all over again?"—a statement suggesting how anxiety-provoking the sessions are for the majority of parents. For the parents, listening to the tapes may be comparable to reviewing the experience of a troubled dream.

Finally, the therapists' give their impressions of the whole experience, including some thoughts about the family dynamics as well as about each family member. We note things that the client, having been so anxious at the time, may have missed. We stress again to the client that the overlooked events can be recaptured by listening to the session tapes.

I have noticed, by the way, that the client-therapist relationship is strengthened after the family-of-origin session. There is more intimacy and a peer-like quality to the relationship, stemming from having gone through the experience together. But it is interesting to note that sometimes there is a wide discrepancy between the way the therapists viewed the session and the way it was perceived by the client. There have been occasions where we thought the family-of-origin session went poorly and the client said it was "great," as well as vice versa. I recall one in particular where I thought that the father, who had been hospitalized frequently for psychosis, was off the wall during the session, whereas the client said, "Wasn't that session wonderful? That was the clearest I've ever seen my dad."

Incidentally, I have often been asked whether any of the family members who come to family-of-origin sessions are psychotic, and of course the answer is yes. I must say, however, that in this context psychotic family members usually pull themselves together during the sessions and instead of playing the role of mental patient, they are father, mother, brother, or sister. I have also seen "senile" parents or grandparents be quite lucid during sessions. Some of these old people have Alzheimer's disease, but there is something about the context that enables them to pull themselves together.

Results of Baker's Study

Before reporting further clinical findings of the family-of-origin sessions, it would be appropriate to cite the results obtained in a systematic follow-up study cited earlier. Baker (1982), studying the effects on the marital relationship of the family-of-origin sessions, received follow-up questionnaires from 71 clients who had been seen in marital or couples group therapy with Framo. A self-report, researcher-designed questionnaire was utilized. All clients had entered therapy conjointly for marital problems, and 84% reported improved relationships with their partners following the therapy. Forty-three of the 71 clients had family-of-origin sessions and they reported greater improvement in their marriage than those who did not have the sessions: 76% reported improved relationships with mothers, 55% improved relationships with fathers, 60% improved relationships with sisters, and 52% improved relationships with brothers. Almost two-thirds of the family-of-origin group indicated the contacts with original family members had changed for the better overall, and over three-quarters were in contact with a family member with whom they had not been in contact prior to their therapy. This latter finding suggests that family members other than actual participants in the family-of-origin sessions become affected by the process and that these "spreading effects" may suffuse throughout the extended family systems.*

Since the clients had originally entered therapy for marital difficulties, these data reveal possible wide-ranging benefits from this intergenerational approach. Furthermore, the follow-up study was based largely on clients who had been out of therapy for several years (some as long as nine years after therapy termination), and it is noteworthy that the positive changes in the family relationships lasted as long as they did. Long-term follow-up outcome studies are scarce in the family therapy literature; most outcome studies are done at the end of the therapy, a time when clients are most likely to report positive results. This study, however, does have shortcomings: the sample

---

*In a book in preparation on a full length family-of-origin consultation, after the family-of-origin session, the father took his son on a journey across the country, seeking out all his relatives (Framo, Weber, & Levine, in press).

size was limited, the data were based mainly on clients' self-reports, and family interaction data were lacking. Laham (1990) reworked Baker's data in a replication study and found that all of the subject sample reported "good" or "moderate" marital adjustments following the family-of-origin intervention.

Beyond Statistics

Aside from the limitations of this particular study, systematic research on a complex, multilayered phenomenon like psychotherapy often conceals as much as it reveals. There are certain therapy experiences which go beyond statistics or scientism. Consequently, it is believed by this author that the flavor and essence of what happened as a result of the family-of-origin session is best communicated by a phenomenological, clinically impressionistic approach that captures the human responses. Here is a sampling of remarks made by clients at the therapy session after the family-of-origin session:

"It was the most difficult thing I've ever done, but the most helpful."

"I feel like I have a family again."

"Before the session I felt I was my mother and she was me. Now I feel more separate as a person."

"In a funny kind of way I feel liberated or freed."

"Some nameless dread that was always present in my family seems to have been removed by the session."

"I was afraid of my father through most of my life, but now he not only doesn't intimidate me anymore, but I feel sympathetic toward him."

"I'm glad I got to know my sister better."

"I thought that my brother, who needed it, got the most out of the session."

"My dad, who said practically nothing during the session, and who never calls me, afterwards has been calling me every day."

"I was really surprised that my Dad talked as much as he did."

"I never realized before how much deprivation had been present in my mother's life, from her own family."

"I particularly appreciated the way you two [the therapists] han-
dled my parents, with respect and empathy."
"I feel better about my family, myself, and my wife and kids."
"I don't hate my parents anymore."
One client humorously said, "I still hate my parents, but now I
hate them on a more mature level."

Not all immediate reactions to the family-of-origin sessions are
favorable. Some people are angry afterwards. One of the reasons
there can be an escalation of hostility during and after the session is
that unspoken dormant conflicts, which had been disguised or
expressed through symptoms, become more explicit and open.
Sometimes a client is disappointed in the outcome; one client said, "I
thought it would cure me." I get occasional reports that a mother was
"very upset" afterwards, and from time to time I hear that family
members are sorry they came to the session. There are times that the
client reacts to the sessions with apparent indifference, and there are
occasions when a client "acts out" in a detrimental way right afterwards (for example, making an abrupt life change without delibera-
tion). These proximate negative responses will be discussed at length
in the next chapter on "Difficulties, Limitations, Pitfalls, and
Contraindications."

Short-term and Long-term Reactions

A distinction needs to be made between short-term and long-term
reactions to the session. I regard the short-term reactions as a stage in
an ongoing process. It usually takes a while for the material from the
family-of-origin sessions to be assimilated. One cannot tell what the
outcome of these sessions will be, based on short-term negative or
positive reactions.

CASE EXAMPLE

A conference participant approached me after my workshop stating that she was in a relationship that meant a great deal to her,
but she was "messing it up." She went on to say that she hated her

father, hated all men as a matter of fact, and she had not seen her father for the last 13 years. She then said that she had been listening to my presentation and she wondered whether it might be helpful to contact her father and have a family-of-origin session. She had six brothers and sisters and her parents were divorced. I told her that if she could get them all to come in, I would see them without charge provided I could videotape the session and use the tape for educational purposes. I forgot this conversation quickly because I never thought she would follow through, but a week later she called to tell me her whole family was coming in. We learned in the session that the father had been a brutalizing alcoholic who drove all his children out of the home when they became teenagers. However, for the first time, the children heard the details of his upbringing: His mother was a prostitute and he was raised by a grandmother who was very cruel, always threatening to put him, "the little bastard," into an institution.

Following the family-of-origin session, the client asked to see me; she was quite depressed after the session "because I cannot reconcile my hatred all these years of my father with that poor pathetic person I saw in the session." What this woman was struggling with, of course, was her attempt to integrate the internalized representation of the father with the real person who was her father. Her depression was short-lived as she came to terms with her ambivalence. There were two major outcomes of her sessions which occurred several months later: The father, who had been an outcast of the family, began to be included in family events, and the client's relationship with her boyfriend improved.

Indirect Results and Spreading Effects

The beneficial effects of the family-of-origin session are often indirect, subtle, and unexpected. One client's sister did not attend the session because she "did not believe in families." I had suggested she be sent a copy of the session tape. The client wrote to me several months later: "My sister, who did not attend the session, is now a participating member of the family, which was not true before." A client who had been in and out of mental hospitals interrupted this pattern and got a job for the first time in her life following her family-of-origin session; it is interesting, however, that she did not connect this event with her session.

Intergenerational work can be especially helpful to families where a prior, calamitous divorce had left many scars, such as unending bitterness and cutoffs. These sessions can help bring about an emotional divorce between parents who have been destructive to each other since the divorce, and the adult children can work out a way of having contact with each parent, without feeling disloyal to the other parent.

There can also be "spreading" effects of the session involving extended family members not seen. A number of people have been stimulated to search out relatives following the sessions.

CASE EXAMPLE

The father of a client was urged to see his brother from whom he had been alienated for many years. He said, "I do not want to die without having made peace with my brother. Because of my parents' will, he felt he was cheated out of the inheritance, and the last time I went to see him he slammed the door in my face, so I'm afraid of being rejected again." I persuaded him to try again, which he did, taking along his son, and this time his brother hugged him. The client reported later that his father was very grateful that he got his brother back, and the client was glad that he got an uncle in the bargain. The client went on to say, "All the aunts are now calling each other up, trying to figure out what happened."

Upset mothers. One problem I have had difficult dealing with is that several times I have been requested to see "upset" mothers alone after the family-of-origin session. Ordinarily, I have no problem with this, but I came to realize that sometimes the family was trying to get me to handle the mother instead of dealing with her themselves. Usually, these mothers are the kind that the family find "impossible" to deal with. I have managed this dilemma by seeing the mother with at least one other family member. In this way I resolve the conflict between my conceptual orientation and my need to respond to human distress. Following the family-of-origin sessions we sometimes see other subsystems of the family (e.g., mother and daughter, only the siblings, only the parents, two brothers, father and son, etc.).

Effects of Sessions on Marriages

From my theoretical viewpoint, the family of origin sessions should have an effect on the marital relationship—either to improve the marriage or, in cases of "hopeless" marriages, to enable the partners to end them. As a rule, the marital relationship of the couple improves, especially if both partners have had family-of-origin sessions. Because energy has been freed up by the session, and because their transference meaning has changed, the mate and children benefit. In fact, this is one of the major payoffs for the spouse, which helps make his or her exclusion from the session more palatable. There are, to be sure, some instances where the family-of-origin session could have deleterious repercussions on the marriage or, indeed, no observable effect on the marriage at all.

A few clients in Baker's study (1982) reported that the family-of-origin sessions helped them as individuals and that relationships with parents and siblings improved, but that their marriage did not change. It would be worthwhile to study systematically the circumstances under which marriages improve following the intergenerational intervention and when they do not. In any event, most marriage relationships do change for the better following the family-of-origin sessions. And couples in therapy who had been living together, and were reluctant to commit themselves to a legal relationship, tend to get married after the family-of-origin sessions.* Some of the mythologies get cleared up and the transference distortions that occur in the marital relationship become lessened. Partners often report that they can now "hear" what the spouse has to say, and they are more able to discriminate between their projections and those of their partners. Their separate realities become more known to each other. Some are now able to clearly identify the connection between

---

*In the movie *Memories of Me*, the man is unable to commit himself to the woman he loves until he is able to work out a relationship with the father from whom he had been estranged (MGM/United Artists, 1988).

material gained from their family-of-origin session and what they expected from a spouse. For instance, one man "discovered" in the family-of-origin session how much he had striven all his life for his father's admiration. His secret agenda of marriage was that it was a wife's job to devote herself to his occupational advancement so that his father would take pride in his accomplishments. This marital expectation and demand created havoc in the marital relationship, especially since his wife's goal involved getting *her* father to extol *her* attainments. The following case history illustrates how family-of-origin and marital dynamics are interconnected.

CASE EXAMPLE

Suzie, age 26, and Joe, age 27, entered marital therapy after they had separated. Suzie had left Joe because she was frightened of his periodic rages. Suzie had her own difficulties, such as having a low tolerance for conflict and suggesting that marriage was akin to playing house; for instance, she had to get up in the morning before Joe so he would never see her without makeup. Her problems were not that deep, however, and were rather easily worked out in the couples group, especially when she learned from other couples some of the realities of married life.

Joe was another story. We discovered early that he and his father had been having violent arguments for many years. Joe had been in "family therapy" as a youngster, but the family therapy consisted of each member of the family being seen separately. He described his father as rejecting, cruel, uninterested in him, and always putting him down. Their arguments were so built into their relationship that when Father had a heart attack and Joe went to see him in the hospital, they had another argument. Mother was described as the peacemaker and his sister as not being that involved in the family conflicts.

Joe was very resistant to bringing in his family, saying it would not do any good and, besides, why give his father another chance to put him down—this time in front of the therapists? He acceded, finally, but only because he wanted to prove to the therapists just how unreasonable and rejecting his father really was. Besides, he predicted his father would refuse to come in. But Father quickly agreed. In the family-of-origin session Joe and his father immediately went at each other. We stopped the argument and engaged the father in dialogue with us. As the session progressed it became obvious that this father was desperately trying to reach out to his son and longed for a better relationship with him. It seemed to be Joe who had too much invested in nursing past hurts. During the session Joe expressed disappointment that the therapists did not take his side against his father, but later said that basically he was pleased we had not done so.

Another pattern that became apparent was the role of the mother in all this. She said that early in her relationship with her husband she felt she could not tangle with him, so she avoided conflict with her husband and let Joe deal with him, playing the game of, "Let's you and him fight."

A week later I got a call late in the evening from the father who said the family was having a confrontation on their own, and they felt like they were on the brink of a breakthrough, but could not quite make it. He asked if they could come right over. In this session, for the first time, father and son really listened to each other. Also, for the first time, Joe and his sister learned about their father's own family background and what he had had to struggle with in his relationship with his own father. Mother finally let Joe off the hook by beginning to deal with her own conflicts with her husband. Father and son hugged each other. After several weeks, Suzie, astonished at the absence of Joe's rages, suggested they live together again. When the therapy ended both said they felt truly married for the first time.

Further Clinical Findings

Some parents and siblings are already in therapy elsewhere when they come to family-of-origin sessions, or they enter either marital or individual therapy afterwards. The clients, who are usually the responsible ones of the family, are relieved that the parents are getting the help they have long needed. Individual therapy can help people integrate the family transactions with intrapsychic material; the complex interchange between the introjects and the external objects can be explored more intensively in the one-to-one therapy situation. It is as if these individuals are freer to examine themselves now that some of the family myths and realities have been exposed and dealt with.

I should mention that when clients terminate either marital or couples group therapy and state that while they are not yet ready to have a family-of-origin session, they will have the session in the future, it has been my experience that they rarely follow through. The context or momentum that is created in the therapy motivates them, and without this context the incentive fades.

As stated previously, ordinarily some time has to go by before the effects of the family-of-origin sessions will be felt and noticed by the family. The consequences of the sessions generally cannot be determined accurately immediately after the session. For example, one client seemed quite indifferent to his family-of-origin session just after it was held. Several months later, when I was trying to get another resistant client to bring in her family, this fellow told her in the couples group, "You really ought to do it. I now have the best relationship with my mother that I ever had." It takes time for the events of the sessions to filter through the preconceptions, to undo the misunderstandings, to enable one to re-examine the relationships in the light of new experiences, and to let go of old beliefs. The delayed effects of the sessions can be manifested in subtle ways: more open discussion of former taboo topics, more frequent contact between family members formerly out of touch, and the most significant of all human dimensions, a deeper sense of trust of each other. Based on my experience with many family-of-origin sessions, I think the fact that a family gets together at all—no matter what transpires in the sessions—has a powerful, deep impact on a primitive level. Following these sessions, the family can never again be exactly the same.

Further results and clinical findings of these sessions and their meaning and significance will be given in the chapters on Theoretical and Clinical Implications.

6

Difficulties,
Limitations, Pitfalls,
and Contraindications

COMPETITION AMONG FAMILY THERAPY SCHOOLS

If one were to examine in simplistic fashion the development of any field of endeavor, the following stages might be postulated:

1. The stage of observation and discovery of phenomena.
2. The formulation of theories about the observations.
3. Organization of the observations into categories.
4. Splitting of the field into various theories or schools.

The history of various movements (Kuhn, 1962) reveals a repetitive pattern of unstructured unity and then division into various groups, sometimes resulting in denunciations between the different factions, especially between the early founders and the later innovators. The family therapy movement has been no exception to this sequence of events, except that the rivalries are more or less friendly ones.

The early workers in the family therapy field are like a family; they are sometimes jealous of each other, they compete to be number one, but they also care for each other. In contrast to the bitterness that developed between the psychoanalytic originators (Freud, Jung, Adler, Rank), as far as I know there are no major family therapy figures who do not talk to each other. Unlike psychoanalysis, which stemmed from a single towering figure, the family movement developed independently in various places, thus naturally giving rise to different viewpoints. The family therapy pioneers were highly creative charismatic individuals who, being mavericks within their own profession, needed to establish their distinctive professional identity and stake out their own domain. It is difficult to separate ideological differences from issues of territoriality. I personally believe that therapists find a way of working that is comfortable for them and then they build a theory on those methods.

In any event, at the present time we now have a dozen or so family therapy schools, each of which tends to be insular and competitive with the others. The adherents of one school are not likely to even read articles or go to conferences of the other schools. Within the family therapy field what has been called "the battle of the brand names" has developed, whereby the various family therapy schools make claims of success without substantiation and they overpromise what their methods can do. In an excellent and long overdue article, Schwartz and Perrotta (1985) recommend that family therapy models not only need to temper their claims, but also have an obligation to report qualifications, warnings, side effects, failures, problems, limitations, and guidelines about their methods. They suggest that the various models should state the conditions under which their methods are effective, with what kinds of families and what kinds of therapists. They make the insightful statement that "the very potency that can make a method an effective clinical tool also creates the potential for its misuse" (p. 25). These authors have affirmed my long-held belief that all therapy schools have a responsibility to cite the shortcomings of their approaches. It is in this spirit that this chapter will describe the failings, dilemmas, hazards, doubts, unpredictabilities, traps, and concerns involved in this intergenerational procedure. It is very important to me to write honestly about my work.

The initial application of any treatment method is always accompanied by enthusiasm and usually by clinical success. I suppose if this were not so, there would never be room for innovation. Since describing this method in my early paper (Framo, 1976), I now have a more sober appreciation of the formidable difficulties in the preparation and conducting of these sessions. I regard family-of-origin "therapy" as the major surgery of family therapy; like major surgery, there are risks in the procedure and there can be untoward side effects. The word "therapy" in the previous sentence is placed in quotes because I do not regard family-of-origin sessions as treatment in the strict sense of the word. The parents and siblings, who are present at the request of the client, did not come in as acknowledged clients seeking help. Rather than labeling these sessions "therapy," I prefer using the term "family conferences" or "family consultations." Moreover, although I do not see personal friends for therapy, I have on occasion conducted family-of-origin sessions for friends.

When a friend who is having marital problems calls me for therapy, I state that I would be very willing to listen as a friend, but the personal nature of our relationship precludes a therapy relationship. The family-of-origin experience, from my point of view, lies outside a regular therapy contract. Since my role is that of facilitator or negotiator rather than a therapist in the brief and limited encounter between the friends and their families, I do not experience the conflict of a dual relationship.

I do inform the individual clients in advance of the sessions of the possible risks involved in the family conferences. They are told that some disturbing family secrets may be revealed, that strong feelings may be expressed, that family members may become temporarily alienated from each other, that their expectations of the session may not be fulfilled, and that, among other disappointments, the parents and siblings may not behave as they had hoped. As the session starts, I tell the family that sometimes people become upset, angry, or tearful as the family issues unfold, but that I see these possible emotions as a stage the family may go through and that the overriding goal is to improve the family relationships. In the midst of these admonitions, of course, the clients and family members are also reassured that the therapists will be fully there to deal with whatever comes up.

As stated earlier, some families come in not knowing that *all* the relationships in the family will be discussed. Despite our having instructed the client to tell that to their family, some families are not informed, so they are surprised or annoyed to discover they are not there just to help the client with his or her problems. Consequently, when this situation comes up, we have to be very explicit, early in the session, about the purposes of the meeting. Moreover, I give the family members control over what they disclose and tell them that it is up to them to decide what is and is not off limits. All of these "informed consents" are advocated by those who have explored the ethical considerations of doing psychotherapy, particularly family therapy (Everstine et al., 1980; Margolin, 1982; Widiger & Rorer, 1984).

SHOULD ALL FAMILY MYTHS AND SECRETS BE EXPOSED?

There are aspects of bringing in families of origin and creating the situation that promotes dealing with the "truth" in the sessions that personally concern me. Parents communicate early to their children about the kinds of information they can handle, so the children tend to tell them what they want to hear. Some parents give the message, "Lie to me because I cannot handle the truth." In the family-of-origin sessions this cover of denial is often stripped away, and family members can become very uncomfortable as family myths get dispelled.* Myths such as the following can be exposed in these sessions: the façade of the parents' marriage that never fooled the children; Grandmom's suicide that was always called an "accident"; Mom's alcoholism disguised by her taking her "medicine"; Dad's "heart attack" which he's been about to have for thirty years; Father's hidden prison record; the "good" son's secret life of drug dealing; Mom's diet pills are no different from the daughter's speed pills; the daughter's close friend is her lesbian partner, and so on.

I have wondered whether some truths should remain hidden, whether some secrets should remain secrets. Are some things between intimates better left unsaid? Should the adult daughter tell her mother that her father (Mother's father) sexually molested her? Should the father tell his adult children about an affair that the mother had? Is it necessary for the children to know that their beloved grandfather died from a venereal disease? Should Father's episode of imprisonment for molesting a child be revealed? How about Mom's incest episode with her brother? I recall one instance

---

*O'Neill's classic, sorrowful play about his family, *Long Day's Journey Into Night*, illustrates the anguish surrounding the uncovering of family myths. (O'Neill, 1955).

that involved a woman in a couples therapy. She phoned me to report that her son was not the son of her husband; neither her son nor her husband knew. That was a secret I respected. Of course, there are secrets and there are secrets, and in some cases the revealing of the secret can be salutary. I have seen situations where the revelation of a family secret not only clarified an incomprehensible enigma about a family, but also had beneficial therapeutic effects on the outcome. On the other hand, I have seen great distress in families over the exposure of a secret or family fable; the consequences can linger for a long time. As any therapist will say, the disclosure of a secret or dissipation of a myth is not the therapist's decision, but the client's or family's. This cliché ignores the subtle but powerful effects that therapists and the context have in influencing such decisions, even when the therapist does not explicitly take a stand. (Many years ago, when I was in classical psychoanalysis, I was able to tell how my analyst felt about something by noting his breathing patterns.) Blanket rules about secrets in family-of-origin sessions cannot be made. Decisions about exposing certain family secrets must be made on a case-by-case basis.

MY DOUBTS ABOUT THIS WORK

Other doubts trouble me from time to time about doing this work: By having clients bring in families, who are really coming in out of consideration for the client, are we pressuring people into a kind of therapy situation that they did not seek? If a family had a prior history of perceiving the client as strange, will they view the client's request for a family session as confirming evidence of the client's deviance? Some parents who come in are emotionally bankrupt and when clients finally realize they can get nothing from them, does this reinforce the client's rage, despair, and futility? What can we do about people who recognize that they cannot get much from a parent or brother or sister and are unable to cut their losses?

When I suggest that clients bring in their families, do I promote unrealistic expectations or imply that they will be transformed? When clients are unable, despite great effort, to get their family to attend the session, am I subjecting these persons to another rejection? Is there a risk that this client, whose family would not come in, will retaliate against his family and cut off contact? Does it really do any good for a son to tell his father how distant and remote he is when the father is unable to do anything about it except feel hurt? What is the value of a daughter telling her Mom that she (the daughter) does not enjoy her children because Mom never bonded to her?

Can we always moderate the emotional intensity or blame aimed at a particular vulnerable family member? Is it destructive for grudge addicts, who cannot let go of their hatred and forgive, to bring in their families? On occasion, as we were previously warned by the client, do we indeed open up "a can of worms" with some families? Is it better with some families to "let sleeping dogs lie?" It is one thing for a therapist to promote an abstract principle of self-disclosure or confrontation, but it is something else for families to experience the often shocking reality of such disclosures and to have to live with the consequences later.

CASE EXAMPLE

In one family-of-origin session the members were extremely angry and intent on hurting each other, despite the therapists' efforts to not let the feelings get out of hand. At one point the adult daughter blurted out to her mother that when she was young she remembered coming home early from school one day to witness her having intercourse with some strange man. Her mother retaliated by announcing in the presence of her divorced husband, "Your father set up my affairs with other men because he got his rocks off by my telling him about them." At the end of the session the client felt that she not only had a horrible mother, but had also lost the positive image she tried to hold about her father.

Other clients have felt cheated by the therapist and have terminated the therapy, refusing even to process the session. As one angry client put it, "Nothing new happened. You let my mother do what she always does—take all the attention." We were not able to help this client get beyond this lifelong feeling of being cheated. One wonders, in these kinds of situations, whether we should have put a lid on the families rather than encouraging openness. Can we refine our early assessments and evaluations of families so that revelations with destructive potential can be avoided? On the other hand, how difficult is it for therapists to accept the fact that they cannot help everyone?

NEGATIVE THERAPEUTIC REACTIONS, SIDE EFFECTS, AND OTHER DIFFICULTIES

Questions such as the foregoing may account for negative therapeutic reactions or "deterioration effects" in psychotherapy—that is, worsening of symptoms. Gurman and Kniskern (1978) reported that approximately 5 to 10% of clients' marital or family relationships worsen as the result of marital-family therapy. These findings are consistent with those reported for other psychotherapy modalities. These authors go on to say, however, that symptom relief is not necessarily a primary goal for family therapists. Family system phenomena such as individuation, improved communication, and flexible family interaction are considered to be more important criteria of improvement. Moreover, Gurman and Kniskern rightly state that the worsening of symptoms in one family member could reflect positive changes on the system level: "... *in marital-family therapy, deterioration is not necessarily the opposite of improvement*" (p. 15, italics in original). A clinical example of mine is when, say, a father, as a result of family therapy, converts projective distortions into intrapsychic conflict and becomes depressed; although he is feeling worse, the children and spouse, former targets of his projections, do much better. Individual therapy for the father may then be indicated.

Family therapists, from the beginning, have struggled with the question, When one person in a system benefits from therapy, can another be the loser? I raised this issue in several early papers when I worked with families of schizophrenics (Framo, 1962, 1965). Stierlin (1988) discussed this issue in a more recent philosophical paper about therapists' oscillation between optimism and pessimism concerning change. Examples abound: A marital therapy may end in divorce when one partner really wants out of the marriage; he or she regards the therapy as a success, whereas the partner who was left, who wanted to keep the marriage, regards the therapy as a failure. Or, when the adult daughter tells her mother she is no longer willing to listen to Mom's complaints about Dad, Mom may feel bereft, having lost her confidante.

Displacement of Hostility from Original Family to Spouse

Another possible negative side effect of family-of-origin sessions occurs when the client avoids grappling with the issues with the original family and then displaces the hostility onto the spouse.

CASE EXAMPLE

One man, who spent weeks in couples group expressing his fury toward his parents, did not deal with his anger toward them during the family-of-origin sessions. At the couples group session, right after the meeting with the original family, he suddenly turned to his wife and angrily demanded a divorce. There had been no previous indication that the marriage was in that much difficulty. A simple comment from a group member reoriented his misdirected anger. Further exploration revealed that the more fundamental issue with his family of origin had to do with his need to separate from them, which then got displaced onto his marriage. Many divorces are pseudo differentiation steps or efforts to disengage from old, archaic family-of-origin situations.

Further Comments on the Relationship Between Family-of-Origin Sessions and the Marriage

There are other ways that the family-of-origin experience may have unexpected negative effects on the marriage relationship. Sometimes clients incorporate the family-of-origin sessions into the marital struggles. For instance, one woman concluded, after both she and her husband had had their sessions, that her family was much healthier than his. As might be expected, this statement added further fuel to their quarrels. I have also seen several situations where the marital problems were so intense and so peremptory that the family-of-origin sessions were not considered that significant by the clients. The clients either looked toward the family-of-origin sessions as providing magical solutions to the marital problems, or they were simply too preoccupied with their marriage.

There is another limitation of this method worth mentioning. From my theoretical viewpoint, people attempt to resolve intrapsychic conflicts, stemming from the family of origin, *through* their mate and children. Present marital and parenting difficulties are largely looked upon as elaborations of relationship patterns from the family of origin. I have repeatedly stated that one major purpose of seeing families of origin is to either improve the marital relationship or, in cases of dead or "impossible" marriages, to enable the partners to end the marriage constructively. Although it is rare to find a direct, one-to-one correspondence, in the great majority of cases the relationship between the family-of-origin dynamics and how they are being worked through in the marriage can be discerned fairly easily. There are occasions, however, where the connection between what happened in the family of origin and what is going on in the marriage is obscure or tenuous. Sometimes I simply cannot figure out how the marital problems are related to the family of origin. Several possibilities come to mind for the apparent lack of relatedness between the two. Countertransference issues may have been involved, or some families of origin deal with pseudoissues in their sessions. With some families my diagnostic skills may not have been sharp enough. It is also possible that connections would have been established if the sessions had gone on for a longer period of time. Some families need time to trust and reveal their typical interaction patterns.

Additional Pitfalls and Problems

Some of the pitfalls and blunders in doing intergenerational work have already been mentioned, such as joining the client in criticizing the parents or treating incoming family members as patients who are coming for help. There are also unforeseen side effects. Family members who attended the session may send sarcastic messages to the client afterwards. One woman, after her family-of-origin session, received a "Get Well" card from her mother; another client got an astrological chart from his mother stating, "Beware of those who threaten family ties."

The sessions can also have a negative effect on the couples group. Usually when clients report to the group afterwards how positive the experience was, other group members, who are wavering, decide to go ahead with their session. Occasionally, however, other group members get discouraged when they hear of the turmoil that occurred during another member's family-of-origin session.

Therapists should also not be fooled into thinking that the issues discussed during the family-of-origin session are the real or important ones. Some family members consciously decide before the session that there are certain issues that they will avoid discussing. For example, in a case of sibling collusion and client compliance, one client said that his sisters told him before the session that even though they had many criticisms of Mom, they had agreed beforehand not to mention them during the session. Another pitfall, noted previously, are the outside therapists, who have a parent or sibling of the client in treatment, dissuading or preventing that person from coming to a family-of-origin session. Usually, when the client calls that therapist, the therapist states that he/she cannot take responsibility for the dire consequences such a family meeting could have on their client, hinting that their client could have a psychotic break if they attend the session. It is noteworthy that professional therapists harbor the same irrational fears about intergenerational encounters as everyone else. I myself never contact any of these therapists since I figure that an explanation of family systems thinking over the phone would be futile. Besides, the clients usually overrule the therapists and come to the session anyway. Most people are wise enough to trust their own judgment.

In the early part of this book I discussed the unwillingness and wariness clients have about family-of-origin sessions. I have since realized that eagerness to bring in parents and siblings could be a resistance itself. Typically, these are merged families who do everything together, and the family-of-origin session is perceived by them as another occasion to celebrate their togetherness. Their sessions are usually very active, with much overtalking, and the sessions seem easy for the therapists to conduct. Despite much "insight" about their fusion, however, nothing much changes. On the other hand, there are clients in marital therapy who refuse to explore their family-of-origin relationships at all, much less have a family-of-origin session. Some of these individuals are even reluctant to give a family history, saying they cannot see the relevance of that to their marital problems. When they do give a history, they give such an expurgated account that they make their families sound like the TV family, the Waltons. These clients, by the way, usually open up more about their families when they are part of a couples group.

In addition to the previous kinds of pitfalls and problems that intergenerational family therapists may encounter, there are other sticky situations that will dampen clients' and therapists' expectations about what family-of-origin sessions can accomplish.

Expectations Not Realized

Not all parents are able to acknowledge mistakes or respond positively to their adult children, and even some of those who are ready to do so are blocked from making amends by the intransigence of their children. Not all siblings make up with each other, not all marriages improve, and sometimes no changes are apparent in anybody following the family-of-origin session. Future research may specify favorable and unfavorable conditions for proposing this intervention.

In any event, there is one phenomenon worth discussing—namely, the dashed hopes of some clients or their siblings that, at long last, these sessions will enable them to get something from parents who had never been able to give much. There are, of course, parents who, for various reasons, are emotionally impoverished and depleted. And there are also parents who set too high a price for a relationship or who insist on conditions for acceptance that are unrealistic or unacceptable. For example, "If you want to get closer to me, you must become a fundamentalist like me and give yourself to Christ." Or the father who said to his son, "If you put your wife before me, I will say Kaddish for you" (a Jewish prayer for the dead—a ritualistic disowning). Or the father who said to his son, "If you want my love you must handle your crazy mother for me."

I help the clients and siblings of such parents to give up the dream, work through their grief, cut their losses, and continue to relate to parents, but not at the expense of personal integrity. It is a sad fact of human affairs, however, that the longing for the unreachable parent almost never completely disappears. Many plays, movies, and novels have portrayed this desperate theme. Under these circumstances what the family-of-origin sessions can do is to help the adult children see that they are not loved because they are unlovable; they are not loved because a parent does not have love to give in the form in which it's needed.

Some clients can become disillusioned by family-of-origin sessions that did not meet their expectations or fulfill their fantasies about what the sessions could accomplish. In the book *One Couple, Four Realities* (Chasin, Grunebaum, & Herzog, 1990) there is a description of a session conducted with a woman and her family of origin. Following years of alienation between this woman and her mother, a breakthrough was achieved when they were able to move toward closing the painful gulf between them. When this woman was interviewed one day after the session and was also interviewed six months later, she was euphoric about the improved relationship with her mother. Six years later, however, when she was interviewed again, she deprecated the value of the family-of-origin session. Follow-up therapy from an intergenerational perspective would likely have made a difference in sustaining the early gains. The individual therapist this woman had following the family-of-origin session may either have focused exclusively on intrapsychic material or could even have discouraged her from having much contact with a mother perceived as "impossible." For people who have suffered severe, early narcissistic injuries, family-of-origin sessions can come to represent the "exciting but disappointing object" (Fairbairn, 1952) when raised expectations are not realized.

Misuse of Family Explorations

Exploration of one's own family has become somewhat of a fad among family therapists and, like anything else, such an enterprise can be misused. Beginning family therapists, misinterpreting Bowen Theory, usually do not stop with taking psychological distance and studying their own family objectively: they embark on a crusade to change their family. I caution my students all the time not to try to "treat" their families because they can create all kinds of havoc. Murray Bowen told me that family therapists call him after reading about his work with his own family (Framo, 1972). They say things like, "I'm going home this weekend. What trick can I use with my family?" Although the callers are unaware of Bowen's highly sophisticated moves with his family, based on well thought-out theory and research, they would have had no difficulty hearing his displeasure at such questions.

Handling of Sessions that Are Sabotaged

Earlier I mentioned those rare instances when incoming family members come to sessions with apparent malicious motives. This sabotaging may take various forms: refusing to participate, making sarcastic or demeaning remarks to the therapists, being obnoxious or unpleasant, or even threatening the client with words like, "It was a great sacrifice for me to come here and I did it for you. But if this thing doesn't work, or if anybody in this family gets hurt by what we do here, it's going to be on your head." Under such circumstances it is tempting for therapists to become defensive, to counterattack, to give reassurances that do not reassure, and to forget that there are no villains in families. These events are a real test of the therapists' capacity to allow the sessions to unfold in order for hidden motives behind the noxious behavior to become known. The therapists' own family-of-origin experiences will often influence the emotional reactivity. Another resource for therapists' difficulties in handling these problems resides in the cotherapy relationship. Presumably, the cotherapists have had different family-of-origin experiences; what may stimulate the Achilles' heel of one therapist may pass right by the other therapist.

The Dilemma of When to Introduce the Idea of Bringing in the Family of Origin

Another caveat, discussed earlier in this book, is the dilemma of when to introduce the couple to the idea of bringing in their families for sessions. In my first publication on this method (Framo, 1976), I stated that I brought up the subject at the end of the first interview. At that time I underestimated the intensity of fear and resistance to the proposal. Some clients who feel they have been severely narcissistically wounded by their family perceive the therapist's suggestion as another humiliating assault. Not only did some clients terminate therapy because they did not want to involve their family, but I learned that even with clients who ultimately bring in their family, suggesting it in the first session is too premature. Most people need to get used to the idea, in part because it sounds so unrelated to their concept of what happens in therapy. I now introduce the recommendation when I have a fairly secure relationship with the clients, unless there are clear indications in the early sessions that the clients want to deal with their families of origin.

Therapists' Stresses

Among the difficulties in conducting family-of-origin sessions are those having to do with the stresses they can create in therapists. Managing these sessions is damn hard work, and with some families you really earn your money. Some families put up such a wall of silence that getting them to talk is like pulling teeth. Other families handle their anxiety by immediately attacking the therapists. I once heard a family therapist, who does this kind of work, ask, "How do you save yourself when you have a family who are like a bunch of sharks eating each other and you as well?" Headley, who works with adults and their parents, states, "This technique makes great demands upon the therapist's abilities. . . . Having had much experience with all modes of therapy (individual, marital, family, and group therapy), I find that joint family sessions with older parents and adult children are the most taxing of all. Emotions seem to rise higher—or fall lower—and intensity of reactions seems far more heightened than in any other situation" (1977, p. 184). When sessions are heading toward emotional explosiveness, Headley breaks up the family group into separate interviews. My own preference is to work it out with everyone present. To be sure, the therapists will experience the gamut of transference and countertransference repercussions; they will be on a roller coaster of emotions—fear of loss of control, fury, admiration, guilt, love, helplessness, distress, partisanship, and so on. I do not think that any amount of therapy for the therapist altogether eliminates these "irrational" feelings. These reactions can be minimized and handled, however, by having only certain kinds of therapists do this work.

What kinds of therapists should do family-of-origin work? What guidelines can be offered for determining which kinds of therapists are capable of using intergenerational methods? In addition to the usual requirement that the therapist be a systems thinker and be experienced in a variety of therapies (individual, group, marital, and family), I believe that specialized training and supervision in intergenerational work is necessary. Part of this training should consist of the therapist having a family-of-origin session himself or herself. In my opinion, therapists should not ask clients to do that which they are not willing to do themselves. It is essential that therapists experience the anxiety about dealing with their own family and know firsthand what it is like to struggle through the impasses. Having done so, they can better appreciate their clients' travail. Besides, when they propose the idea to clients and the clients ask, "Would *you* do it?", one can answer, "I already have." (I should hasten to add that I myself have already had family-of-origin sessions with the remaining members of my own family.)

Admittedly, training and supervision in my particular intergenerational approach is not easily available. I have only been able to train a few therapists in this method. Weekend workshops that I conduct around the country, and reading this book, are not regarded as substitutes for supervision of one's cases by an experienced supervisor who observes the trainee conducting family-of-origin sessions, either through the one-way mirror or on videotape.

One problem with going to workshops is that the leader plays a videotape of a session that went the way it is supposed to. Since workshop leaders never play their failures, this videotaped session, of course, has been selected out of many that did not go so well. Workshop participants, including beginning therapists, get discouraged when they find that they cannot get the method to work as the workshop leader did. The key to learning how to do therapy, as I see it, is to have competent supervision. In the absence of formal training, I recommend peer group supervision, which was the only training I got in those early days when there was no one around to train us and we were forced to train ourselves. I also think that mature and experienced therapists may be more able to appreciate the developmental issues that arise from the different life-cycle stages of the parents and their adult children. The book *Family of Origin Therapy* (Hovestadt & Fine, 1987) discusses further concepts and training issues in this area.

The Absent Member Stratagem

One of the ways that therapists inexperienced in this method can be misled is to agree to exclude certain family members from attending family-of-origin sessions. I make it a policy, and so tell clients, that unless everyone in the family, including all the siblings, can be present for the session, it will not be held. Through the years I have learned the necessity of such a rule because the absence of one family member can make a real difference in the outcome. Now, to be sure, if the family shows up without a family member, I do not send them away, especially since they usually have come from several different states. However, I do not let the client know in advance that I will go through with the session if someone is absent. My stance is intended to communicate my respect for the integrity of the whole system. The point is, a therapist who has not had much experience in bringing in families of origin is likely to be seduced into "buying" all the myriad of excuses as to why a particular family member cannot come to the family meeting.

CASE EXAMPLE 1.

A woman from a distant state requested a session and said that one adult son, who had been cut off from the family, was willing to come, but that another son did not want to attend. The latter son said that such a session would only "open old wounds." He said that he had achieved a modus vivendi with his parents and did not want to tamper with that. Besides, he was the one living near his parents and he felt he would be stuck with the fallout from the session, whereas his brother would leave town after the session. So the client asked if we could have the session without that son; I kept to my rule and said no. Everyone finally came to the session, and at the end the mother thanked me for insisting everyone be present.

CASE EXAMPLE 2.

A live family-of-origin demonstration was being planned for a national convention of family therapists being held on the west coast. A woman who had volunteered phoned me to say that she and her family would be interviewed at the conference and that everyone would be there except her brother. She said her brother lived on the east coast but, more importantly, he had "chosen to have nothing to do with the family." I urged her to call him and ask him anyway and she demurred, saying it would be futile because he had been "cut off" from the family for years and was not an important family member. (She was a family therapist and knew the lingo.) After I told her the session would not be held without him, she agreed to ask him. Her brother, after being asked, not only flew to the west coast, but turned out to be the central figure in the family-of-origin session. Had I not seen this sort of thing happen before, I would not have known to be persistent in insisting that everyone be present. A videotape of this family-of-origin session is available to mental health professionals.*

WHAT FAMILIES ARE SUITABLE FOR FAMILY-OF-ORIGIN SESSIONS?

I have given a lot of thought to the question, for what kinds of families are family-of-origin sessions most appropriate? On one level, I

*Masters Series. 1984. American Association for Marriage and Family Therapy. 1100 17th Street, N.W., 10th Floor, Washington, D.C. 20036.

believe that every family could profit from a family meeting where there is an honest exchange about the family relationships. However, even though I have conducted many family-of-origin sessions, I am not yet able to specify the family characteristics of those who benefit the most or least. The usual dimensions of evaluating suitability for family therapy do not seem to apply. I have seen initially unmotivated families gain much from the sessions, and motivated ones go nowhere. Alienated families seem to do as well as fused ones, and social class does not appear to discriminate. I have seen productive outcomes with severely dysfunctional families (with incest, alcohol and drug addictions, physical abuse), and unrealized outcomes in so-called normal families.

Part of the problem in determining guidelines for selecting the types of families suitable for intergenerational sessions is that the family therapy field still does not have a widely accepted system of diagnostic categories for families. The enmeshed-disengaged continuum seems simplistic and incomplete. Data aimed at specifying kinds of families appropriate for family-of-origin intervention await systematic research investigation. The chapter on Clinical Implications contains some speculations on which clinical situations are most and least responsive to this approach.

Considerations Involved in Determining Contraindications

The problem of selection of families is intimately related to the topic of contraindications. Under what conditions should one *not* bring adult children and their parents together for family of origin sessions?

The subject of therapy contraindications is complicated. Some years ago Nathan Ackerman (1966) proposed quite specific contraindications for family therapy:

1. A trend toward irreversible breakup of the family;
2. Dominance in the group of destructive motivation;
3. One parent with a progressive paranoid condition;
4. Parents who are unable to be honest; lying and deceitfulness deeply rooted in the group;

5. The existence of a valid secret;
6. Cultural, religious, or economic prejudice against this form of intervention;
7. Extremely rigid defenses which, if broken, might induce a psychosis, a psychosomatic crisis, or physical assault; and
8. Finally, the presence of organic disease that precludes participation in one or more members. (p. 111–112)

I would suspect that present-day therapists, who consider themselves more sophisticated than Ackerman now, would not rule out family therapy for any one of Ackerman's eight criteria. Ackerman may be wiser than we think, however; it is possible that many unexplained family therapy failures are generated by the guidelines he proposed. Lyman Wynne (1965) was the first family therapist to write a paper expressly focused on contraindications for family therapy, and he dealt with the subject in more general terms: ". . . any 'condition' of the family-therapist unit (including characteristics of the therapist) which makes family therapy inadvisable, though it would be otherwise appropriate, constitutes in a broad sense a 'contraindication' to family therapy." (p. 315).

I myself have wondered under what conditions family-of-origin sessions would be contraindicated. As I said already, I believe that every family could gain from the experience of getting together with experienced facilitators and talking about the important things. From time to time I have questioned whether, with a particular family, the family would have been better off, in the short run, without the session, but I have never been able to develop a policy or make a generalization about when it would be *inadvisable* to have a family-of-origin session. Kramer (1985) gives two examples of contraindications for transgenerational family conferences: if the client has already changed her dependent role in her family, she may decide not to have a family meeting; and, if members of the family of origin have had previous negative experiences in therapy and refuse to come in. Neither of these are true contraindications in the sense that harm would result from the sessions being held.

In the abstract I have considered that there might be family situations that were so malignant that a family conference should not be held. However, it is very difficult to determine in advance, based on the client's account, just what the family is like or how toxic the situation is. When I hear parents or siblings described as cruel, as malevolent monsters, as crazy, as manipulative, as "the personification of evil," as powerful or powerless, poisonous, or even as "perfect," I have learned that these characterizations are based upon the intrapsychic elaborations of exaggerated child-hood perceptions. In other words, I have rarely seen a parent or sibling who was as sick or awful or flawless as they were described. Even taking into account "office behavior" during the session, the relatives described in totally negative terms are usu-ally more interested in working things out with the client than we had been led to believe. Since one cannot consistently evaluate, ahead of time, based on clients' descriptions, the suitability of a particular family for a family-of-origin session, are there other guidelines? Certainly, one cannot appraise the danger a session may bring about by the amount of heat or uproar engendered by interactions during the session. Consequently, for a number of years the only conditions that prevented me from holding a family-of-origin session were either the client not wanting to ask the family to come in or one or more extended family members refusing to attend. But these are also not real *contra*indications.

A True Contraindication

Only recently have I come across a situation that I consider a true contraindication to use of this intergenerational model, although even this condition has qualifications attached to it. I have mentioned previously that I get requests for family-of-origin sessions from people, mostly therapists, who come from distant geographical places. Since these are not regular clients, a long period of preparation for the sessions is not possible. Also, as stated earlier, I have found it advisable to have a session with the out-of-town client prior to the family-of-origin meeting in order to get a family history and develop an agenda. Consequently, I do not know these clients as well as I do those in ongoing treatment. In any event, there have been several instances of conducting such preliminary interviews where it became apparent that the primary motive in arranging the session was to get revenge and punish the parents. On many previous occasions I had heard people express vitriolic anger at their parents during the preparation interview, but their ferocity always ameliorated by the end of the family-of-origin session and everyone would end up in each other's arms. What was unique about these particular clients was that the rage was bottomless and did not diminish by the end of the family-of-origin session; these people were just as unbending and unforgiving of their parents at the end as they were at the beginning. Several experiences like that have led me to consider as a contraindication to family-of-origin sessions those circumstances when there is strong evidence that the primary motivation of the client is to destroy the parents and make them pay. To be sure, it is not always possible to make this determination in a preparation session because, as I said, expressions of anger toward parents are common at these times.

The usual procedure for conducting family-of-origin sessions for out of town clients and their families has consisted of all the family members flying in from different parts of the country and reserving motel rooms. The preparation session with the client alone is usually held just before the meeting with the whole family. One precaution under consideration is to schedule preparation sessions as separate trips in the event more preparation is needed. One then has more time in which to decide whether to postpone or cancel the family-of-origin session should the motive appear to be primarily destructive.

It is also possible that family-of-origin sessions of this sort, where clients are determined to thrash their parents, are a phase of intergenerational work and that additional or more lengthy sessions would bring about more constructive changes. Later events could also bring about positive changes. For example, one client of this kind, who did not soften her bitterness during the family-of-origin session, played the tapes of the sessions for her own individual therapist in her hometown. After the third playing of the tape she finally "heard" her parents try to make amends, and she at least moved into a position of neutrality toward her mother.

I will conclude this section on the difficulties, side effects, and hazards involved in family-of-origin work by describing at length a case where a family-of-origin session set up a storm in the family and, for a while, gave me pause about using this approach. It finally turned out okay, but there were times when I questioned whether it would.

CASE STUDY

Marc and Val were on the verge of divorce when they entered marital therapy. Marc said he felt burdened by Val's dependency on him, and Val could no longer tolerate Marc's outbursts of temper directed at her. Marc came from a family where he felt like an outsider to the threesome of his father, mother, and sister. While preparing for his family-of-origin sessions, he related how his parents always favored his sister, and he had felt like a stepchild in his own family. For example, he related that he had had to earn his own spending money as a child, whereas his sister was overindulged and showered with gifts and attention. This pattern apparently carried over into adulthood since his parents ignored his children and pampered his sister's children.

His sister, Louise, was in individual therapy for seven years with a psychoanalyst whom I knew casually. Louise was in the midst of a horrendous divorce and had made a serious, life-threatening suicide attempt. Just before the family-of-origin sessions, I got a call from her psychotherapist stating that Louise was "very, very sick and extremely fragile" and that although she had advised Louise not to attend the family meeting, Louise had decided to attend anyway. (I have noted, by the way, whenever I have attended psychoanalytic meetings, that psychoanalysts usually say that their patients are "very, very sick.")

During the family-of-origin sessions, Marc dealt forthrightly with his prepared agenda and for the first time spoke of the unfair treatment he felt he had received and of his parents' blind partiality toward Louise. During the session, after I had asked Louise about her relationship with her parents, she answered, "You have no right to ask me that! That's between me and my psychiatrist!" After the sessions, Louise told Marc that I had interfered in her private therapy and, further, she said she wanted the tapes of the sessions. When Marc asked her what she was going to do with the tapes, she did not tell him she planned to play them for her therapist. Marc got very angry; he told her that the tapes were his, at which point Louise ordered him out of her house. Marc then went to his parents' house and his parents insisted he give the tapes to Louise. They had a vehement argument, during which Marc learned that his parents were colluding with Louise to secretly turn the tapes over to Louise's psychiatrist.

Marc, again feeling that when the chips were down his parents would automatically take Louise's side, became furious, told his parents to keep the tapes and "stick 'em," and he stormed out of the house, saying he never wanted to see them or Louise again. Marc was distraught afterwards; his wife Val said that she had never seen her husband cry before. Louise's psychiatrist then called me to say she was right all along about advising Louise not to attend the family session. (I could picture her at a psychoanalytic meeting talking about the irresponsibility and recklessness of family therapists.) I then received a call from Marc's father, who said that Marc needed long-term therapy with a psychiatrist—he emphasized an *M.D.* psychiatrist—and he concluded the call by saying, "Thank you for losing me a son."

Marc's father was a prominent attorney, and I envisioned at that point a huge malpractice suit. Well . . . I remember confiding to a colleague that maybe this family-of-origin stuff did not always work. It took an experience like this for me to realize that this intervention sometimes shakes up the roots of a family tree, and there can indeed be unforeseen side effects from stepping into certain family situations. Actually, after the immediate crisis was over, it did not turn out so badly. I had told the father that family ties are pretty strong and family members do not ordinarily stay alienated. After we helped Marc tone down his emotional reactivity, he went to see his parents on Father's Day and he gave his father a gift. Marc had come to realize that he could not penetrate the threesome of mother, father, and daughter, but he *could* have a one-to-one relationship with each. There were further developments. Marc and Louise made up. Louise's psychiatrist called me to say that the family session had helped Louise make some movement in her individual therapy after all. The interesting outcome to this is that a few weeks later Marc's parents visited Marc and his children and took these grandchildren to the circus.

7

Theoretical Implications

OBJECT RELATIONS THEORY

The theory that provides a basis for understanding the present intergenerational approach is the object relations theory of Fairbairn (1952); its application to marital relationships, as exemplified by the work of Dicks (1967), and my extension of this theory (1970), relates the internal object world to the transactional operations between closely related people. My work attempts to integrate dynamic and systems concepts, and intrapsychic and interpersonal dimensions, thereby providing a conceptual bridge between the personal and the social. I stress the interlocking, multiperson motivational systems of intimate relationships and suggest that family members collusively carry psychic functions for each other. People in close relationships reciprocally become a part of each other's psychology, forming a feedback system that regulates and patterns their individual behaviors.

In a previously published theoretical paper, "Symptoms from a Family Transactional Viewpoint" (Framo, 1970), I explored the relationship between the intrapsychic and the transactional. I proposed that intrapsychic conflicts stemming from the family of origin are repeated, defended against, lived through, or mastered in the relationship with one's spouse, children, or any other current intimate. Marital partners in particular can have severely distorted transference reactions to each other, sometimes creating outwardly bizarre marital expectations and behaviors. The attempted interpersonal resolution of inner conflicts is fundamental to the profound distress and misery that we see clinically in couples and families who come for help.

The following is an abbreviated synopsis of object relations theory as it relates to the family-of-origin work described in this book.

1. Fairbairn (1952) postulated that the human being's need for a satisfactory relationship constitutes the fundamental motive of life. This view is contrasted with Freud's theory of instinctual gratification as being primary. That is, Freud viewed persons in the environment as being used for the purpose of discharge of drives, rather than for the inherent pleasure of attachment or relationship. For Fairbairn, pleasure is derived from the object-seeking, and aggression is a reaction to frustration when the specific sought-after object denies satisfaction.

In the early months of the infant, when the circumstances are fortunate and the care is loving and reliably supplied, bonding and a sense of basic trust are established, providing the foundation for coping with life (Bowlby, 1969; Erikson, 1964; Winnicott, 1960). Under unfavorable conditions—gross neglect, being unwanted, abuse—the infant is overwhelmed with primitive terrors. In order to survive, the child must keep the vitally needed attachment and at the same time control affects that are singularly devastating—an awesomely frightening experience of imminent disintegration and death.

2. Fairbairn considers separation anxiety to be the basic anxiety; anxiety about separation becomes the prototype for all future losses, perceived and real. When parents' behavior is interpreted as rejection, desertion, or withholding, the rageful infant, unable to give up the external figure or change it in outer reality, incorporates the needed-hated object in order to control it in the inner psychic world. These internal objects are retained as introjects, as psychological representatives of external objects. The inner objects will then serve as models and templates for future close relationships.

3. In Fairbairn's model of the mind, the internalized "bad" object is split into its exciting, needed aspects (libidinal object) and its frustrating, rejecting aspects (antilibidinal object), both of which are repressed. "Good" objects are retained as satisfying memories, and the ideal object, the nucleus of the original object divested of its exciting and frustrating elements, can be safely loved by the central

ego as a desexualized and perfect object. (The ideal object is personified by the idealization of a parent or romantic object. Children's
fairy tales also deal with these universal themes of "good, bad, and
ideal.")

4. The complex interchanges between internal and external
objects are modulated and organized by the actual experiences in the
original family. The child internalizes actual characteristics of the
parents and their marital relationship, as well as distortions based on
his/her own perceptions; these become incorporated into the self-
structure of the child. Those children who are raised in a relatively
secure family context, without major trauma or loss, will be able to
have healthy self-esteem, ideals, and goals; they will be able, in
Freud's words, "to love and to work."

In contrast, those children whose parenting figures have been
physically or psychologically unavailable or abusive or who have
experienced massive scapegoating, malignant double-binding and
deceit, parentification (Boszormenyi-Nagy & Framo, 1965), mystification (Laing, 1965), or gross injustice will be tied to an inner world
of bad objects (Seinfeld, 1990).

The internal objects—guilty, hungry, anxious, rageful,
conflictual—remain as "internal saboteurs" or warring forces in the
inner world. Brutal or perverse behaviors toward the young child not
only create fears in the child of destroying the needed parent object
by one's own aggression (Klein, 1946), but also gives rise to the ultimate dread of abandonment.

> The power of life-sustaining family relationships ties is much
> greater than instinctual or autonomous strivings. . . . For the
> sake of approval by the parents, and because abandonment has
> such disastrous consequences, the child will sacrifice whatever
> ego integrity is called for in order to survive. If the price of
> acceptance is to absorb unrealities, accept an irrational identity
> or role assignment, be persecuted, be overindulged, be scape-
> goated, be parentified or what have you, this price will have to
> be paid; to be alone or pushed out of the family either physically
> or psychologically is too unthinkable. (Framo, 1982, p. 53)

5. During the individual's course of development external real fig-

ures are assimilated in successive strata or by fusion into the internal object world.* The extent to which individuals have to rely on their inner world of bad objects ascertains whether further splitting occurs and the degree of central ego impoverishment. The consequences of the internal drama are manifested in relationships with real people. Some individuals have such massively lethal experiences in their early years that they are unable to bond or sustain any kind of relationship with others. They suffer fragmentation and disorganization under the stress of threatened loss, and their bottomless demandingness, remoteness, or aggressiveness turn people away from them. In conventional diagnostic terms they are called psychotic or borderline or severely narcissistically injured.

However, all human beings exist along a continuum of the capacity to love and to develop an intimate, trusting relationship (everyone's Achilles' heel). Even those at the mature level of development have some degree of narcissism, sense of entitlement, regressive expectations, symbiotic yearnings, primitive hostility, and difficulty reconciling ambivalence. These characteristics require special conditions in order to be manifested, such as a marital relationship. To some extent everyone tends to view their intimates in terms of their own needs or as carrying their own denied, split-off traits. Life situations are not only unconsciously interpreted in the light of the inner object world, but *active unconscious attempts are made to force and change close relationships into fitting the internal role models*—the central problem in marital difficulties.

6. The foregoing helps decode and makes more understandable some apparent relationship predicaments and puzzles. The inner psychological splitting of which Fairbairn spoke can have real relationship counterparts; individuals seek representatives of their libidinal and antilibidinal objects in their external relationships. Attempts are made to dispel and ameliorate painful intrapsychic conflict by interpersonal choice, but the inner object world can guide choices that may intensify the pain. Some individuals are

---

*Actually, object relations theory has little to say about what happens to the internal objects over time as the individual goes through life—whether they are fixed from the early imprinting, or whether they do change as a function of life experience. Do positive experiences with significant others enrich the "good" internal objects? Do negative ones reinforce "bad" inner objects?

only attracted to those who, it is guaranteed, will only bring them grief and frustration (The Rejecting Object). The Exciting Object is personified by the partner (or parent in the present day) who is *almost* reachable, who tantalizes and promises but never delivers. Still others live in an unrealistic world of denial and are unable to see problems or shortcomings in their intimate relationships (The Ideal Object).

7. Marital partners select each other on the basis of rediscovering lost aspects of their primary object relations, which they had split off and which, in their involvement with the spouse, they reexperience by projective identification (Dicks, 1967). The partner chosen by the emotional radar must stimulate the re-creation of the childhood dream of unconditional love; at the same time, the prospective mate must be enough like the bad inner object to allow for the penetration of old hatreds. *People usually do not select the partner they want; they get the one that they need.* A partner is chosen who, it is hoped, will enable one to cancel out, replicate, control, master, live through, or heal, in a dyadic framework, what could not be settled internally. Consequently, one's current intimates, one's spouse and children, are, in part, stand-ins for old images, the embodiments of long-buried introjects.

8. It is my thesis that the family-of-origin consultation can have great power in producing positive change and flexibility in the individual and in the marital and family systems. Instead of working through one's introjects, or exorcising one's personal demons via the relationship with the therapist, when the adult person meets with his/her parents and brothers and sisters, and everyone deals with the significant personal and family issues of the past and present, the problems are taken back to their original sources, thus providing a direct path to etiological factors. As the old family conflicts are reviewed, early experiences of the adult children are relived and assessed from the perspective of the grown adult; traumatic incidents (deaths, illnesses, desertions, etc.) are re-examined, childhood misunderstandings and misperceptions are clarified, and transference distortions are explicated. Dealing with the real, external parents (who are the original transference figures, as well as objects being reprojected upon), loosens the hold and intensity of the internal objects and exposes them to current realities.

When "good" external objects become available by the transactions of these family-of-origin sessions (changed perceptions of parents and siblings) such mechanisms as splitting, projective identification, and denial lose some of their charge and the "bad" internal objects can be gradually released and surrendered (Seinfeld, 1990). The context of the family-of-origin sessions gives permission for the family members to confront each other with painful, difficult issues that had always been avoided; the safe setting allows the frank interchange on forbidden topics to occur. A combination of getting to know the parents as real people, confronting and reproaching them without losing them, realizing what the parents had struggled with in their lives, coming to terms with their shortcomings, forgiving them, and expressing love to them—all of these events help free up psychic energy which can then be invested in contemporary relationships.

The parents, relieved that they have reached new understandings with their adult children and that they are not going to lose them, are more able to relate to their children as separate persons in their own right. On a family system level the sessions usually repair family cutoffs, lessen family anxiety, have spreading effects on extended family, and result in a closeness-distance balance among family members that is more voluntary than obligatory.

9. By exploring past and current issues with parents and siblings and by experiencing them in a new and different kind of way, the original client is then in a position to examine how those family transactions are related to his/her intrapsychic or marital struggles. On an intrapsychic level the family-of-origin sessions can foster a reorganization of the inner universe of mental representations, often resulting in healthfully changed perceptions of the self. The split-off, disowned aspects of the self (originally based on parental introjects), which had been projected onto the intimate others, are more open to being owned and reinternalized. Interpersonally, the spouse and children can then be related to in a more appropriate fashion since their transference meaning has changed. As can be seen, the relationship between the intrapsychic and the transactional constitutes the core of this theoretical approach.

TOWARD A THEORY OF THERAPEUTIC CHANGE

Why do family-of-origin sessions usually have such potent effects on family systems, on individuals, and on the individuals' parental and marital relationships? Elaborating on the foregoing list of theoretical implications, the following series of conceptual formulations are proposed as a theoretical model of therapeutic change, with particular reference to the intergenerational experience described in this book.

Recontouring of Internal Objects

It is first proposed that the experience of the family-of-origin session shifts the balance of good and bad objects in the internal world of the family members. Recapitulating some aspects of object relations theory (Fairbairn, 1952), in the early months of life the young child splits the parent figure into the libidinal object—who protects, comforts, loves unconditionally, and gratifies the wish for regressive fusion—and the antilibidinal object—who rejects, abuses, neglects, withdraws love, threatens abandonment, and is hostile and critical. Those children who have been subjected to threatening experiences with parent figures will be subject to two potentially devastating fears: closeness signifying obliteration and separateness signifying abandonment. The parents, who themselves had experienced actual or threats of separation and loss in their early years, regard the child's growing autonomy as a rejection of themselves. Zinner and Shapiro (1972), in discussing restitution of loss, state that the concept of projective identification not only implies that individuals project a split-off part of the self onto an intimate other (usually, a negative, dissociated aspect of the self) and has identified with that projected self (thus serving a defensive function), but also that projective identification serves a restorative function: it brings back to life the parents' own lost objects in the form of the offspring. Jaffe (1968) suggests that children may be perceived not only as the parents' parent but as the child the parent once was, resulting in the child being both parentified and infantilized.

Parental behavior toward the child can also take the form of physical and psychological abuse. Most parents, of course, love their children, but the woe that parents inflict on them, wittingly and unwittingly, is infinite—ranging all the way from benign double-binds, martyrlike behavior for which the child has to pay, to intrusiveness, by using the child as the battleground for the marriage, exploitation, humiliation, shaming, scapegoating, physical abuse, and child murder. Sheloff (1981), who explored the opposite of the Oedipus myth (the Persian myth of Rustom and Schrab where the father unwittingly kills his son), examined the basis of hostility of parents to children, essentially the punishment of the younger generation by the elder. The symptoms that develop in the young or adult child reflect the end stage of a relentless family process (Framo, 1970). Any textbook on psychopathology is replete with categorizations of the manifold ways that people can express their distress: depression, violence, withdrawal, disharmony of affect, narcissism, addictions, physical disorders, delusions, the inability to relate to others, and so on. (As an aside, it is curious that mental health education, diagnostic systems, mental health laws, grants for research, etc., are based on symptoms, which are, after all, a minor piece of an intricate complex.) Some adolescents and young adults become so disillusioned with their families that they renounce or give up on them and turn to gangs or friends as family (Lindsey, 1982).

In any event, as the child moves through the developmental phases, the introjects and their accompanying affects, which are repressed, unconscious and timeless, remain stuck in the internal world where they are relatively impervious to external events. To be sure, an incalculable number of events intervene between childhood and adulthood, but the foundation for perceiving and interpreting these events has been laid early on. The individual is inexorably tied to the internalized bad parent figures, because without them there is nothingness, depersonalization, fragmentation, and fear of dying. Bad parents are better than none (Guntrip, 1969).

Interpersonally, the young adult seeks out and shapes those others who offer the potential of repeating and working through the early experiences. In order to preserve the original libidinal object (the loving or hoped for aspect of the parent) the split-off, bad, antilibidinal object is found in the intimate others (Seinfeld, 1990). (Thus we can account for some people idealizing a parent and beating or murdering a spouse.) Under very special circumstances, however (e.g., death of a close other, a life-threatening illness, undergoing a divorce or other situation of great stress, in dreams, being in an intense relationship with a spouse, child, or boss), the defenses against the early introjects are slackened, and the internal objects emerge and reactivate in some form. They can also be manifested, of course, in the individual psychotherapy situation, being reprised with the therapist via the transference. The point is that the internal objects are usually stimulated, re-enacted, and recontoured by the transactions with the parents, the original representatives of those introjects, during the family-of-origin sessions.

Reprojection Process

One's parents in the present are not the parents of yesteryear; indeed, they never were. The parents of today are perceived by their adult children through the astigmatism of their childhood views of the parents and by how those perceptions have been metabolized by later life experiences. The parents are not only the original transference figures, but are also reprojected upon from the perspective of the adult child's current transference distortions, resulting in a kind of double transference. In this connection, Anthony (1971) states,

> To have family therapy with one's original family is a radically different experience from having it with one's family of procreation. In the first type of situation, the patient is confronted by the external representation of his internal family. In the second type of situation, the external family may be the recipient of transferred feelings from the internal family. The matter is not quite as clear-cut as stated, since transference, in its psychoanalytic sense is no respecter of persons, and almost anyone or anything can receive transferred emotions. This means that a person may transfer from his internal objects to the actual latter-day members of his original family. To any particular member of the family, therefore, he may, at one and the same time, experience both transference and interpersonal feelings, adding complexity and confusion to his emotional life. (p. 373)

The above quotation can help explain why parents can be so bewildered by an offspring's attacks and bitterness. When an adult sees his father cry, he may wonder, "Is this the father of my childhood?" The parents themselves may no longer fit the inner objects since, over time, they may have undergone internal changes that their children know little about.

Double transferences, moreover, also go in the opposite direction—from parents to adult children. Not only do parents transfer to their young children from *their* families of origin and generational history, but intervening experiences create newer transferences to their adult children. One may hear statements like the following in family-of-origin sessions: "Mom, when are you going to stop treating me like a child?" or "Dad, I can no longer be your confidante about your marital problems." During these sessions the family members attempt to maneuver the others into behaving in a way that is congruent with their internal objects. When the other person behaves differently than previously perceived, the dissonance creates the opportunity for change. As can be seen, tracking the complexity of transference phenomena in family-of-origin sessions is a convincing challenge.

The Role of the Therapists

The male-female team of consultant-facilitators creates a safe setting of acceptance and openness; they offer the support, protection, and control that will contain and handle the emotional exchanges, underground irrationality, fantasies, secrets, and fears that every family brings to these sessions (Pincus & Dare, 1978). In this secure and protected context, where the therapists' strength can be joined with, the family members can hear and be heard in a way that is new and different. In most cases, changed behavior on the part of the parents (being interested and receptive, really listening and hearing, acknowledging and validating feelings, refraining from old criticisms, etc.) reduces the tenacity of attachment to the bad internal objects, and even sometimes allows for their release because the negative aspect of the parent of the past is being experienced as a better parent in the present.

These events do not occur smoothly, without pain, backsliding, angry interchanges, confusion, and untangling of misinterpretations; instant revelations of understanding are rare. (I have always regarded confusion as a good sign in therapy; it means that the old patterns are breaking up and that the new ones are not yet available.) As the cotherapists balance the conflicting demands and expectations, highlight the contribution of each family member to the others' lives, nurture the family's inherent resources, and introduce hope into long-standing stagnant contexts, all family members earn credit and entitlement (Boszormenyi-Nagy & Krasner, 1986).

Since they are not dealing with their own parents, the therapists can respond to the parents as ordinary human beings, divested of their magical power. The therapists' reacting to the parents as real people makes it easier for the adult children to do so.

During the course of these sessions—as past and current issues are faced; as self-disclosures take place; as the system is opened up; as family members do not disintegrate when told the truth; as past hurtful memories are confirmed, demystified (Laing, 1965), and dealt with sympathetically; as family myths and legends are demythologized (Byng-Hall, 1973, 1988; Ferreira, 1963); as systemic rage is let go; as sibling issues are dealt with; as the parents become more real as persons—the cotherapists create an atmosphere that allows for reconstructive changes to take place within the individual family members as well as in their relationships with their spouses and children.

The Role of Apology

Another key factor in helping bring about positive change in these sessions is the role of apology.* The technique, mentioned before, of having each family member tell every other family member what he/she likes and appreciates about that person, helps pave the way for amnesty and for warm feelings to emerge, even in the midst of apparent recrimination. When a parent, for example, apologizes for a past injustice or maltreatment, or if an extenuating circumstance for a wrong is explained, there can follow not only an easing of long-

---

*This concept was suggested by Felise B. Levine.

held grievances, but a reorganization of the internal world of the adult child and a resultant rise in self-esteem. One client said, in response to a parent making amends, "Hey, maybe I wasn't such a rotten kid after all." Another client said that this was the first time she felt heard and understood by her family. This change is comparable to the beneficial effect that can occur when a therapist apologizes to a client for a mistake that the therapist made in therapy (Goldberg, 1987).

Boszormenyi-Nagy (in Boszormenyi-Nagy & Krasner, 1986) states that when a parent apologizes, not only is the child's self-esteem raised, but the self-esteem of the parent is elevated as well. That is to say, when a parent who has exploited or parentified a child in the past atones in the present, the child is credited and the parent earns entitlement, thereby helping to balance the emotional ledger and increasing the ethical fairness. An exonerated parent is then free to give more. Although I have stressed the role of parental apology, parents can feel rejected by their children, too. Indeed, the adult children in these sessions occasionally express the wish to make amends to a parent or sibling they have wronged.

Changing the Family Rules and Legitimizing Family Disloyalty

One of the most powerful forces in families is the injunction against breaking the rules and customs of the family. Every family has its own unique rules, such as "parents must be respected," "we do not air our dirty linen outside the family"; "the children do not deal directly with the father; they must go through mother"; "Mom's alcoholism must never be noticed or mentioned"; or "In this family anger is not allowed." These codes are not written down and are rarely explicit, but family members discover very quickly that a rule exists when they break one. In family-of-origin sessions the family rules are not only revealed by the overt and covert interactions, but they are usually put on transitory hold by the therapeutic interventions. For example, when the therapists ask the adult children to address father directly, or someone brings up the taboo subject of a parent's drinking, or someone gets angry, the change in the family rules arouses intense anxiety.

Closely allied with the phenomenon of family rules, which are often institutionalized into family myths, is the critical concept of family loyalty. Boszormenyi-Nagy and Spark (1973) view the loyalties which bind the family together as being central in understanding family dynamics. These loyalties, or shared expectations, are sustained for the maintenance and survival of the family group and are enforced by guilt induction or threats of abandonment, as well as by positive feelings of love and allegiance. Some families require greater pledges of loyalty than others do, and families vary considerably along the dimension of what constitutes disloyalty.

As a matter of fact, there are parents who unconsciously perceive as betrayals their children growing up and leaving them one day, with the children perhaps even transferring their devotion to someone else. Seemingly disloyal acts (leaving the family in a rage, committing a crime, developing psychiatric symptoms, joining a cult, forming a disastrous marriage that quickly breaks up so the adult child must return home) are often, paradoxically, disguised affirmations of basic family fealty. The invisible bonds of loyalty to the family of origin exercise their irresistible influence throughout one's lifetime.

It is suggested here, however, that one of the reasons change can take place in family-of-origin sessions is that *the context legitimizes disloyalty.* In this setting it is permissible, okay, and sanctioned that the family rules be breached, that family myths be exposed, that honesty take precedence over self- and other deceit, that channels of communication be changed and made more congruent, that colliding loyalties and alliances be revealed, that hidden longings or aversions be verbalized, that double-binds be commented upon, and that positive feelings, which had been blocked or not recognized, be allowed free expressions. The safe surround of the family-of-origin sessions permits the temporary suspension of the old family realities so that some new ones can take their place.

Changes on the Individual System Level

As stated previously, it is proposed that as a function of the family-of-origin encounter, changes can take place in the systems of three levels: the individual, the marital and parental system, and the system of the family of origin. With respect to the individual, as a function of facing the parents and siblings with one's vital issues, the person ends up recognizing that being rebellious, passively compliant, or cut off, are not the only available choices, that being close does not have to lead to suffocation, and being separate does not signify desertion or being forsaken. In object relations terms, there is an attenuation of splitting, an expansion of the central ego (leading to more wholeness), less denial, a shift in the equilibrium of internal and external objects, an increased capacity to tolerate and contain ambivalence, and since there is a more balanced perspective of the parents, there is less need to be frightened of being *like* a parent.

Greenson's classic paper on "The Struggle Against Identification" (1954) illustrates how some people are terrified of becoming like a negatively valued parent. This fear can impel some people to live their entire lives as a refutation of the parent, thus creating new problems. The experience of the family-of-origin session can weaken this massive defense so that the individual is less compelled to be *unlike* a parent and therefore is more free to be his or her own person. Moreover, being sympathetic to a parent helps with the introject of that parent. Most of the adult children in these sessions come to recognize that it is in their own self-interest not to hate a parent; they have sensed that when you hate a parent you hate yourself.

In addition to changes in attitudes toward parents and siblings as a result of family-of-origin sessions, individuals are usually able to relate more appropriately to their spouses, their children, their friends, and even to their colleagues in the work situation. Some individuals become more successful in their careers, or change careers.

Changes on the Marital System Level

Gordon (1982) speculates on why these sessions are effective in detoxifying troublesome marital relationships. He states,

I suspect, however, that the key factor is working through the idealization of the family of origin—idealization present in even the most embittered individuals. Somehow within the context of (family of origin) sessions the individual can more objectively observe the original family's operations. They have a greater sense of the frustrations and hurts that come about and give meaning to their over-sensitivities and fears within the context of their marriage. The costly idealizations of one's family of origin means displacing the bad object onto a spouse or child. By replacing appropriate anger and ambivalence onto the original frustrating love object, the intensity of the transferences and projective identifications onto one's spouse becomes significantly diminished. (p. 330)

The family-of-origin sessions are indeed useful in helping the partners to reinternalize that part of the self that had been projected onto the spouse, resulting in these individuals being able to manage their ambivalence and aggression in a less destructive way. The sessions also help the partners to balance in better proportions their autonomy needs versus their needs for the relationship; they struggle less with the question, "How much do you owe others, and how much do you owe yourself?"

If marriage is, in part, an attempt to heal past conflicts that existed with parents and siblings, then marriage can be the beneficiary of those past conflicts being ameliorated. Many adult children in family-of-origin sessions rediscover admiration, appreciation, and love of a parent or sibling, and these feelings sometimes transfer to the spouse. Moreover, since individuals incorporate aspects of their parents' marital *relationship* as well as characteristics of their individual parents, they can discover, in family-of-origin sessions, that the parents' caring of each other was stronger than they thought and that the love had been concealed behind their disputes. On the other hand, adult children can finally realize that attempts to help their parents' cheerless marriage are futile, and they can give up trying to be marriage counselors to their parents. Then, just as the adult child does not have to work so hard at being *unlike* a parent, so that person does not have to try so strenuously and artificially to create a marriage that has to be so different from the parents' marriage. Allowing themselves to be happier than their parents opens up many more life options.

There are innumerable people in this world who are unable to leave marriages which they experience as desperately unhappy.

Some cannot leave for reasons which are apparently realistic: they have young children, they have no money, and no where to go. Still others want to get out of their marriage, but cannot; friends wonder why, despite such suffering, emptiness, or mutual destructiveness, such couples stay together. Being tied to a disliked partner and unable to leave that relationship is not sex-linked; men as well as women can be locked in by emotional enslavement. Speculating on why unhappily married people stay together, Dicks (1967) says that "social values and duty to the children apart, there is a need in each partner to wring out of the other the response that signifies to the unconscious the typical interaction model with the internal object or objects which have come to be vested in the marital relationship" (p. 269). Guntrip (1969) affirms this clinical finding by pointing out that, "patients cling tenaciously to their *external* bad objects because they represent *internal* bad objects whom they feel incapable of leaving" (p. 342).

Since primitive attachments to inner objects become disengaged or moderated in family-of-origin sessions, it is not surprising that some clients, following these sessions, are able to take a step that would have previously seemed unimaginable: end a hopeless marriage. In family-of-origin sessions some clients discover that their family could meet the needs formerly provided by the spouse. If the client is fighting an old battle with a new enemy, when that old adversary is tamed, the new enemy is no longer needed. The spouse is no longer invested with deep object relation meaning since the transference models are changed.

Since both partners are dynamic agents in the field of marital forces, impinging and being impinged upon, the marriage relationship has a better chance of improving when both partners have family-of-origin sessions. Positive changes in a relationship can, of course, take place when only one partner undergoes intrapsychic change, whether from life experience, individual psychotherapy, or the intergenerational experience. The redistribution of introjects, resulting in the maturation of one person, is likely to have a reverberating effect on the mutual projection system (Zinner, 1976). When the recipient of a projection no longer "cooperates" in the projection, the projector is left hanging with the projection. When one person's demons have been laid to rest, the marital game may lose its flavor, resulting in divorce. However, while some divorces are unnecessary, some divorces need to take place.

Changes in the Family-of-Origin System

In addition to changes in the individual and marital systems following the intergenerational encounter, favorable corrections and regenerations can occur in the original family system. After these sessions, the family-of-origin relationships are usually more free and less guarded; there is a diminished need for the guilty hiding of secrets, and needs are more openly expressed. Other positive changes that can occur are less rigidity of roles, clearer boundaries, more direct communication channels, less use of pathological scapegoating and parentification, and fewer family and individual dysfunctions (parents' alcoholism, a sibling's drug addiction, psychosomatic disorders, etc.). Family members who had previously not had contact with each other continue to keep in touch, and siblings renew and strengthen their relationships with each other (particularly helpful when the parents are unable to give). The parents and adult children are usually more able to view each other as separate and real persons. The parents' marital relationship sometimes improves, and the parents, now more able to face death since they *tried* to work out things with their children, may even be able to live longer. There is abundant evidence that the lack of satisfactory relationships with significant others, leading to loneliness, has serious medical consequence (Lynch, 1977).

There are suggestions that the family-of-origin sessions have *spreading* effects. Parents are sometimes stimulated to make peace with their own cut-off siblings, and the brothers and sisters of the client are often motivated to do something about their own marriage or their children. Some parents take more interest in their grandchildren. Other parents, who were paralyzed with anxiety and were unresponsive *during* sessions, are able to come through for their children in later weeks.

A FINAL COMMENT

The reader may have gained the impression that I regard the family of origin as the only determining influence on people's lives, and that psychopathology and disturbed marriages are the inevitable fate of disordered families of origin. Indeed, many people who have had terrible family backgrounds may believe that they are doomed as prospective mates or parents or that they will never be able to sustain an intimate relationship. People hold onto their old family inside them, but also worry that the negative legacies from that family will carry over to their children's family of origin.

In actual fact, the traumas of early family life do not necessarily shape one's future (Vaillant, 1977).

While it is true that the family of origin is the most powerful force in organizing and framing later life experiences and choices, there are indeed many other influences which impact on the human being and which may even counteract the deleterious effects of one's family. Among such factors are the following: positive experiences with someone outside the immediate family, such as a grandparent, aunt or uncle, a teacher or mentor, good friends; group supports; special skills or high intelligence that the individual has, such as artistic talents, skills in sports, school successes that create opportunities outside the family; inherent personality traits or temperament that enables the individual to better handle malevolent family processes; developmental, life cycle, or serendipitous events that modulate or attenuate pathological family forces; economic, social, ethnic, or spiritual influences; the fortuitous selection of a spouse who fits one's needs; and unknown variables that occur as a function of being human in a changing world.

Individuals can sometimes attenuate the damage resulting from severely disturbed families by the healing of a good marriage, by the experience of having children, by supportive friends, by vocational and other accomplishments, and by other means. Furthermore, due to later auspicious experiences in living, some individuals are able to influence their family of origin in a favorable way. Sometimes adult children can "raise up" their parents.

8

Clinical Implications

Most psychotherapists tend to believe in the myth that the most significant events of peoples' lives occur in the treatment office. In fact, there are a host of factors extrinsic to the therapy situation that are relevant to the course and outcome of relationship problems. With respect to intergenerational intervention, I have not discussed the critical importance of the reality considerations involved in the relationships between adult children and their parents. I refer here to such practical factors as: how often the adult children and their parents see or keep in touch with each other; the economic status of all concerned; the geographical proximity to each other; the extent to which adult children or parents give financial or other help to each other; whether the parents are divorced, widowed, retired, or dead; whether one or both parents are alcoholic, institutionalized, disabled, missing, or in prison; the affectional ties between them; value discrepancies between the generations; the sibling relationships; the quality of the in-law and extended family relationships; and problems of ailing or aging parents. Space considerations prevent any further discussion of these important matters, some of which will have strong effects on the clinical effectiveness of family-of-origin sessions. The reader is referred to the following references for information on these relevant considerations: Bank & Kahn, 1982; Brubaker, 1983; Cicirelli, 1981; Flomenhaft & Kaplan, 1968; Herr & Weakland, 1979; Johnson & Bursk, 1979; Kahn & Lewis, 1988; Leader, 1979; Mancini, 1990; Sussman, 1960; Troll, Miller & Atchley, 1979; Uzoka, 1979.

By bringing in clients' families of origin I attempt to introduce preventative antibodies into the culture of the family. My approach to intrapsychic and relationship problems is to deal with basic processes rather than with the superficial manifestations of system breakdown in the form of symptoms. Using symptom removal as a criterion of improvement is relatively easy and clear-cut. Much more difficult an undertaking is the evaluation of the gradual, subtle, and perhaps more in-depth system changes within the family. The most important and meaningful data about families are the most difficult to obtain because these data tap the deeper crosscurrents of family life such as fusion versus differentiation, closeness-distance balance, clashing of need systems, shifts in loyalties, intergenerational influences, and mutual projective identifications.

The next section will focus on the following clinical implications of involving the family of origin in the treatment of individuals and couples:

1. Evaluation of this intergenerational method as a form of therapy;
2. Research suggestions;
3. Recommendations and caveats to family therapists who conduct family-of-origin sessions;
4. Comparison to other intergenerational family therapists;
5. Speculations on why adults are so fearful of having sessions with their families of origin;
6. What family-of-origin sessions can accomplish; and
7. Personal associations.

EVALUATION OF THIS INTERGENERATIONAL METHOD AS A FORM OF THERAPY

In the absence of hard outcome data, I feel incumbent to transmit my clinical impressions, based on many years of experience with this method, of some indications, limits, and conditions for the therapeutic effectiveness of this work.

1. From the outset, I must state that I do not consider the family-of-origin encounter to be a routine procedure, a complete form of

therapy, or an all-purpose method to be used in all or even most clinical situations. It is a highly specialized procedure. Intergenerational exploration is not even necessary for the milder forms of marital dysfunction, since conventional marital therapy techniques will usually suffice (Framo, 1980).

Further, it needs to be emphasized that family-of-origin work, in the sense in which it is used here, is not an emergency procedure. It is not crisis intervention and is not aimed at expeditious symptom removal, the rescue of a marriage in crisis, the achievement of instant intimacy, or the quick resolution of long-standing conflicts that have existed between family-of-origin members.

This intervention is a carefully planned method whereby clients are prepared to face parents and siblings directly in order to deal with the vital past and present issues between them. Clinical experience with this method has indicated that shifting the original family system by small but pivotal increments can gear by multiple ratio and lead to significant long-range changes in relationships. These changes can take place in the family of origin, in the extended family, in the marital system of the clients, and intrapsychically in the individual systems.

However, I do not expect that a four-hour meeting of parents and adult children will drastically transform family or marital interactions and styles that have existed for many years; the individual personalities will not be extensively altered. Not only do these shortcomings exist, but the resistances in clients to having family-of-origin sessions are enormous, the sessions are difficult to organize, arrange, and conduct, and the sessions themselves are a formidable enterprise that tax and challenge therapists' skills and personal value systems.

2. But having said all of that, I do believe, as stated in the beginning of this book, that one session of an adult with his/her parents and brothers and sisters, conducted in this special kind of way, can result in more beneficial therapeutic effects than the entire course of a psychotherapy. Although I have had the reputation of doing long-term family therapy—probably based on the book *Intensive Family Therapy* (Boszormenyi-Nagy & Framo, 1965)—the family-of-origin intervention may be the *ultimate brief therapy.*

As described in this book, family-of-origin work covers a range of formats, extending from sessions I conduct with clients in ongoing individual, family, or marital therapy to the one-time intensive experience for clients who are either self-referred or referred by another therapist for a family-of-origin consultation. Each of these categories is meaningful and productive, but in different ways.

Generally speaking, self-referred families who specifically request these family meetings in order to deal with issues with each other seem to get the most from these sessions. These families are highly motivated to straighten out matters between them, and they come to sessions well prepared.

Although the method almost always has substantial positive effects when used as a one-time-only procedure with motivated individuals and families, clients who need to be persuaded to have the sessions usually report how healing the experience is. Initial resistance on the part of clients appears unrelated to outcome. That is, clients and families who are initially very opposed to undergoing the procedure, as well as those who just go along with the idea, frequently derive great benefits, especially when the clients are well prepared for the sessions by the therapists.

The potency of the therapeutic effects of this intergenerational method is increased when the procedure is integrated with individual or marital therapy. The therapy done prior to and following the family-of-origin sessions is an integral part of a process that relates current relationship problems to old ones. Some family members, following the family-of-origin consultation, choose to pursue individual exploration of their introjects, while others may feel no need for further therapy.

Those clients who are in individual or marital psychotherapy with another therapist and who are referred for a family-of-origin consultation are returned to their therapist for continuing work. This particular use of the method as an adjunct treatment has great potential, not only for enriching the ongoing therapy, but also for abbreviating the treatment. Orthodox psychoanalytic treatment may be shortened if the analysand, at some critical point in the analysis, has a family-of-origin session and makes distinctions in the continued psychoanalysis between the fantasy internal objects and the real external family members. *One can speculate as to whether the length of all psychotherapies can be reduced by appropriately timed family-of-origin sessions.*

3. Some schools of family therapy (Strategic, Structural, Systemic) claim that attending to the *origins* of dysfunctions will not lead to change. Ruminating about the past and gaining "insight," by themselves, are indeed likely to be unproductive, especially when this endeavor is not undertaken under the guidance of a skillful, empathic therapist. One unique aspect of bringing in the actual original family is that it is real, immediate, and action-oriented. It bypasses resistances that occur in other forms of therapy, it clarifies faulty memories, translates obsessive speculation into interaction, and directly intervenes into the heart of the family matters that have existed in the past and their legacies in the present. It is the link between the past and the present that I emphasize.

4. The experience of just getting together as a family in a protected context and dealing with matters of importance have a nonspecific effect that stirs the family mystique on a primitive level and constitutes a *seeding* operation that can reap later benefits. Many of the positive results do not appear until long after the sessions are over (e.g., a warmer, more sympathetic feeling toward a previously feared or hated parent; a more mellow, involved father; a less demanding mother; a changed perception of one of the siblings previously viewed as a ne'er-do-well; a settled feud between brothers or sisters, etc.). Moreover, those interventions that have salutary effects and interrupt pathogenic relationship patterns in this generation may carry over into succeeding generations.

5. In evaluating this method as a form of therapy, there is another consideration that applies to all psychotherapeutic situations. I share with most therapists the mistaken belief that our methods or techniques are received by clients in the way they are intended. In truth, I believe that clients take from therapy inputs what they need; they reinterpret interventions according to their own needs, expectations, fears, fantasies, and wishes (Silberschatz, Fretter, & Curtis, 1986). Families, too, have their own system-rule filters that determine what will or will not get through. This phenomenon helps to explain how sessions that the therapists thought were great are responded to by clients with indifference or as being unproductive, whereas sessions that the therapists perceived as awful or meaningless are sometimes responded to by clients enthusiastically as the best ones.

6. Intergenerational family therapy has unique properties com-

pared to other forms of psychotherapy, some of which are listed
here:

- The original transference figures are being dealt with in
  vivo.
- Family members who come in do not acknowledge themselves as patients seeking help.
- Family members who attend sessions have usually trav-
  eled long distances to get to the sessions.
- The process of preparing for these sessions usually stimulates changes in both the family of origin as well as in the
  family of procreation. Even simply raising family-of-
  origin issues with clients who never have the family-of-
  origin sessions can bring about changes in that family.
  Indeed, sometimes the family has done so much work
  prior to the sessions that the sessions themselves are
  anticlimactic.
- The spreading effects on the extended family can be far-
  reaching because parents' relationships with their own
  original family members (usually siblings) are frequently
  opened up and improved. The client's sibling may go
  back to his/her spouse to deal with an issue heretofore
  avoided, resulting in a more viable marital relationship. (I
  have called this phenomenon "marital therapy by proxy.")
- By bringing in families of origin a therapist can get to see
  people who, while they may have a great impact on
  others, are often not the kind of people who would ordinarily go for psychotherapy. Therefore, one can possibly
  have an effect on a segment of the population that therapists do not ordinarily see. This intervention, then, can
  have public health implications. In addition, by doing this
  work, a therapist can get to see nonclinical subcultures
  that might not ordinarily present for treatment in one's
  practice (e.g., I have seen Amish families, prominent families, and even a bonafide Mafia family).

7. There are some family clinical situations that appear to be especially responsive to intergenerational exploration, just as there are

those about which there is less expectation of positive outcome. Before presenting examples of both, I need to stress that the results of family-of-origin intervention depend on a multiplicity of interlocking variables, including family variables, therapist variables, the interaction between the two, as well as reality factors extrinsic to the sessions themselves. Among such family-therapist variables are the fit between the family and therapists on values of social class, ethnic group, religion, politics, and lifestyles and the extent to which the family and therapist team can like or "connect" with each other. Therapist variables concern such factors as whether the therapists have attempted to deal with their own family-of-origin issues, therapists' skills and experience doing different kinds of psychotherapies as well as the therapists' capacity to tolerate such family characteristics as scapegoating, deceit, stonewalling, angry outbursts, and chaotic communications. Extrinsic variables could be the current realities of the relationships between the family members, referred to earlier; whether a family member is in psychotherapy with someone else; health, economic, and geographical considerations; and so on.

CLINICAL SITUATIONS MOST RESPONSIVE TO INTERGENERATIONAL INTERVENTION

With these cautions in mind, the following are examples of those clinical situations that will respond particularly well to family-of-origin sessions:

- Couples who are unable to make a commitment to their marriage, or to separate, until issues are worked out with a parent or sibling;
- Individual or marital therapy that has hit an impasse and cannot move forward until the clients go back and deal with their families of origin;
- Premarital couples who have severe doubts about marrying and are fearful of commitment;
- Adults, usually in their 30s and 40s, who have reached the developmental stage where they have moved beyond their rebellious or autonomy struggle with parents and are

searching for a different, more personal way of relating to them.

- Parents who were physically or sexually abused as children and who are fearful of repeating those patterns with their own children;
- Families where there has been a bitter divorce in years past and the parents and adult children are still suffering from the aftereffects (Wallerstein & Blakeslee, 1989). Family-of-origin sessions can help the parents to finish their emotional divorce, settle old accounts, and thereby free up their adult children;
- Individuals who have had repeated divorces and who recognize that working out issues with original family may interrupt their divorce pattern.
- Families where the adult children note a pattern of being unable to form lasting, satisfactory, or committed intimate relationships until issues are worked out with the family of origin;
- Alienated families with a history of cutoffs, sometimes to such a marked degree that the members do not go to weddings or even to funerals of other family members;
- Families where one member, usually an adult child, is intensely motivated to bring about change and settle family discords or achieve more closeness with a parent before it is too late;
- Families where there has been incomplete or aborted mourning over losses, resulting in various kinds of individual, marital or parenting dysfunctions (Paul & Grosser, 1965);
- Individuals who are open to exploring the connection between symptoms (e.g., depression, alcoholism, suicide attempts, drug abuse, psychosomatic disorders) and events in the original family;
- Families with intrusive, smothering mothers and distant fathers, where the adult children are trying to push the mother aside and reach the remote father. It is said that mothers love too much and fathers not enough;
- Adult sons and daughters who yearn to get closer to their

distant fathers and get to know them. When these hereto-fore inaccessible fathers respond, there are long-term beneficial effects (Framo, 1990; Osherson, 1986). Mothers and daughters have their own special relationship bonds and distinctive painful conflicts, as do mothers and sons, fathers and daughters, as well as fathers and sons. These gender and generational combinations have their own unique characteristics. These important dimensions of family relationships have been explored further in such publications as *My Mother, Myself* (Friday, 1987), *The Invisible Web* (Walters, Carter, Papp, & Silverstein, 1988); *Finding Our Fathers* (Osherson, 1986), and *Men in Therapy* (Meth & Pasick, 1990).

• Parents who request family-of-origin sessions in order to resolve issues with their adult children; and

• Sessions just with siblings in order to share memories of their deceased parents and, on occasion, to deal with past traumas such as child abuse, incest, or parents' alcoholism. These sessions usually strengthen the sibling subsystem, the only family they have.

CLINICAL SITUATIONS LEAST RESPONSIVE TO INTERGENERATIONAL INTERVENTION

The foregoing list is by no means exclusive, any more than are the following examples of situations that seem to be less amenable to family-of-origin intervention:

• Family-of-origin sessions organized primarily for the purpose of getting revenge on a parent or sibling. The overriding motive is one of vindictiveness;

• Families where members have made a pact, prior to the sessions, not to deal with anything important, or they have decided beforehand to avoid certain issues with specific members of the family e.g., agreeing to avoid any criticism of Mom;

• Families characterized by long-standing and severe

pathologies such as virulent double-binding, disorganization of family experiences, mystification, gross invalida-
tion of one or more family members, a history of explosive violence, drastic distortions of meanings, tangential
thinking, flagrant dishonesty, and so on. Some family
members could be diagnosed, in conventional terms, as
borderline personality disorders, or psychotic;

- Situations where the family members collude to keep a
significant family member away from the session (Sonne,
Speck, & Jungreis, 1962), or, when one family member
refuses to come to the session;

- Those clients who have unrealistic expectations of what
the sessions can do and who fantasize that everything that
has always been wrong will magically be made right;

- Those clients who passively comply with the therapists'
urging to have the sessions but who are basically not motivated to deal with family-of-origin issues;

- Partners who are so overwhelmed with their marital crisis
that they are unable or unwilling to get involved in issues
with parents or siblings; The crisis (e.g., around a recently
disclosed affair) is so acute and consuming that the marital
therapy largely consists of putting out the immediate fires.
These clients do not want to even look at connections
between their experiences in their family of origin and their
present perceived calamity: "Hey Doc, the problem is not
with my mother; the problem is with my wife."

- Families who are so fragile, brittle, or frightened that they
cannot deal with any issues of consequence. Some of
these families have dark secrets or very loaded issues (e.g.,
incest);

- Family-of-origin sessions where the clients have not been
well prepared or the timing of the sessions is premature;

- Families who come in with the expectation that they are
only going to be discussing the problems of the client;

- Couples whose marriages have improved or individuals
who are not hurting so much are disinclined to work on
family-of-origin issues.

RESEARCH SUGGESTIONS

Although I have long since moved away from clinical psychology's view of individuals as existing in a vacuum, and I have moved toward a systems view of individuals in context, my early background in psychology compels me to emphasize the importance of research. I decry the split that has occurred between clinical psychology and academic psychology and have long advocated the application of systematic research methods to clinical problems (Framo, 1972). Clinical theories need to be operationally stated and put in the form of testable hypotheses, and the variables need to be manipulated by rules that permit the data to confirm or to disprove the hypotheses by other than clinical anecdotes. Only in this way can laws of broad applicability be abstracted from the individual instance.

Assessment of intergenerational relationships as well as quantitative investigations of family-of-origin methods have been undertaken by Baker (1982); Bray, Harvey, and Williamson (1987); Bray and Williamson (1987); Bray, Williamson, and Malone (1984); Fine and Norris (1989); Hovestadt, Anderson, Piercy, Cochran and Fine (1985); Laham (1990); Mazer, Mangrum, Hovestadt and Brashear (1990); and Wilcoxon and Hovestadt (1983).

What follows are some suggestions, based on my clinical experience with the family-of-origin method, of possible research studies on this intervention:

1. What are the short- and long-term effects of family-of-origin sessions on the individual family members, on the marital and parental relationships, and on the relationships within the family of origin? Outcome studies could be conducted which relate the effects of family-of-origin interventions to variables emphasized by other family therapy schools. For example, do family-of-origin sessions bring about increased differentiation of family members (Bowen Theory); shifts in family loyalties and fairness (Contextual Theory); changes in family structures and boundaries (Structural Family Therapy); fewer sequences of dysfunctional behaviors (Strategic

Family Therapy); or more congruent, open, empathic communications (Communication Theory)?

2. How are introjects modified by this intervention (e.g., measures of self-esteem before and after family-of-origin sessions)?

3. Do family-of-origin sessions have an effect on symptoms manifested by any of the family members?

4. What are the effects of this intervention on the children of the client or on children of the client's siblings?

5. Does this intervention have spreading effects on extended family members not seen (e.g., marital relationships of the siblings, or parents' relationships with their own siblings)?

6. Are emotional and physical cutoffs repaired by this intergenerational method?

7. Do alienated families of origin develop more cohesiveness, and do fused families become more differentiated following these sessions?

8. At what point in ongoing individual or marital therapy should family-of-origin sessions be held?

9. What should be the length and spacing of these sessions in order to obtain maximum benefit? Treatment outcome studies can systematically vary these variables.

10. Family-of-origin scales are steps in the right direction (Hovestadt, Anderson, Piercy, Cochran, & Fine, 1985). However, I believe that measuring instruments should be based on observation of family members interacting with each other rather than having each member respond separately to a questionnaire (Framo, 1965b, 1972).

11. In addition to changes in the relationship between the adult children and their parents, do the family-of-origin sessions have any effect on the relationships between the adult children and their own children?

12. Under what circumstances do marriages improve following intergenerational intervention, and when do marriage relationships worsen or not change at all?

RECOMMENDATIONS AND CAVEATS TO FAMILY THERAPISTS WHO CONDUCT FAMILY-OF-ORIGIN SESSIONS

Most of the following suggestions and admonitions have been mentioned previously in this book but are presented herewith, in no particular order of importance, in summary fashion:

1. The incoming family in family-of-origin sessions should be treated with respect and appreciation of their anxiety. They cannot be approached as patients who have requested help for their problems.
2. Never join the adult children in attacking or criticizing parents. Even those who are furious at parents will ultimately be grateful toward the therapists who are supportive of parents.
3. Clients must be instructed before the family-of-origin session to tell all family members that *all* the family relationships will be discussed in the sessions, not just the problems of the client.
4. Therapists must be sensitive to ethnic issues in these sessions in terms of how the family takes to therapy with outsiders and how acculturated the family is and should also be sensitive to such ethnic considerations as respect for elders, duty, gender roles, traditions, values about rearing children, marital power, and so on (McGoldrick, Pearce, & Giordano, 1982).
5. There are spouses who enter marital therapy who are quite unable to examine their contribution to the marital problems. They cannot take responsibility for their own experience and view their own negative behaviors as logical reactions to their partner's perceived noxious behaviors. These people are especially resistant to the suggestion that they bring in their family of origin. Some of these individuals may refuse to even relate a family history because to do so might imply that they themselves play a part in the disturbed marital drama. One client said, "How in hell could my family have anything to do with the insulting, control-

ling, and humiliating actions of my wife?" With these kinds of clients therapists may have to comfort themselves with the fact that they cannot help everyone. Other techniques such as behavioral marital therapy or strategic, paradoxical techniques may be useful with such resistant clients.

6. Do not allow incoming family to use the sessions in order to criticize the spouse of the client. This maneuver diverts from the main purpose of the sessions.

7. Therapists who have control issues, who lock horns with the parents and battle with them, are likely to lose the family and the client.

8. Therapists whose experience has largely been with treating individuals are likely to have difficulty making the transition to the whole family. Child therapists, in particular, may find it difficult to see the parents' point of view.

9. There are occasions when family members, prior to the sessions, jointly decide or agree to avoid discussing certain topics. This plan creates a dilemma for therapists who do not want to participate in the collusion. The sessions can feel "phony." However, since it is the family members' choice to do this, the therapist must respect their decision.

10. Family-of-origin sessions are likely to be unproductive when a spouse has the sessions in order to please his/her partner, or requests the sessions in a desperate effort to save a failing marriage. The client must have issues he/she wants to work out with parents or brothers and sisters.

11. This intergenerational method is not set up for quick fixes. The changes usually take time, are subtle, and may require an intimate knowledge of the family that only a family member can observe. The changes may go unnoticed unless attention is called to them. One cannot judge enthusiasm or lack of enthusiasm on the part of the family members as indicators of the effectiveness of family-of-origin sessions. These sessions often contain inputs that germinate later, and what may appear as uneventful sessions, may in fact have strong favorable repercussions many months down the road. In contrast, some dramatic sessions may not fulfill their promise.

12. Therapists should not allow the family to focus too much on the therapists (e.g., their feelings about the therapists or questions about therapy). This diversion is usually a function of family members' anxiety about dealing with each other.

13. Clients with severe narcissistic wounds may be disappointed because they feel that someone else in the family got more from the sessions than they did. Clients may also feel that the therapists failed them because their expectations were not met. Some of these clients may express rage toward the therapists. These kinds of clients need special preparation for sessions by indicating that the needs of all the family members will be attended to and that some fantasies cannot be fulfilled. Longer periods of preparation and extended family-of-origin sessions may be indicated for such hypersensitive people. As Lansky (1981) has indicated in his work with the "narcissistically vulnerable couple," it may be necessary for the therapists to keep to a minimum family members' interaction with each other and encourage more direct and empathic communication between the therapists and each family member.

14. It is necessary for therapists to balance support of parents with the adult child's need for validation of memories of past injustices and emotional injuries.

15. Although it is clear with some clients that they cannot make progress (either with intrapsychic or marital problems) without first working out certain issues with their parents and siblings, there are other clients for whom family-of-origin sessions, while possibly useful, may not be necessary (e.g., superficial marital problems).

16. It is important to stress that the sessions will be canceled unless *all* the family members are present. Although this stance is not always literally held to (e.g., medical emergencies), having the family and client believe that the sessions will be canceled will likely bring in a reluctant family member who would not ordinarily attend.

17. Because the expenses for travel, lodging, and therapy combined can be rather high, I usually suggest that all the fam-

ily members contribute to the costs, to the extent that each can afford to do so.

18. Further individual therapy following the family-of-origin sessions is indicated for certain clients. Some clients are motivated to integrate the results of the family-of-origin sessions with their intrapsychic conflicts. Others, unable to face the reality that they will never get the parents they always wanted, will need further help in finding ways to get their needs fulfilled elsewhere.

    Those clients who seek out individual therapy with another therapist should be advised to select a systems-oriented individual therapist inasmuch as some individual therapists may negate the advances made from the family-of-origin sessions (e.g., by discouraging contact with parents or siblings). Those clients who continue with marital therapy after the family-of-origin sessions are more open to explicating the relationship between old themes and how they are being played out in the marriage.

19. Some clients, for various reasons, are unable to get their family to come in. On these occasions I find it productive to use the Bowen method of sending clients home and coaching them on how they can change the rules of the system by making a differentiating move (Bowen, 1978). For instance, I suggested to a woman, who had an overly close relationship with her mother and a distant relationship with her father, that on her next visit home she invite her father to lunch and get to know him better. This invitation upset her mother, who said, "Why on earth would you want to talk to your father?" Further coaching enabled her to effect a closer relationship with her father without alienating her mother.

20. It is a good idea to include a spouse, sibling, or significant other when gathering a family history from a client while preparing for a family-of-origin session. This "outsider" usually can give useful, objective information about the client's family of origin; outsider accounts are frequently more revealing than those of the client.

21. It is not appropriate for the therapists to become directly

involved with getting the family of origin to come in. Such efforts promote the opportunity for resistances to be strengthened. It is the client's responsibility to get the family in and to negotiate with the family about the travel and lodging arrangements.

22. The cotherapy team relationship must be continually monitored; cotherapy conflicts, left unresolved, can give rise to a variety of therapy problems (Sonne & Lincoln, 1965).

23. Those clients who are in individual therapy elsewhere and are referred by their therapist for a family-of-origin consultation must be returned to their therapist. Do not participate in the acting out of a client who wants to transfer to you. Further, I prefer not getting information from the referring therapist about the client; the agenda for this family-of-origin consultation is based on information obtained from the client. With the family's permission, the client may play the taped family-of-origin sessions for the referring therapist.

24. Sessions should always be taped (audio or video). Some family members will never listen to the tapes; these people feel they were there for the moment in the sessions and do not want to go back to the experience. In some ways it is like not wanting to relive the anxiety of a dream after it has been analyzed. Other family members get a great deal out of repeated listenings of the sessions. Certainly, copies of the tapes should be sent to family members who could not be present.

25. One must be prepared for the resistances of outside therapists who are seeing a member of the family. Some of these therapists will advise their client not to attend the family-of-origin sessions because the experience would be "too upsetting" for the client or would "interfere with the psychotherapy." I do not deal directly with therapists who are resistant to this intergenerational approach. Instead, I prefer working out resistances with the client. In my experience, any attempt to convince a nonsystems-oriented therapist about the value of family-of-origin sessions is likely to be futile. These therapists do not recognize that family-of-origin sessions would enrich the therapy they are doing with their client. Most of these clients, incidentally, overrule

their therapist. I do believe that most clients find a way to get what they need. Sometimes they are wiser than their therapists.

26. There are some people who actively forbid their partners to have anything to do with their family of origin, and in some cases these partners comply, because to do otherwise would threaten the marital relationship. Family-of-origin sessions under these conditions are not likely to take place.

27. Therapists who use this intergenerational approach also need to be prepared for last minute cancellations of family-of-origin sessions. In addition to the many forms resistances can take in conventional family therapy (Anderson & Stewart, 1983), this form of intergenerational work has unique resistances of its own which can come from many more sources.

28. If any of the adult children in the early phases of the family-of-origin session start confronting one or both parents with heavy issues, the therapists should divert to safer issues, such as the sibling relationships. These premature confrontations could threaten the parents and set a tone of defensiveness. Such confrontations, if they do occur, should come up later when there is more security in the situation.

29. Since a primary goal of family-of-origin sessions is to have the family members face each other directly to deal with their issues, a guiding principle for therapists when these behaviors occur is to pull back, let it happen, and intervene only enough to keep the process going constructively.

30. Those people who request family-of-origin sessions who are not regular clients and are therefore unknown should be seen for at least one session in order to get a family history and prepare an agenda. Otherwise the therapists could end up working in the dark.

31. Follow-up resources and therapist referrals should always be offered to family members from out of town who request further help.

32. At the end of the sessions, the family should be offered follow-up sessions should they need and request them. Some families are strongly urged to return, but logistical prob-

lems, especially for out-of-town families, may be insurmountable. In my experience, about 10% of families return for additional family-of-origin sessions.

33. Sessions should end on a hopeful note, with the therapists commenting on the positive resources in the family and indicating that the healing process that has been started in the office will continue in the future. To the extent that is possible, the therapists should try to help the family members feel good about themselves and their family when they leave and also to have more realistic expectations about what they can and cannot get from one another.

34. Family-of-origin sessions can be very stressful for therapists. Therefore, the care and feeding of the therapists are important considerations. Most therapists have developed ways of avoiding burnout. With respect to these sessions, having a cotherapist alleviates some of the anxiety, but the best antidote for stress in this situation resides in the therapists' own self-awareness and process of working out significant issues with their own families of origin. Then the therapists are less likely to introduce their own issues into the situation and are more able to handle the family's irrationality.

COMPARISON TO OTHER INTERGENERATIONAL FAMILY THERAPISTS

This discussion of the work of other intergenerational family therapists is restricted to selected aspects of their methods and how they are related to the intergenerational approach described in this book. By no means am I attempting to give a comprehensive account of their theories and methods.

Murray Bowen

Murray Bowen, who died in 1990, was a colleague and friend of mine for over 30 years. For a personal account of our relationship, see Framo (1989, 1991). Bowen, of course, was the first family theoretician and therapist to call attention to the importance of intergenerational forces and patterns in family life. Bowen Theory is probably the most comprehensive and influential in the family therapy field (Bowen, 1978; Kerr & Bowen, 1988; Papero, 1990). With respect to treatment issues, Bowen rarely brings in his client's family of origin. Rather, he sends clients home for short, frequent visits, having coached them in their differentiating efforts beforehand.

The Bowen approach consists of supervising clients on how to get "outside" the emotional system of their family of origin, how to view their family with more objectivity, and how to respond to their own thinking rather than the emotional field of significant others. Clients are coached to establish a person-to-person relationship with each parent separately—a person-to-person relationship being defined as one in which it is possible to talk to the parent as a person—and to talk to the parent about the self as a person. This goal is similar to my approach of having family-of-origin members talk face to face in sessions about the important matters. The Bowen rationale suggests that if the client takes a special "I position" stance, along with continued relating to the family, that person will develop a more differentiated self. And when one person in the family differentiates, others in the family are likely to do so. Bowen stresses that he does not view getting involved with extended family as a therapeutic method.

Further, he raises the intriguing question as to whether one can bypass the presenting problem of clients and work directly on family of origin. He states,

> . . . families in which the focus is on the differentiation of self in the families of origin automatically make as much, or more, progress in working out the relationship system with spouses and children as families seen in formal family therapy in which there is principal focus on the interdependence in the marriage. My experience is going in the direction of saying that the most productive route for change, for families who are motivated, is to work at defining self in the family of origin, and to specifically avoid focus on the emotional issues in the nuclear family. I am not yet ready to say this, but I do have a group of people who are working at this in which there is a more disciplined effort to avoid focus on nuclear family process. If this current impression

eventually proves accurate, it has sweeping implications for theory and for the clinical practice of family therapy. (Bowen, 1974, p. 93)

My own belief is that it is necessary to work with the *integration* of family of origin and nuclear family issues, partly because of my theoretical convictions and partly because of the practical reality that most individuals, couples, or families will terminate if they feel that are not getting help with their immediate, pressing crises. On the other hand, I do try to get to family-of-origin issues as soon as practicable.

Ivan Boszormenyi-Nagy

Ivan Nagy and I go way back (to 1957, actually); we were among the early therapists who started seeing families, and we worked together for 13 years. We spent many mind-stretching, rewarding hours exchanging ideas about theory and therapy and we collaborated on one of the first books in the family therapy field, *Intensive Family Therapy* (1965). One can detect suggestions of our common roots in each of our present concepts and methods, but although our thinking overlaps in some respects, our theoretical paths and practice have become somewhat divergent. Different aspects of the intergenerational process are emphasized by each of us.

Numerous and exciting discoveries came out of our early experiences in treating whole families, but I will just mention a prototypical one that illustrates the antecedents of our now distinct approaches: When we started working with schizophrenics and their families, we initially felt bewilderment and even anger toward parents who did such awful things to their children. Later, with more experience, we recognized that whatever destructiveness or overburdening parents put on their children was once done to the parents themselves, as it had been done to their parents, and so forth. I extracted from such experiences the observation that children would pay any price to be accepted by their parents, including the price of irrational role assignment or even psychosis. In my major theoretical paper I wrote,

This writer postulates the theory that the universal human conflict between autonomy and reality on the one hand and the
need to be accepted by others on the other hand would have to
be included in any comprehensive explanation of the development of psychopathology. The power of life-sustaining family
relationship ties is much greater than instinctual or autonomous
strivings. (1970, p. 163)

Such observations presaged my object relations-based conceptualizations and their clinical application in the form of family-of-origin
work. Ivan Nagy moved in a different direction.

Nagy's Contextual Theory has been developed along the existential dimension of relational ethics, encompassing such constructs as
fairness, the sacrifice of autonomy in favor of loyalty to the family of
origin, emotional indebtedness and accounts, entitlement, crediting,
and trustworthiness between family members. His therapeutic
approach is aimed at determining the distribution and chain of
unfairness in the system; balancing the give and take and emotional
ledgers between family members; having people be held accountable
for unfair behaviors and correcting them; diminishing displaced
destructiveness; rearranging loyalties following the equilibration of
merits; assisting in the earning of entitlements and credits; establishing trust and the giving and receiving of rights and obligations; and
attempting to restore good faith in the interest of future generations
(Boszormenyi-Nagy & Spark, 1973; Boszormenyi-Nagy & Krasner,
1986, Van Heusden & Van Den Eerenbeemt, 1987).

Although it may seem that our conceptualizations are far apart,
Nagy's thinking and mine do intersect. Among the assumptions we
share are that individual or relationship difficulties emerge from patterns of dysfunction transmitted from one generation to the next;
that allegiance to the family of origin supersedes self-determination,
truth, and commitment to one's nuclear family; that in order to preserve the good image of the parents, unrealistic expectations and
revengeful behaviors are displaced onto spouses and children; that
people need to face their parents with their grievances over real or
felt mistreatment so that the deeper positive feelings can be
expressed; and that forgiveness ("exoneration" in Nagy's terms) of
parents, even of parents who exploited or brutalized, can emerge

from an appreciation of the parents' life struggles. When these intergenerational dialogues take place one can achieve wholeness with oneself, which gets translated into more salutary relationships with one's spouse and children, thereby aborting in this generation repetitions of self and other victimizations, positively accruing to the generations to come.

Carl Whitaker

Although he decries the value of theory (Whitaker 1976a), Carl Whitaker does have a philosophy which guides the seeming chaos of his unique therapy. Whitaker's psychotherapy has been reacted to with amusement, ridicule, wonder, awe, confusion, envy, and admiration. His use of story, fantasy, play, dreams, myth, primary process, and allegory probably gets closer to the truth than reality-based interpretations. Underlying his various techniques of absurdity, non-sequiturs, and sometimes straight, wise talk, he touches on certain universals of the human condition, dealing with generic themes of life and death.

Among Whitaker's beliefs is the one relevant to this book—that it is necessary to include three generations in working with couples or families (Whitaker, 1976b). He believes that including the extended family increases therapeutic power, just as inviting a consultant or a cotherapist to join the therapy promotes a growth experience for the clients and the therapist. Whitaker pushes for family-of-origin involvement and is explicit that the grandparents be invited in as assistant therapists or consultants, not as patients. He adopts the stance that the therapy he is doing with the parents is failing, and he needs all the help he can get.

In more recent years, he and his wife Muriel have conducted marathonlike family networks over a period of two or three days in a spalike setting. They include in sessions all the extended family they can get, embracing even involved nonfamily members, including previous spouses, uncles, aunts, the boss, or even the neighbors. Spouses and children of the adults, as well as grandparents if they are alive, are always included; and although sometimes the family of origin of only one of the parents come, the Whitakers prefer to have both families of origin present. It is interesting to me that in his recent book, *Midnight Musings of a Family Therapist* (1989), Whitaker titles one of the sections, "Battle Plan for a Three-Generational Family Reunion," suggesting, as I have found, that some of these family-of-origin sessions have the characteristic of family wars.

The reader is aware that my goals in arranging family-of-origin sessions differ somewhat from those of Whitaker. From my perspective, when family-of-origin members try to work out their painful, hard issues of both the past and present with each other, face to face, the presence of spouses and children inhibit or even muck up that frightening endeavor. From my point of view, the best way to help children is to help their parents straighten out their own selves, their relationship, and their priorities. I think these goals have the best chance of being approached by the parents, separately, working out hidden and overt conflicts with their own parents and brothers and sisters. I think it would be difficult for an adult son if his wife or children were present to feel free to tell his dad that they must close the gulf between them before his dad dies; the son's past history with his father was part of their generation with its own private world and unique meanings.

Despite these differences between us, however, there is a remarkable degree of congruence between our observations about the things that can happen in these sessions and the changes the experiences can bring about. Whitaker writes,

> The parents usually discover in this real-life confrontation that the grandparents are much different from their introject of 20 or 30 years earlier, which may enfeeble the control residing in that introject. . . . I must stress here that in many years of utilizing this extended family consultation I have never seen it harmful, although occasionally grandparents are angry afterwards. Also, I have never seen it fail to be useful. Many times I can't understand why, but I grow more and more convinced it's always helpful. . . . Including the third generation increased the power of our intervention in resolving the identified patient's symptoms, as well as helping with the multiple family problems. . . . The objective of such a conference is to resolve rifts in the family . . . the discovery that one belongs to a family, and can call on

blood connections makes a great deal of difference to people who feel isolated. . . . Often the discovery of the grandparents by the grandchildren may evoke forgiveness and a group spirit. . . . Each generation group may come to admit that it is only possible to belong to one's own generation, so that role expectations are eased, and new roles developed. . . . Some members may even begin to make tentative forays into a new adulthood. Roles become flexible. Teenagers can contribute wisdom, oldsters can dare to be irresponsibly childlike, men can be tender, and couples freshly loving. Grandparents may become fun playmates for the first time . . . frequently loyalty debts and covert alliances are altered. . . . Discovering that one belongs to a whole, and that the bond cannot be denied, often makes possible a new freedom to belong, and of course thereby a new ability to individuate. (Whitaker, 1976b, pp. 188–192)

If I did not know Carl had written the foregoing, I would have thought I had written it myself.

Donald Williamson

Donald Williamson has developed a singular intergenerational theory and method with the goal of equalizing the political power structure that exists between adults and their older parents (Williamson, 1978, 1981, 1982a, 1982b). He aims to eliminate the intergenerational intimidation that is inherent in parent-child relationships, an intimidation that is "sourced ultimately in the primitive fear of parental rejection and exposure to death" (1981, p. 442). He claims that parental vulnerability, especially in older parents, may be the ultimate intimidation. Williamson believes that parental rights should be terminated. He states,

This means that the older parent no longer has any special position or privilege simply because of his historical role as biological and psychological source. Neither duty or obligation is intrinsically required or owed. . . . The adult generation can offer support without assuming emotional responsibility or burden for the welfare, the happiness, or the survival of the aging parents. And this support may be offered "spontaneously" rather than "indebtedly."(1981, p. 442)

Williamson's methods are oriented toward the adult client establishing a peer relationship with parents, who then become "former parents." He says, "The essence of being an adult is to have given up the *need-to-be-parented*. . . . The purpose is not to confront, chastise or get rid of parents. Nor is it to demand or need them to be in any way different. Being able to embrace the first generation exactly as they are, and to value this, is the very essence of giving them up *as parents*" (italics in original) (p. 444).

In order to effectuate these aims, Williamson has developed a series of procedures in order to "terminate the intergenerational hierarchical boundary." His clients, who seem to be largely self-selected (as mine often are), write an autobiography, relate family histories, are placed in small groups, audiotape letters and phone calls to parents, have face-to-face conversations with parents while on home visits—all of which are considered as preparatory to the three-day in-office consultation with the clients and parents (siblings are not included). One of his procedures involves having clients call their parents by their first names.

I have some difficulty giving a fair critique of Williamson's work. On one level I sense that he has hold of something very important. Renegotiating power imbalances can have weighty implications not only for adult and older parent relationships, but also in all hierarchical relationships (e.g., supervisor-supervisee, doctor-patient, male-female, etc.). Moreover, there is no question that the loyalty obligations and emotional bondages that exist between adults and their parents can have all sorts of symptomatic consequences. Some of Freud's early patients manifested the pathological results of having to devote their lives to taking care of sick parents. In the present day there are many adults emotionaly enslaved by alcoholic parents who phone in the middle of the night, demanding to be taken care of. Indeed, there are many "adults" who remain childlike vis à vis their parents. For instance, in one couple I saw, the wife reported that her husband, when they had dinner with his parents, would have his father cut his meat for him. Many of these people, of course, transfer this dependency onto their spouse after the parents have died.

Yet, I have to part company with my colleague, Don Williamson; I believe that there is much more to older parent-adult relationships than the power dimension, and I think he does not fully appreciate the emotional bond that exists between the two generations. In the family-of-origin sessions that I conduct, the parents usually step down from their throne and come to be perceived as less intimidating; the parents become more real, but they do not become *former* parents. I do not believe that parents can *ever* become exparents, and I think that calling parents by their first names is unnecessarily distancing. For me, one's mother and father will always be one's mother and father, and no amount of theoretical persuasion, however well intentioned, can change the magic in the words "Mom" and "Dad." I suspect that the differences between Don and me on this point grow out of our own family-of-origin experiences. After all, Don has an Irish background, and mine is Italian—and you know how those Italians are when it comes to family!

Focusing largely on the adult child's efforts at individuation by converting parents into "former" parents, Williamson makes little mention of how he deals with the pain of the parents during this process. There seems to be less attention to the needs of the parents, to their claims, to the system effects of the "loss" of the "former" child. That is to say, does one member of the family profit at the expense of other members of the family? This concern about the requirements and interests of *all* the family members, which has existed since the early days of family therapy, is epitomized in Boszormenyi-Nagy's concept of "multilateral partiality" (1973, 1986).

Another aspect of Williamson's work that I can resonate with is his emphasis on getting to know the parents as persons. Williamson's work has spawned an instrument to measure intergenerational processes according to his conceptualizations (Bray, Williamson, & Malone, 1984).

Norman Paul

Paul does not seem to have developed (at least in his writings) a formalized, routine procedure for face-to-face meetings between adult clients and their families of origin, although I'm sure, as a family therapist, he conducts such meetings. Nonetheless, an intergenerational orientation permeates all of his work. His work seems more focused on the internalized images of the family-of-origin members, rather than on the actual relationships with parents and siblings.

Paul was the first family therapist to stress the importance of death, loss, and grief as omnipresent forces in family life, and he has demonstrated that aborted or incomplete mourning often results in seemingly unrelated symptoms, both intrapsychically and interpersonally, even years after a significant loss (e.g., depression, drug abuse, sexual difficulties, divorce, etc.) (Paul & Grosser, 1965; Paul & Paul, 1975; Paul & Paul, 1982).

Paul postulates that there are two aspects of how one views the self in relation to experience. One is the subjective aspect (perceptions, feelings, judgments) experienced with the self, and the other is the observable self, the self others see. He developed some innovative techniques to help people gain access to data about their observable self. He makes creative use of videotape by using split screen pictures of different aspects of the self, and he has superimposed photographs of, say, of one's father onto one's own photograph (an uncanny experience). By exorcising the early introjects from the family of origin, the client becomes a student on himself and closes his own "credibility gap"— that is, the gap between the two experiences of self (Paul, 1976).

Paul uses explicitly sexual films and stressor tapes, has referred clients for the EST experience (to help them get in touch with childhood experiences and have them become more responsible for their own experience), and guides temporary separations for couples in distress (Paul, 1980). In more recent years, Norman Paul and his wife Betty Byfield Paul have been exploring marriage and divorce as expressions of a person's quest for selfhood.

Virginia Satir

The late Virginia Satir (always known, belovedly, as just "Virginia") made so many contributions to the family therapy field, and to the world, that it would be impossible to enumerate them. I will just focus on one imaginative method she developed that is relevant to the present topic. Most people do not associate Virginia with this work, but her Family Reconstruction Technique is certainly an intergenerational method of great power (Satir & Baldwin, 1983; Nerin, 1985).

Briefly, the technique consists of a person being in a group and selecting members of the group to role play different members of the family of origin. After constructing a family history and family map, the individual reenacts important family events with the stand-in significant figures. Virginia used psychodrama, guided fantasy, body sculpting, and role playing to enable people to revisit old learnings and recognize how they do not fit present contexts. During the process past hurts are revived and worked through, old family rules and beliefs are reworked and retained or discarded for their present usefulness, and parental behaviors are seen in a new light.

As can be seen, these outcomes are similar to those obtained from my own methods. Some clients are able to make significant breakthroughs utilizing the great power of the Family Reconstruction Technique alone, whereas others have used that procedure as a rehearsal for family-of-origin sessions with their real family. I do believe that dealing with the actual parents and siblings lends a different, more realistic quality to the experience.

Lee Headley

Headley's intergenerational methods and goals appear more similar to mine than those of any other intergenerational theorist and practitioner (Headley, 1977). The differences between our two methods are minor (e.g., she does not routinely include siblings in family-of-origin sessions). Her work has been referred to frequently throughout this volume.

Jeannette Kramer

My friend Jan Kramer focuses on the interfaces between clients and their families of origin and between therapists and families, but also on the interface between therapists and their own families of origin (Kramer, 1985). My own paper on this last topic dealt with how treating families revives the ghosts from one's own family (Framo, 1968). Kramer put this paper into clinical practice by running, for a number of years, what she calls Therapist's Own Family Groups, wherein therapists explore their own families. She utilizes a variety of techniques in her work with clinical families and therapists, including genograms, experiential approaches (Gestalt, redecision therapy, sculpting), as well as making use of the self of the therapist. I particularly admire her courage in relating her own family-of-origin history so that others could learn from it.

Other Theorists and Therapists

In addition to the foregoing, there are others whose work is relevant to the intergenerational approach: Haas (1968), who independently published a paper remarkably similar to my 1976 paper; Hovestadt and Fine (1987), who edited a book on various aspects of family-of-origin therapy, including chapters on assessment, training, and teaching a course on this topic; Lieberman (1979), who wrote a book that explains the importance of transgenerational influences upon the family members; and Titelman (1987), who edited a book where therapists followed Bowen Theory in studying their own families.

I have also found the work of object relations family theorists and therapists to be most valuable in conceptualizing intergenerational work (Klein, 1990; Scharff & Scharff, 1987; Slipp, 1984; 1988). Several theoreticians from a psychosynthesis and spirituality framework have related such concepts as life force, empathy, forgiveness, love, and renewal to family-of-origin work (Kramer, 1988; Mandelbaum, 1990). In addition, a number of popular books written for the general public have been published on intergenerational themes: Bloomfield (1983); Halpern (1978); Hoffman (1979); and Schenck and Schenck (1978).

SPECULATIONS ON WHY ADULTS ARE FEARFUL OF HAVING SESSIONS WITH THEIR FAMILIES OF ORIGIN

Despite my years of experience observing clients' deep anxieties and resistances toward bringing in their families of origin, I am still struck with the intensity of their fear, which in some people borders on the ineffable. Their dread at the prospect of all of the family members meeting together in this unique setting and telling each other the truth is almost palpable, something like condemned prisoners going to their execution. To be sure, there are exceptions, such as those people who request the experience, although even these individuals manifest varying degrees of apprehension. As a matter of fact, when I observe an absence of anxiety, I know that the sessions will not be very productive.

This phenomenon not only has clinical-treatment consequences, but conceptual implications as well. I have come up with some speculations about the reasons why people are so fearful of having sessions with their families of origin. These conjectures, listed in no particular order, are based on client statements and my clinical inferences:

- There is the fear that the process will destroy, drive insane, or kill the parents. This apprehension is the residual of the primitive, impacted rage everyone carries over from early childhood experiences.
- Fear exists that the family of origin will be torn asunder by the disclosures in the session and that the family members will never again talk to each other.
- There is what I call the "last chance" hypothesis. Everyone needs to believe that their parents love them. What if you find out in the session that your parents do not love you? You went for broke and took the risk of taking that last chance; it is better, without the session, to live with the *belief* of being loved. (Only once did a client discover in a family-of-origin session that he was not consciously loved. His stepmother told him she never loved him. Rather than being upset by this disclosure, however, he was relieved because it validated the feeling he had had for

years that she had pretended she loved him and had denied the pretense.)

- On the other hand, what if you find out in the session that you *were* and *are* loved? *Then* what will you use to explain your problems? After all, we explain away our difficulties by reciting the theme that if we had only been loved, our lives would have turned out differently.
- If you have the session, you could break up your parents' marriage, and who would want to be responsible for that?
- Dark family secrets (incest, criminal records, psychotic breaks, etc.) could be revealed by the proceedings, and everyone would have to live with this family shame.
- You might *lose* your family; they might cut you off and abandon you. Or, there is the fear that you will lose what little you do get from a parent or brother or sister.
- Fear exists of loss of control in this situation as to what might be revealed. In individual therapy you can pretty much determine what will be disclosed, but with everyone in the family free to bring matters out in the open, the context is fraught with danger. Who knows what might come out?
- There is the fear of your coveted role in the family being threatened, or your family's image of you being affected. If your family idealized you as the family hero, as perfect and "really together," you would be loath to change these perceptions. On the other hand, family scapegoats, who one would think would like to get out of that role, might resist change; family scapegoats have a way of clinging to their role.
- If you have the session, you may have to give up your bag of tricks and manipulations that you use with the family. They will be on to your game.
- Primitive fears may be rearoused, those fears one had when one was vulnerable and helpless. As an adult one thought those fears had been put to rest and that one had learned to cope with life, but the sessions could revive them.

- You might have to relinquish, finally, your child self, lose the nurturant mother and your wish for fusion with her, thereby becoming defenseless in a harsh world.
- Disengaged family members may fear that they may have to meet obligations previously warded off (e.g., taking care of an infirm, hated parent, an alcoholic brother or retarded sister, or an irresponsible sibling or parent who cons money from family members). For some people, increased closeness threatens to expose them to a vulnerability to criticism they had previously created "impervious" barriers against.
- Fear exists of being sucked back into an overly close family with intrusive, smothering parents who cannot tolerate individuality or separateness.
- If the session "fails," it could all fall on you. Your parents and siblings could say, "If it hadn't been for you forcing us to come to that damn therapy, we would have been all right." You might feel responsible henceforth for the mental health of all your family members.
- There is the fear that if you have the session, you might fall apart, be overwhelmed, fragment, or disintegrate.
- The sessions could start a process of new expectations which you might not be able to sustain, and whose consequences are unforeseen.
- There is the fear that the therapists will be co-opted by the parents and be fooled or taken in by them.
- You fear that if your "true self" emerges in the family meetings, your therapist, who has been your special ally or "good parent," might not like you anymore.
- There is the fear that your memories, feelings, or perceptions will not be validated by the family and that you will end up feeling crazy again.
- There is the fear that the family, after having been opened up, will be left bleeding on the operating table.
- Your present pain is known. Why trade that familiar path for untracked territories which could lead to greater anguish? "The devil you know is better than the devil you don't know." There is the fear of the unknown.

In my judgment there probably exists a generalized, natural aversion to family-of-origin work, not only on the part of the general population and clients, but including psychotherapists, even family therapists. Usual reactions to the fantasy of dealing with parents face to face in a personal way are extreme because the potential release of the bad internal objects is a terrifying experience. This kind of instinctive resistance to possibly confronting parents is comparable, as I see it, to the automatic repulsion people have about their unconscious.

Considering all the foregoing fears and possible dangers, why should anyone have family-of-origin sessions? The answer: Because the great majority of the aforementioned fearful events almost never happen, and also because the following rewards make the effort worth the risks.

WHAT FAMILY-OF-ORIGIN SESSIONS CAN ACCOMPLISH

Some of the following can happen as a result of family-of-origin sessions:

- Family-of-origin sessions are a kind of rite of passage. The parents are at a middle age, stock-taking stage where they are reassessing their lives and their relationships with their children. The adult children, now having moved beyond their adolescent, rebellious phase, and having experienced what it is like to raise children, are also re-evaluating their relationships with their parents, and their siblings as well. Both generations are ready, then, to deal with and get beyond past and current loaded issues between them. Matters of psychic survival can be at stake. The intergenerational encounter creates the opportunity for forgiveness for alleged wrongs, for mutual understandings, compromise, acceptance, and resolution.
- The parents get to see their children as adults, and the adult children get to know each parent as a real person rather than as a role. Instead of being mysterious fantasy

figures, the parents become, for the adult children, more human, palpable, and even peerlike. Divested of their magical power, the parents need no longer be unrealistically idealized or denigrated. The adult children come to recognize that the parents were beset with problems of balancing life's demands like everyone else, and that they did the best they could with what they had to work with. This awareness brings about the realization that some day their own children will view them as they viewed their parents.

- Old conflicts and feuds between siblings can be dealt with, as the adult children review events in the family history. They can express opinions long held in private: Who got the dirty deal? Who was the favorite? Who got more and who was cheated? Rifts between siblings are usually healed in these sessions by the mutual sharing, more accurate reading of intentions, and reinterpretations of past events. Brothers and sisters are always grateful that they got an estranged sibling back, and the parents are relieved that they can die without leaving a divided family.

- In these sessions past misunderstandings and misperceptions can be discussed, clarified, and straightened out. The family members are freed up by the disentangling and understanding of motives and intentions. Family myths can be exposed, deciphered, and neutralized. Past losses and traumas can be more openly discussed and delayed mourning dealt with.

- Adult clients usually report after these sessions being "liberated" or "emancipated." They discover that they could express a need or confront or challenge the parents (or an intimidating brother or sister) without those significant others dying, collapsing, or going crazy. They learn that the family can receive honest, open opinions and feelings without threatening abandonment; this experience is tremendously relieving. And since the "bad object" turns out not to be so bad, the old pains, betrayals, and hurts can be annulled, the barriers to expressing positive feelings can be reduced and then expressed as that universal, poignant statement everyone wants to say or hear: "I love you."

- Clients report, after family-of-origin sessions, feeling better about themselves, more whole and integrated. The events of the sessions (e.g., apologies by parents or siblings for past injustices; letting go of old rancors; feeling more validated and affirmed; feeling not so weird about one's views about the family and its members; making atonement for one's misdeeds; feeling less vulnerable and more empowered; clarifying of misperceptions; looking at a mother, father, brother, or sister with new eyes; being accepted despite one's challenges of the family rules) realigns the internal organization of introjects, resulting in a rise in self-esteem and feeling more real and genuine.

- Psychological symptoms in individual family members are sometimes abated or eliminated following these sessions. Such symptoms as depression, anxiety, withdrawal, rage reactions, rigid compulsivity, isolation of affect, substance abuse, phobias, underachievement, overachievement, marked self-centeredness, psychosomatic disorders, and the inability to sustain an intimate relationship have all been benefited by family-of-origin sessions.

- In these sessions the family members may say things to each other that have been said many times before, but in this context they get *heard*. The family members become more aware of the impact they have on one another.

- Family-of-origin sessions offer the opportunity for men to heal what Robert Bly (1990) calls their "existential grief" about their distant relationship with their fathers. When grown men abandon their complaints and grudges about how their dads were rarely around and were not there when they *were* around, they are invited to listen to their fathers and learn what their fathers' lives were all about. Instead of concentrating on what they did not get from their fathers, men can discover the good things they got and can still get.*

Fathers, who have been work-oriented all their lives, have expressed their soft, vulnerable feelings only to their wives, but never to their children. For the first time the children may see a father cry, especially when he associates to his relationship to his own father. Although children do not like to see their parents upset, the adult men come away with an expanded definition of what it means to be a man. The father, in effect, has given himself and his son permission to be an intimate partner and parent.

• One of the most important things that usually happens in these sessions is that the adult children come to realize that the parents can only love the way they can love, not necessarily the way the children want them to. They give up the fantasy of what the parent *should* give and settle for what the parents *can* give. The family members find out what they can and cannot get from each other. Knowing these limits helps them get on with their own lives.

• Usually people feel that they must *have* their parents before they can give them up and commit to another relationship. In some families the adult children come to recognize that the parents' life experiences have made them emotionally bankrupt. These parents have nothing to give. When the adult children realize that it is not their own "unloveableness" that made the parents unable to give to them, they can be helped to stop pursuing the dream of that which can never be obtained. They discern, painfully, that they have to know when to let go and get their needs filled elsewhere. They may choose to maintain contact with their parents, but they reduce their expectations.

• The family of origin, following these sessions, can never again be exactly the same. The original family members

---

*Two videotaped family sessions illustrating this theme were conducted by me as part of the Master's Series for the American Association for Marriage and Family Therapy: *Longing for Dad* (1986) and *Follow-up: Finding Dad* (1989). These tapes are available from the AAMFT, 1100 17th Street, N.W., 10th Floor, Washington, D.C., 20036.

are usually more open with each other about their dissatisfactions, satisfactions, or needs; boundaries are more defined; communication channels more direct; cutoffs repaired; there is less fear and secrecy, more flexibility of roles, less scapegoating, and the family members usually like each other more.

- The family-of-origin sessions promote a chain of therapeutic, spreading effects to extended family members not seen, such as restoration of alienated relationships between the parents and their siblings (the client's aunts, uncles, cousins), beneficial effects on the marital relationships of the siblings, improved relationships between the siblings and their own children, and even improvement in the work situation and careers of the family members.

- Settling important matters with parents and siblings releases psychic energy for investments in oneself, one's partner, and one's children. Those clients who had been overly attached to their original family (either consciously or unconsciously) usually loosen these ties and are more committed to their nuclear family. And some parents, after having dealt with their adult children about their concerns, are more able to relate to their grandchildren. Family-of-origin sessions can either help create a more viable and realistic marital relationship (especially if both partners have these sessions) or, in cases of hopeless marriages, they can help the partners to end the relationship more constructively. Some unnecessary divorces can be prevented by these sessions. Parents will do less destructive projecting onto their children.

- Spouses are usually more sympathetic to partners who have had family-of-origin sessions. When they listen to the tapes of the sessions, they come to realize what their partners had to struggle with in their original families. This knowledge not only makes the partner's behavior more understandable, but also increases the empathy that is necessary for a healthy marriage.

- Partners sometimes report that their spouses have helped them get a different perception of a parent or sibling, usually a more sympathetic one. For example, one client said, "My wife helped me see how I reject my mother and how I don't appreciate her good qualities." In my own case, my wife has helped me give up trying to educate my brother and sisters and pushing them to pursue goals that were important to me, not to them.

• The parents, having instilled in their children a set of obligations and expectations, can also release them from these expectations and obligations. They can give unambivalent permission for their children to be loyal to others as well. The opportunity exists for the adult children to come to terms with parents before they die. They will then not have to suffer unending grief and guilt over committed and uncommitted crimes after the parents are gone. With past bitterness dissipated, the adult children are now able to nurture their parents, pay back emotional debts, and help make their remaining years relatively happy ones.

• The parents, the older generation, are sometimes the ones who get the most out of the family-of-origin experience. Though they initially approach the sessions with trepidation—and in the early phases are on guard against anticipated criticisms—as the family transactions unfold, they come to see that old misunderstandings and feuds can be set right and that there is a second chance for them and their children. By the end of the sessions, the parents are grateful that there is hope that they can be a family again. Deep sadness over long-standing alienations is often relieved—alienations between them and one or more of their children or among their children. The parents can then accept approaching death less hampered by paralyzing regret or hopelessness. Other salutary side effects of these sessions for the parents that I have seen are: symptom relief, improved relationships with their own parents, if they are still alive, with their siblings, and even at this late stage the parents can experience a better marital relationship with each other.

9

Case Examples of Family-of-Origin Consultations

Consistent with the philosophy of this book, before presenting the case examples of family-of-origin consultations, it is necessary to place them in context. Not only do family-of-origin consultations ensue from diverse clinical problems (usually marital and family relationship problems as well as intrapsychic conflicts), but there is variability in terms of who actually attends these sessions.

Most of the family-of-origin consultations that I have conducted have been for clients who initially entered treatment for marital problems. For this reason, the only full-length, extended case example presented herein will describe how the family-of-origin consultations were integrated into this long-term marital therapy case.*

Following the long-term case, short case vignettes will describe:

1. A family-of-origin consultation for a client I saw in individual therapy (more infrequent since individual therapy constitutes only a minor portion of my practice).

---

*Although practically all the marital therapy I do is short-term (between 15 to 20 sessions), some cases lend themselves to long-term work. There are certain intrapsychic and marital interaction material that will only become visible over long-term treatment. If the couple are motivated for long-term intensive work, I believe the opportunity exists for reconstructive change to occur both in the individual and marital systems. Further, I suspect that the knowledge we have about marital systems is more likely to be complete and reliable if based on long-term marital therapy.

2. A family-of-origin consultation for a self-referred family from out of town. The consultation included both parents, even though the parents had been divorced for years.
3. A family-of-origin consultation for a sibling subsystem, since both parents were dead. These self-referred adult children were struggling with the aftereffects of abusive parents.

DETAILED CASE EXAMPLE: INTEGRATION OF A FAMILY-OF-ORIGIN CONSULTATION WITH LONG-TERM MARITAL THERAPY

Kevin and Susan were in an acute crisis when they entered conjoint marital therapy. Kevin, 47, was a successful attorney, and Susan, 46, was a medical technician. The couple had been married for 25 years and their three children, two sons and a daughter, were all married and had children. Both Kevin and Susan were attractive and articulate, and their strong motivation for therapy was evident. For example, they quickly picked up on the therapists' suggestion that they audiotape the therapy sessions and listen to them afterwards.

On one level Kevin and Susan were hurting badly. They were despairing, angry at each other, felt unappreciated, misunderstood, betrayed, were bewildered about what was happening to them, and frightened that their accustomed world was collapsing around them. On another level they conveyed the kind of easy familiarity and look of partners who had been together a long time, who basically loved each other, and they revealed, by their hand-holding and manner, that there was no way they were going to end this marriage.

My wife and I, as a cotherapy team,* connected with them easily and knew that remediation of this relationship was largely a matter of time. We could tell that time was something they were willing to give (unlike many couples who come in wanting quick therapy fixes, like quick oil changes and fast junk foods). We also soon realized, as the difficulties unfolded, that some tough times lay ahead.

---

*I acknowledge with appreciation the invaluable contribution of Dr. Felise B. Levine, my wife, who was not only a creative co-therapist with this couple and the subsequent cases, but also provided some of the ideas expressed in this account.

Kevin had just discovered that his wife had been having an affair with someone whose identity she kept secret. He had found out about the affair by looking at her appointment calendar, which Susan had left around. The emotional pain of this husband was intense, visible, and deep. He kept asking, almost in rote fashion, "How do I live with this? How can I get over it? How do I trust again? I thought I knew her. Who is she?" An organized person in the midst of this personal calamity, he had desperately read every book he could find on infidelity, looking for answers. His anger and rage were contained, partly because he did not want to confirm Susan's view of him as being hostile and mean, but also because he did not want to lose her. Occasionally he expressed anger toward the past lover of his wife, a safer target.

Susan tearfully explained that she had felt neglected for years by Kevin, that he was a workaholic, and he had frequently threatened to leave her and find someone else. She said that he had often pushed her away and "he even told me to find someone else, so I did." She said her husband had two personalities—Mr. A and Mr. B. Mr. A was loving, warm, romantic, and wonderful, and Mr. B was mean, critical, nasty, devalued her, controlled her, and had ferocious temper outbursts that demoralized and immobilized her. Susan saw herself as good, well-intentioned, helpful, and always doing for others, a view shared to a large extent by Kevin. She said, "When Kevin is nice to me I melt and I'd do anything for him, but when he unleashes his fury on me, I want to run away from him."

Susan indicated that her unfaithfulness was totally out of character for her, and that she herself did not fully understand why she did it. She indicated that the sexual part of the relationship was not important to her because at those times she dissociated herself from her body. It is interesting that at no time during the long-term therapy, despite pressure from Kevin, did she ever discuss any details of the nature of the relationship with the other man or the meaning it had for her. She tried to give the impression that the affair, in part, represented a way of getting her husband's attention, like the proverbial mule getting hit by a two-by-four. Although she claimed that another motivation was to fulfill her needs to be loved, the concept that an affair is also a very hostile act was quite out of her awareness. When Kevin was tortured by his preoccupation with the sexual aspect of her affair, she had to reconcile his fantasies with her own knowledge of what the affair was actually like.

When they made passionate love during this period Kevin would ask her such questions as, "Did you do this with him? Was he better than I am?" Susan was kind in trying to reassure him about his sexual attractiveness, minimizing the pleasure of the affair. Since there were indications that the relationship with the lover had not been all that satisfactory and that the sexual aspect had not been central, she did not have to lie. Besides, as far as we could tell, the lover had served as a temporary way station back to her husband. When questioned, Kevin admitted being turned on by the exciting-painful fantasy of his wife being locked in sexual embrace with another man, but at the same time the image horrified and sickened him.*

The couple went through roller-coaster periods of agony and ecstasy. They had the best sex they had had in years and felt the kind of romantic feelings they had experienced in the early years of their marriage. Still, Kevin made Susan's life hell with periodic barrages of recriminations and questions that kept her up all night. Susan said that no matter where they started, no matter what issue they dealt with, it always came down to the affair. He played detective with what few clues he had about the lover's identify, and pressured her to tell him who the man was, saying he could only trust her again if she would give him the man's name. Susan refused to tell him who the lover was, perhaps viewing the disclosure as her last chance to have some degree of control in the situation, and also because she was afraid of what Kevin would do if he knew. At one point, however, when he threatened to leave if she didn't tell him, she gave him the man's name and then felt defeated. Fortunately, the revealing of the name did not make that much difference or have any untoward effects.

For some people, like Kevin, sexual unfaithfulness of the mate is their worst-case scenario, and the most primitive passions of jealousy, revenge, depression, murderous rage, and anguish are aroused. Sometimes, also, Kevin manifested a kind of mourning and grieving, tied in with the theme of lost love. Such extreme reactions are usually a function of earlier, unconscious rejections being stirred up.

---

*I once wrote a paper where I described this paradoxical phenomenon: "Husbands' Reactions to Wives' Infidelity," in Framo (1982).

What was particularly galling to Kevin, as he kept making connections, remembering and reinterpreting past events, was his recollection that Susan's affair occurred at just the point when he had already cut back on work and was more attentive as a husband. In other words, according to Kevin, she acted out at just the time when things were getting better between them. This issue rankled him for a long time, and even when we got past the affair crisis in therapy, he would bring it up. This usually restrained man often fought back tears as he struggled with the question, "Did I push her into that affair with *my* behavior?" The question was usually followed up with, "But dammit, no matter what the provocation, she had no right to hurt me this way, when things were better between us."

At this stage of the therapy, the partners had quite different agendas. For Susan, the affair, while regrettable, was over, and she was prepared to start a whole new marriage with Kevin. For many weeks, however, Kevin remained overwhelmed by his obsessive thoughts and flood of feelings about the affair. When he was not questioning Susan he was questioning himself, saying he was rocked by these events to the very foundations of his personality. Susan's reactions to his pain were mixed. She felt his suffering, was contrite and guilty, and at the same time, in her "little girl" voice, defended her past actions.

The issue of trust was a critical one, something Kevin said he had struggled with most of his life. Kevin, of course, worried about whether Susan would ever have another affair and he was not reassured by her reassurances. She did say, "I finally have the husband I wanted, so why should I turn to anyone else?" With some prompting from us she did say that if he ever slipped back into his old ways she would leave him before she would have another affair.

It took some time for the therapy to move beyond the management of the crisis. When they wondered whether they could ever get past the effects of the affair and have a marriage, we gave our honest appraisal that we could see the basic caring and bonding that existed between them. However, we also told them that at some point each partner would have to examine self and his/her own contribution to the marital difficulties, as well as how their personalities interlocked. This process, we told them, would be difficult but rewarding. Once the intensity of feeling was lessened, the partners were gradually able to develop an observing self, which enabled them to start understanding what had happened in their lives and their marriage. By reducing their anxiety and giving each partner a sympathetic hearing, they came to trust us, and that also helped.

Although both partners were, on one level, very different, they shared similar sensitivities and fears of rejection and abandonment. The couple had reciprocal emotional reactive systems; one or the other would be depressed, and as soon as one partner looked distressed, the other would comfort. They were hypersensitive to looks of approval or disapproval from each other, and scrutinized each others' facial expressions carefully during sessions. The course of the therapy, like all therapies, and like marriage, followed a zig-zag, up-and-down, fluctuating course. In between warm, positive, loving exchanges there would be periods where each partner felt criticized by the other, which in turn created defensiveness and counterattack and then apologies for hurting the other.

There were times when Kevin excused his rages by saying to Susan, "Compared to what you did to me with the affair, my anger is nothing." When he implied that henceforth he had a blank check in the future for whatever aggression he expressed toward his wife, we had to point out that this threat was a form of emotional blackmail and would not get him the kind of marriage he wanted. Kevin was the sort of client who really took in therapists' observations, and this behavior stopped as we began to examine the roots of his lifelong anger.

Kevin, despite his hurt and anger, was more motivated to come to grips with the warring demons within him. (Susan did not present herself as internally conflicted, a situation that presented a therapeutic challenge later.) One aspect of his obsessiveness about Susan's affair was that basically he had always seen himself as "bad" and had viewed Susan as "good," so the real betrayal for him was the discovery that the good Susan was not all that good. Part of the reason the affair held such a grip on him was that, from his point of view, for the first time in the history of their marriage he was not totally the bad guy.

He ambivalently embraced both roles of victim and aggressor and was uncomfortable with both. Kevin related that he had always been concerned about his rage outbursts and he had been worried that the way he intimidated his wife would drive her away. He began to wonder if indeed he had a need to punish or control people, to make others pay for some deep, ill-defined sense of injustice. For some time, however, these revelations were interspersed with bitter and sarcastic jabs at his wife, recriminations that stemmed from his deep sense of heartbreak, shame, and Susan's breach of faith.

Kevin's family history helped to explain who he was. He said that the greatest tragedy of his life was the death of his mother when he was 16. He felt she was the only person in this world who understood and loved him, and he was inconsolable and bereft when she died. Somehow, he connected the bereavement about his mom with his grief about the affair. Like the mother who died and left him, Susan had abandoned him during the affair.

After his mom's death, Kevin said, everything changed. As the oldest child in his family, the responsibility for his four siblings fell on him, especially since Dad collapsed into helplessness after Mom's death and drank heavily. Whenever Kevin mentioned his father, his face hardened and got a haunted look. He described his father as "always angry, and I could never please him." He said his father beat him cruelly and frequently and was always critical of him, drunk or sober. When asked whether he had anything positive to say about his father, he said he could not think of one thing. When pressed, he finally said, "My father loved my mother and often brought her roses."

Kevin said that in later years, after he was married, his father would show up on his doorstep asking for money. "He had become a bum and a 'user.' He wasn't interested in me or my family. He wanted money so he could buy liquor." On two occasions Kevin had to commit his father to mental institutions because "alcohol had affected his brain." Kevin described the experiences of committing his father as "the toughest things I ever had to do in my life." Kevin said he grew so disgusted with his father that he refused to give him any more money. He said, "I grew callous toward him, and he dropped out of sight. After some years the police came to my house saying my father had died in a fire and they wanted to know how to dispose of the body. I told them, 'I don't give a damn. Put him in Potter's field with the rest of the bums.'"

It is curious that people with the most traumatic family backgrounds often do not see any connection between past disturbing events and their subsequent functioning. Kevin looked surprised when I related his previous anger excesses toward his wife to his rage about the years of abuse, rejection, and exploitation by his father. When I connected the two he said, "Well, what am I supposed to do, find his grave and yell and scream at him for what he did to me?" He could see that he had expressed inappropriate anger to his children when they were young, and he said that he had tried to overcome that behavior when he realized he wanted to be a better father than his father had been.

It had become apparent to us (the cotherapists) that a family-of-origin session for Kevin could be very helpful. His abiding bitterness and periodic temper outbursts were at least partly the heritage of an unconscious identification with the physical and emotional abuse meted out by his father. When my therapy orientation about bringing in the remaining members of his family was suggested to him, he was initially quite resistive. He did not see much point to the idea because the "past was the past" and besides he did not have much to do with his brothers and sisters.

When we asked about his siblings, we learned that it was Susan who had kept in touch with them; she was the switchboard between Kevin and his family. As a matter of fact, Kevin's siblings lived with the couple during various periods of their lives. It was noteworthy that we learned more about Kevin's family from Susan than from Kevin; he was not only reluctant to talk about his siblings, but I got the impression that he wanted to deny that he was part of the same family.

We learned from Susan that he had two brothers and two sisters, that all the siblings had lived disorganized, chaotic lives; two of the siblings had alcohol and drug problems, one had been in jail for robbery, and one had been into "really weird stuff" but was now a born-again-Christian. Susan said that his siblings were always reaching out to Kevin, but he was not very responsive to them and had held them off at a distance.

Susan joined the therapists in encouraging Kevin to at least call his siblings and see if they would be willing to come in. He reported in a later session that he did indeed call each one and, much to his surprise, they all were not only willing to come in, but were eager to do so. He agreed to having the family-of-origin sessions, saying something like, "Well, since everybody thinks I ought to do it, I guess I will, but I doubt anything will come of it."

The following main themes emerged from Kevin's family-of-origin sessions:

- It was apparent that Kevin's brothers and sisters had Kevin on a pedestal that was out of reach for them. He was regarded as the successful one who had "made it." All the siblings yearned for recognition from him, and they were so pleased he had called them to this family meeting.
- They agreed that their mother had been the glue that had held things together, and that her death was not only devastating but was followed by the family's disintegration.
- Following the loss of Mom, the kids were farmed out to various people, and the siblings told stories of feeling abandoned by Dad, who moved in and out of their lives. The difficulties they had in later life (drugs, breaking the law) were attributed to the instability of the parenting they got from various people after Mom died.
- The siblings acknowledged that Dad had been rougher on Kevin than on the other kids, and that Dad was a dapper, irresponsible, charming, con-artist who was destroyed by alcohol.
- The siblings not only saw Dad in a more positive light than did Kevin, but much to Kevin's astonishment they told him that Dad had kept newspaper clippings of Kevin's accomplishments and that Dad had been proud of Kevin. They had brought a scrapbook of the newspaper articles to the session which Kevin was seeing for the first time. Kevin now had concrete evidence that his father cared for him, although he commented bitterly, "Why didn't he tell me instead of others?"

    The siblings had also brought in a wedding photograph of their mom and dad, as well as a collection of love letters between Mom and Dad. They were so glad that they could do something for Kevin as a kind of payback for all he had done for them as the oldest, responsible one. (As mentioned earlier, from time to time they had stayed with Kevin and Susan when they were in need.)

- Kevin's brothers and sisters said they, too, had some anger toward Dad, but that they felt terrible that Dad had been "buried like a dog," and they wished he were buried with Mom.

- The sibling subsystem did some work between the two family-of-origin sessions. Kevin read over the letters his parents had written to each other and could not get over the fact that Dad had kept newspaper clippings about him.

- At the second session Kevin was confused, an indication to me that his lifelong, fixed beliefs about his dad were beginning to unravel. He then reported that the previous night he could not sleep undisturbed until after having a very vivid dream. He said, "*I dreamt that I brought roses to my father's grave.*" He did not make the connection to his previous statement—the only positive thing he could say about his father was, "*My father loved my mother and often brought her roses.*"

- I then told Kevin the story of a client of mine who had been physically and psychologically abused by her cold, unloving mother. The client reported that after her mother died she was determined to give her mother an expensive funeral, her formula being, "I will give to you what you never gave to me." She said that following this ironic, uncompassionate repayment, she then planned to curse her mother loudly at the conclusion of the graveside ceremony. I told Kevin that this woman said to me, "My spending all my money on an expensive funeral was going to be my revenge on my mother. But when the time came for me to curse her, I couldn't. All I could do was cry."

- Kevin reacted to this story by tearing up and experiencing the grief about his father that had been long suppressed. When the cotherapists expressed the idea that Kevin might be more at peace with himself if he could find some way to forgive his father, Kevin had great difficulty reconciling that yearning with the bitter memories of the mistreatment at the hands of his father.

- We then proposed that the family find Dad's body, rebury him with Mom, and place roses on the grave. Perhaps, we said, this ritual could help lay to rest the hurtful past.

- The final phases of the family-of-origin consultation concerned the relationships between the brothers and sisters in this disengaged family. Kevin's siblings felt rejected by Kevin and told him so, and Kevin was able to acknowledge his distancing. One of the characteristics of families that avoid closeness is the fear that intimacy spawns obligations. There was an implication that for Kevin to become more involved with his siblings meant that more would be expected of him. On the other hand, he paid a price for being cut off from his roots. The gift from his siblings—the shift in Kevin's perception of father—enabled him to tell his brothers and sisters that they should all keep in closer touch with each other, and he said that he wanted to be more a part of their lives.

A perennial question for mental health theoreticians and practitioners is, how do people overcome and integrate a past where they were rejected and brutalized by those who should have loved them. How does one deal with the heritage of such maltreatment—low self-esteem, the rages towards parental stand-ins, the distrust of others, and so forth? Positive relationships with others, such as trusted spouses, good friends, a mentor, warm relationships with siblings, and even a favorable relationship with a therapist, can help repair the damage. What can also benefit is the kind of reinterpretation of past traumatic events that the family-of-origin experience can promulgate.

In Kevin's case, I believe that the knowledge that his father, despite the harsh treatment, did on some level care for him enabled Kevin to undergo some internal reorganization. In Fairbairn's sense, Kevin was able to belatedly incorporate a piece of the good object from his father, which in turn enabled him to grieve the loss of his father and even partially forgive him. He had found some goodness in his dad with which he could identify. Further, getting reconnected with his brothers and sisters helped. In any event, in the weeks following the family-of-origin sessions, Susan reported that Kevin's rage reactions had diminished considerably. Occasional reminders of the affair still brought up for Kevin feelings of anger and betrayal, but these infrequent episodes seemed appropriate.

Since Kevin's contributions to the marital difficulties had become attenuated by this time, and his Mr. B had become somewhat pacified, we turned our attention to Susan, whose defensive structure in some ways proved more formidable. When questioned, she denied any negative thoughts about anyone but Kevin's Mr. B, and when we asked, "Don't you ever get angry?" she replied, "No" with a puzzled expression that indicated that she did not understand such a question. When Susan said, "I never hurt anyone in my life," my co-therapist said, "Yes you did. You had that affair and that really hurt Kevin." The good relationship we had with this couple enabled us to present them at times with bitter truths.

Susan became more understandable when we got some history on her family. She described her family as "sweet and close." When she spoke of her mother one could almost see the halo over her head; her description of her mother was that she was eligible for sainthood. She said in her family there had been no anger, no disappointments, no distress—that it was a happy, normal family. She said she had a younger sister and brother and her father had died five years previously.

Kevin partially confirmed her mother's saintliness, but also disclosed that her father had been an alcoholic and frequently angry, that her brother was a drug addict, and that her sister was repeatedly involved with abusive men. Susan minimized Kevin's disclosures and dismissed summarily the idea of her having a family-of-origin session, saying her mother was too old and ill, and besides, she did not want to sully her mother's image of her (Susan's) marriage as perfect. We abstained from any pressure to bring in her family, recognizing the inflexible signs that attempts at persuasion would be futile and counterproductive at this time.

Susan's Pollyanna defense of denial was powerful and daunting. She saw the world and people (except for Kevin's Mr. B) in vague, unrealistic, benign terms, rather than as they really were. Any unpleasantness either did not exist or was explained away. In many ways Susan was indeed unselfish, thoughtful, generous, upright, warm-hearted, kind, and always doing for others. So how can one question such goodness? Since she seemed too good to be true, we enlisted Susan's cooperation on embarking on a discovery of who the real Susan was. My cotherapist started the journey with an astute observation which had a long-term impact on Susan: She said, "It seems to me that you are competing with Mother Theresa."

Susan's naive trust, optimism, and selflessness were highly valued by Kevin (which had made her sexual unfaithfulness all the more incomprehensible to him). Those innocent, beneficent traits were the very ones Kevin felt that he lacked, and by the mechanism of projective identification he participated vicariously in her goodness. Like all couples, Kevin and Susan's choices of each other as partners were motivated by the wish to find someone who could complement, negate, or reinforce an internal representation (introject) of a parent figure. Intimate partners work out old agendas *through* their spouse. For Kevin, Susan had alternately been the good mother and bad father. Like his mother, Susan was loving, unselfish, and kept the family together; like his father she had a knack for hurting him and for making Kevin feel he was always disappointing her.

By the same token, it had become apparent to us that Kevin's Mr. B—the rageful, mean person—represented a dissociated aspect of Susan's personality. Again, by the mechanism of projective identification, she projected this disowned part of herself onto Kevin *and then fought it in him.* Kevin had not only carried his own "badness," with its resultant guilt and shame, but also was carrying Susan's "badness" as well. Conversely, Susan's defensive clinging to her altruistic image served Kevin's internal dynamic purposes. Both partners, then, were colluding with one another in mutual projection, provoking the other to behave in a way that fit their internal perceptions and enabling each to participate vicariously in the other's behavior. This collusive process between them helped create their fusion and at the same time brought about their circular arguments and alienation.

Helping the partners become more aware of the foregoing

entailed some risk, especially for Susan. For Susan to come to grips with the "monster" inside her, which was being obsessively attended to in Kevin, even when his rages had subsided, could create intense anxiety in her and create new defenses. She was now defending herself against assaults that were not happening. She said, "I only become 'Mrs. B' in response to his 'Mr. B.'" This unacceptable part of Susan was so anathema to her that she began to speak of "taking a rest from therapy." However, she had gotten to the point where she could see the painful effect her infidelity had on her husband, and there was dawning recognition of the hostile nature of the act. Susan was not yet ready to own her disowned hostility, which is probably why she talked about termination.

We cotherapists could see that they had made much progress: the intensity of emotional reactivity about the affair had diminished considerably; they were communicating more openly and honestly; they had begun to understand their irrational expectations of each other and of the marriage; they had come to appreciate each other's position more; and they had deepened their love for each other. We were concerned about them, however, and even though we thought the potential existed for deterioration in their marital relationship, we did not discourage their termination at this point.

As it turned out, that termination was a hiatus in treatment. They returned to therapy five months later, and matters between them were very different this time. Unlike before, Susan was brimming over with anger. She was angry about Kevin, about people at work, at friends, at the world. Kevin was somewhat depressed and upset by her new-found aggressiveness. We told them that in some ways her behavior was a blessing in disguise. Whereas previously Kevin had been worried that his wife might have another affair, we told him that her getting in touch with her own anger was a built-in safeguard against her expressing it through an affair.

The intensity of her anger frightened her; in a sense, she had overcompensated and had now *become* the embodiment of Kevin's rages. She had her own Mrs. B. It took some time for her "monster to be tamed" as we put it; for a while she alternated between little-girl petulant complaining and adult assertiveness. As Susan became more assertive, this meant facing issues she would not allow herself to face before. What this shift meant was that more conflict was created between them—this time not over the affair, but over preaffair issues they had avoided.

Those were the issues that had helped precipitate the affair. At one point Kevin said jokingly, "Look at this. We come to therapy to save our marriage and now we fight more." I translated that statement by saying, "This time you're fighting over the real issues, and you're fighting better. Besides, sometimes things seem to get worse before they get better." Among their real issues were: whose needs were going to be taken care of; who gives more; threats of abandonment; jealousy; and a power struggle focused partly on a redefinition of gender roles.

The couple began to deal with issues of control: Susan told Kevin she had allowed him to manage her in a way she could no longer tolerate. She had always felt like the powerless one in their relationship. For example, a gender issue came up in the form of Kevin saying, "I always let you work didn't I?" Susan responded, "What do you mean you *let* me work? Does that mean I need your permission?" (At this point I could see and appreciate the feminist position that some men inappropriately assume a paternalistic position toward their wives and are hurt that this benevolent attitude is not appreciated.) Susan and Kevin were moving toward a more equalitarian relationship, and neither one was sure they liked it.

Because of the changes she had undergone, Susan was now ready to bring in her family of origin. It was interesting to observe the strong motivation she had in contacting all her family members and in making the logistical arrangements. This effort was in contrast to all the excuses for not having the sessions when she did not really want to do it. In her family-of-origin sessions, which her mother, sister, and brother attended, it became apparent that Mother was indeed perceived by all as saintly.

However, the siblings saw the deceased father differently than did Susan. They said he was harsh, angry, and depressed much of the time ("Mr. B" in effect). The sister said this perception of Dad was indirectly supported by Mom, who used to say, "Don't make Daddy mad." Susan was the only one to describe Dad as "loving."

One of the clearest themes of the sessions, however, was how Mother's "goodness" was really a burden for all the adult children, because they all wanted to be as good as she was and found it impossible to do so. Anyone who tries to live up to perfection will always fall short. What saved these adult children in this session occurred when Mom herself disputed her exalted position by telling them how difficult life had been for her at times (especially with her husband's alcoholism), and that she had made mistakes and had shortcomings. Mom even confessed to having a hidden alcohol problem herself, which prompted Susan's siblings to discuss their problems with drugs and alcohol.

Susan's role as protector of the parents was shaken by her mother's disclosures. She had identified with a perceived angelic mother, and when her mother became more human and more real, Susan had permission to become more real. One final finding of the family-of-origin sessions was that Susan's siblings implied that after Mom's death she (Susan), as the successful one of the family, was expected to take care of them. It is noteworthy that Kevin's siblings perceived him similarly.

For a while after her family-of-origin sessions, Susan had difficulty integrating her two selves. The old ways no longer worked and the new ones were not yet available. She missed her old, happy, starry-eyed self; Kevin missed her previous self also. Still, having seen her mother's realness, Susan became more real herself, and we cotherapists were pleased to see a genuine, more empowered person emerge.

Susan's mother's physical condition got worse and the doctor's reports were not hopeful. Susan then went through a period of regression as she took care of her dying mother. She stayed up with her mother night after night, giving her oxygen and feeding her. During this crisis she was most distraught, and although her brother and sister spent some time with Mom, it was Susan who took the main responsibility for keeping her mother alive.

However, a positive aftereffect of the family-of-origin sessions was demonstrated: Susan was able to allow her "dysfunctional" siblings to come and help take care of Mother. This was the first time these adult children were treated as responsible family members, because the more Susan overfunctioned, the more they underfunctioned. By encouraging Susan to allow her siblings to give to Mother, we were helping Susan to become more healthfully selfish. (After all, people who overgive usually end up being resentful over being taken advantage of.) The "spreading effects" of family-of-origin sessions were evident by the fact that following these events, Susan's brother entered a drug treatment program, and her sister terminated an abusive relationship.

After her mother died, Susan became quite depressed and berated herself for not having done more for her. Kevin, who really liked Susan's mother, also felt the loss and was very supportive of his wife at this time. From week to week we noticed that Susan seemed to age perceptibly; her face looked more like her mother's. After I made an interpretation to her about regaining her loss and canceling it out, in the form of "If I can't have her, I will *be* her," it was fascinating to observe the youth returning to Susan's facial features over time. The death of Susan's mother had brought the couple closer together, and the passage of time helped assuage her grief.

We had seen this couple for about two years, excluding several breaks in the treatment. Improvement in their marital relationship was becoming more and more apparent. Signs of empathic understanding and appreciation of each other were making more frequent appearances. For instance, Susan said at one point, "Kevin is the organizer, the planner, and the worrier in this marriage and if you're not careful, he'll plan your life for you. Yet, he gets things done and makes things work in our lives and I like that." In complimentary fashion, Kevin said, "I have always appreciated Susan's social outgoingness and emotional generosity because those are qualities I lack."

As mutual discussion about termination took place, we cotherapists noted the changes that had taken place. Kevin was certainly more at peace with himself; his demons were more at rest. But as a private person he still did not trust easily or confide in others. Susan was much more real, more able to assert her needs as an adult, and more able to face up to the realities of the world. Part of her missed her old fanciful self. Insofar as the marital relationship was concerned, the partners not only knew each other better, but liked each other more (in addition to loving each other). Trust had been painfully reestablished.

Instead of being thrown by the others' negative behavior, being hurt, disorganized, or becoming defensive, they had learned to focus on what the partner was experiencing and on understanding what was going on in the other. Although like all married couples they argued and fought on occasion, they were managing their conflicts better. In the face of their differentness, they were better able to meet each other's needs. Their hypersensitivity to approval or disapproval from each other had diminished. In addition, Kevin had begun to be more actively available to his children and grandchildren.

To what extent did the family-of-origin sessions contribute to their improvement? These intergenerational interventions provided a direct route to etiological factors—the parental introjects that had so heavily influenced their lives. Kevin's incorporation of his father's abuse as a disowned aspect of his personality was expressed in his marriage. Susan's split-off hostile self, the introject of her father, was acted out in the form of an affair.

Dicks (1967) has written of couples having a "shared internal object." Kevin and Susan also shared an internal good object of sanctified mothers, which to some extent probably provided the basis for their love of each other. In her family-of-origin sessions Susan found that her Pollyanna denial of the pain in her family could no longer be maintained. Kevin's discovery that his "bad object" was not totally bad enabled him to belatedly forgive his father and bury him with sorrow, literally and metaphorically. As a function of the redistribution of their internal psychic economies, self-esteem was raised in both partners, and there was less use of pathological projective identification. That is to say, the partners were more differentiated, less fused, and each had come to own to a greater degree their own motives, wishes, and needs.

Finally, a word about the role of the cotherapists with this couple. As a husband-wife cotherapy team, we were able to be gender sensitive and resonate with the different ways that males and females experience life. In a more personal sense, we all had been through a lot together—they had come to mean a lot to us and we to them. Over the many months of our work together, a strong bond and sense of trust had been established. Unlike our work with other couples, we felt more free to be open about our marital struggles when the self-disclosure was relevant to what they were dealing with. But, we noticed, that we used as examples only those conflicts we ourselves had worked out successfully.

Some time ago a student asked me an important question: "What are the characteristics of clients you've had that improve in therapy?" After some moments of thought I replied honestly: "They are probably the ones that I liked."

CASE VIGNETTE: FAMILY-OF-ORIGIN CONSULTATION FOR A CLIENT SEEN IN INDIVIDUAL THERAPY

Mark, a 26-year-old single male computer specialist, presented himself as a "sexaholic." He said he felt compelled to visit prostitutes, massage parlors, and sex video stores, after which he would feel "rotten and disgusted" with himself. The compulsive sexual addiction was accompanied by a mixture of great excitement, anxiety, and then revulsion. Insofar as relationships with women friends were concerned, he said they were usually sexual in nature and that he belonged to what he cynically called the "4-F Club," which he translated for me as, "find 'em, feel 'em, fuck 'em, and forget 'em." During sex he would imagine he was having sex with a different woman than the one he was with, or he would imagine he was a past lover of the woman. He said, "I don't like who I am, so I play roles," indicating he was like a chameleon who would adapt to whatever emotional coloring was necessary to get along and fit the situation. He could not just be himself and he could not have the woman be who she was.

Mark said that after having sex with a girlfriend, even one he liked, he did not want to stay with that person and would want to flee. When I asked him what he thought the woman was feeling when he fled, he seemed puzzled by the question, as if the woman's response had never occurred to him. He said that some women had dropped him, and as he put it, "I did not always score," but his charm and good looks always enabled him to get another woman.

One positive sign for therapy was that he was distressed by his behavior and occasionally felt remorse, saying at one point, "I want to live up to my values and be authentic," and adding, "I guess I've treated women pretty shabbily." Occasionally he suffered depressive episodes and panic attacks. He was also afraid of AIDS, saying, "I could die, or if I get it, I could pass it on to someone else and be a murderer." Mark said, "This is not the way of life that I want. I want to be able to love someone and be loved and have a family someday, but I don't know if that's possible for me." He was terribly preoccupied with the question of whether he was capable of love. I could sense the anguish in this troubled man over that vital question: If I cannot love, how can I be human?

After a few therapy sessions, in an effort to control himself, Mark tried abstinence; he stopped frequenting porno massage parlors, stopped viewing hard-core videos, and even avoided looking at women on the street. However he did meet a woman he really liked and decided not to have sex with her—just get to know her as a person. It was a unique experience for him, which he interpreted as real progress. However, he indicated that the relationship could go nowhere, because she was not intellectual enough to please his parents. This statement prompted me to get a family history.

Mark was the oldest of three children, having a sister and brother. His brother, who was in college, was bisexual, and his sister had once been suicidal and had been hospitalized for depression. His parents, both in academic life, were described as "intellectual snobs who still smoked pot after the kids stopped and acted like it was still the 60s." He was closer to his mom and was intimidated by his dad, whom he felt had strong but inexplicit expectations of him. Mark said that in his family people did not confront each other, emotions were not expressed, and rational discussion was emphasized. He said his father gave the illusion of democracy in the family, but things had to be done his way.

Yet Mark said his parents were "very liberal—too liberal as a matter of fact. My brother and sister agree that we were given too much freedom and had no guidelines or limits set for us." He went on to relate that once, when his sister was only 15, she had sex with an older man with the knowledge and, he thought, approval of his parents. Mark described a laissez-faire attitude that his parents had about the children: the kids were told, "Do what you want to do" and they had to make their own decisions about right and wrong.

He admired his father but did feel that the family revolved around not hurting Dad's feelings. In one session he reported a dream of being very angry at his father because his father was a superstud and he (Mark) could only compare unfavorably to his father. In that dream his father was "fooling around with my girlfriend." Mark had the idea that his father might have had affairs, but he was not sure about that.

Considerable anxiety was provoked in Mark when I suggested he bring in his parents and siblings for family-of-origin sessions. He said he was quite sure they would refuse to come in and, besides, it would be too embarrassing for him to disclose his problems to his parents. By way of preparation for such sessions, I suggested he invite his dad out to lunch and that they talk about sex. When Mark recovered from his shock at such a suggestion, he became intrigued by the idea and said, "I'll do it!"

Mark later reported that he had indeed met with his dad and he had disclosed his problems to him. His father had always seen *him* (Mark) as a "stud," and until Mark told him how disturbing his life-style was, Mark had the impression that his father envied his free sexual life and "catting around." Mark had directly asked his dad if he had ever had an affair, and his father denied ever having done so. When Dad asked Mark how he could help him, Mark asked if he would be willing to come in for sessions with all the rest of the family. Father demurred, saying "I think we can do it ourselves." Since Mark was unconvinced of the value of bringing in his family he, too, thought they could do it on their own. I told him I thought that was a great idea and suggested he call a family meeting in the family home at the forthcoming holiday when they were all together.

The holiday came and went without the family meeting taking place. Mark began to wonder whether it wouldn't be better to bring them into my office where, as he put it, "an objective professional would be in charge." He said, "My family doesn't have serious problems, like I imagine a lot of the families have that you see, but I can see it's much too anxiety-provoking to tell each other personal things or the truth without having somebody there who wouldn't let it get out of control." I gave Mark a copy of the article I had written on the subject (Framo, 1976) and suggested he send a copy with a letter to each member of the family. When Mark requested that there be a preparation session with his brother and sister before bringing in his parents, I agreed. As it turned out, because of scheduling problems, that session could not be held before the family session. He prepared for the family-of-origin sessions in individual therapy, without his siblings.

As the date of the family-of-origin sessions got closer, Mark became more anxious and resistive to bringing in his family. He "forgot" to come to several of his sessions, apologizing each time. He came to one session in great distress, saying he had "slipped" and had gone to some "sleazy" massage parlors. I discovered that just before this behavior he had found that his father had lied to him. His sister told him that Mother had confided to her that Dad did have an affair and that at one point she had contemplated divorce. Mark was very angry at his father about being lied to, and now he was determined to have the family session. I had to slow him down, indicating that these sessions were not productive when they were only fueled by anger. I held off having the family session until he settled down.

The early phases of the first family-of-origin session were painful for the parents, and it was necessary to give them support. Although Mark was quite anxious, he brought up the issues on his agenda and was self-disclosing about his sexual preoccupations, his worries about not living up to his values, his self-doubts, his inability to sustain an intimate relationship, and his perception of his father as all-powerful. Although Dad knew some of these disclosures from the prior meeting with Mark, he was flabbergasted. He said, "Mark, you were my godlike son, and *you* were the powerful, virile one, not me. I have felt insecure all of my life." (It could be speculated that Mark was acting out in exaggerated fashion his fantasies of his perception of Father as superstud. From the material developed in the family-of-origin session, Father had not been much of a Lothario. It is likely that Father experienced Mark's sexual exploits vicariously.) Following some face-to-face interchanges between Father and Mark, Mark said he was so pleased that he and Dad could stop playing roles, could take off their masks, and be real with each other.

Mark then mustered the courage to bring up the issue of Dad's affair and how he had felt betrayed and disillusioned by his father's lie. What he was saying, in effect, was "How can I live an honest life if you are not straight with me?" Initially Mom was angry at Mark's sister for revealing this information that had been given in confidence. Mother then decided to give the facts. She said Dad had come to her and told her about the affair, and his being honest about it enabled her to get beyond her anger and hurt. Dad said to Mark that he was too ashamed to tell Mark the truth. Mom said she wanted the children to know that despite their marital problems, she and Dad really loved each other. Mark was relieved to learn that Dad was not a chronic philanderer and had not been duplicitous to his wife, and all the children were pleased to hear this declaration of love.

This degree of openness led to a discussion of the long-standing concerns of the children, which had had such far-reaching effects. It started with the sister crying about her previous suicidal episode and telling the parents that when she had gone to them to ask if she should enter a hospital, they had responded with, "If it makes you happy to go into a hospital, that's okay with us." The sister went on to say, "That's the way it always was in our family. Everything was okay with you. You never let us know how far we could go. We never had anything to measure against or any restraints, and it was scary." The other two adult children joined in with similar sentiments, talking about how there had been too much sexual openness, with the parents walking around in the nude, and being embarrassed by the sexual jokes that the parents told.

The parents were surprised by these statements and the strong feelings that accompanied them. They both said that the children had exaggerated perceptions of their looseness and that their expectations of the children were very different from the children's internally set expectations.* They did acknowledge that perhaps they had not communicated clearly their standards and limits of behavior. Dad associated to his relationship with his own father; he said his father had been a strict disciplinarian with lots of rules, and he had decided that he wanted to be more easygoing and liberal when he was a father. He said, "I guess I went too far and got too lax, now that I hear what my kids are saying."

Mom disclosed some aspects of her family background, revealing that she had been the family rebel. This disclosure surprised the children since they had always viewed their mother as submissive. Then in response to our prompting, both parents took a stand: they said to Mark, "It is *not* okay to go to prostitutes. You are at risk for AIDS."

---

*These parents were giving their children the opportunity to reconcile external realities with the transformed internalizations that the children had made of those realities. This phenomenon demonstrates the usefulness of family-of-origin sessions in the midst of an analysis or psychotherapy.

And then they addressed all their children: "It is *not* okay to do what you want so long as it makes you happy. And it is *not* okay to be deceptive in relationships." It was obvious from the adult children's facial expressions that these clear statements were very relieving.

When Mark questioned his parents as to whether they could accept a partner of his who did not meet their intellectual standards, they stated that he misunderstood their hopes for him. The quality that mattered to them in a partner for any of their children was whether that person was loving and caring.

Mark's brother then risked discussing his homosexuality, saying that he appreciated that his family accepted his lover. Dad even disclosed that as a youngster he had had a homosexual experience. The brother said he was gratified that Mark and his sister were accepting of his life-style, and the sister stated her wish that the three siblings be more in touch with each other. The relationship between the siblings, which had always been tentative and guarded, moved toward bonding. There was an agreement, further, that in the future all family members would try to be more straight, open, and honest with each other. This emphasis on candidness was a distinct change for this family, which had previously been characterized by conspiracies of silence, veiled intimations, and unstated expectations, resulting in runaway fantasies and mind reading. At the conclusion of the family-of-origin sessions, the family members were elated and they all hugged each other.

Following the family-of-origin sessions, Mark continued with his individual therapy, and at this stage the goal was to integrate the findings of the family sessions with his intrapsychic struggles. Mark was profuse in his thanks to me for having pushed him to have the family-of-origin sessions when he did not want to have them. He said his family thanked him for urging them to come in when they did not want to. He said, "I feel that we all in our family know each other better. And I can't tell you how great it made me feel that my parents finally made their expectations clear." He was also glad to hear that his dad and mom loved each other, which was somehow relieving. (One interpretation that I did not make to Mark, which one could get for half-price, was that the parents' love for each other released him from the guilt and threat of being an Oedipal winner.)

In subsequent therapy sessions, Mark opened up more about his

sexual fantasies, saying he had had fantasies of older women seducing young men and of teenage boys seducing young girls. I thought
this disclosure was a regression until he said that he trusted me more
since the family-of-origin sessions and knew more that I would not
reject him or be repelled by him. As it turned out, those disclosures
marked a turning point, because they were followed in subsequent
weeks by a series of positive changes. He reported he had stopped
going to massage parlors and had even thrown away his collection
of porno magazines and videos. He said he had even gotten in touch
with some old girlfriends he had exploited, apologized to them, and
asked how he could make amends. When I wondered how the women
responded, he said they were surprised but understanding.

Subsequently, Mark reported that he had met a woman he really
liked, and it did not matter that she did not have an advanced
degree, because she was sincerely interested in him as a person and
he in her. He then said, "Guess what? We slept together, and I was
fully present sexually. I did not pretend I was someone else or she
was someone else. I could be me!" He went on to say, "And this was
the first time I wanted to stay with a woman after sex."

Mark terminated therapy shortly thereafter, having had four family-of-origin hours and 28 individual sessions, over a period of six
months. He spontaneously hugged me when he left. A few months
later he phoned to say he had become engaged to be married.

CASE VIGNETTE: FAMILY-OF-ORIGIN CONSULTATION FOR AN OUT-OF-TOWN, SELF-REFERRED FAMILY OF DIVORCE

Although one person in a family usually makes the initial contact in
requesting family-of-origin sessions, in this case we* heard from four
adult children. One after another there were frequent phone calls
from each, suggesting much anxiety in the situation. We held the
preparation session with all four siblings, while their divorced parents waited outside.

Before the preparation session got underway, the adult children
kept going to the window to observe their parents sitting together on

---

*The cotherapist was my wife, Felise B. Levine, Ph.D.

a bench in a small park. They were amazed. One said, "We just can't believe that they're actually talking to each other. You have no idea what this means to us." The cotherapists did not understand these statements until the family session was underway.

In the preparation session the following information was revealed. The siblings reported that each of them, in their 30s, had been divorced, two of them had divorced twice. One said, "None of us can sustain an intimate relationship." They all ascribed their difficulties with relationships to the extremely bitter and acrimonious divorce of their parents of 17 years ago—a battle, they said, that never ended. Over the years they struggled with divided loyalties, as both parents tried to get them on their side. Most of the children initially sided with Mom because they perceived that she had been cheated by the property and financial settlement. Apparently, during the predivorce struggle over money, Mom had gone to court many times, had made such unrealistic demands, and had hired so many lawyers that the judge lost patience with her and made his decision about the distribution of assets. Dad had to make alimony payments, and Mom got life occupancy of the house; she paid taxes and repairs, but Dad owned the house.

These adult children felt they were pulled into this divorce war. They were more overtly angry at Dad since he was the rejecting one and had also remarried to a younger woman. Mom was resented covertly. One said, "Mom whines and complains all the time, cries poor, drinks a lot, clings to her hatred of Dad, and doesn't like it if we have any contact with him. The toughest part is dealing with her pain because she never built a life for herself. We don't know how to help her anymore."

The siblings stated that they had thought the marital strife would end with the divorce, but it did not. They described how they had come to distrust that any relationship could work, and they suggested that their developmental life tasks had been seriously impeded. "When we started dating and getting seriously interested in someone and wanted our parents to meet the person, each parent would resent us if we introduced the person to the other parent. You can imagine how difficult it was after we were married and the tightrope we had to walk deciding which parent to spend the holidays with."

When asked what they thought could be accomplished by the family sessions, they said that I was known for bringing about reconciliations between alienated family members. They thought that if the parents ended their war they (the adult children) might be freed up from the terrible bind they were caught in. Their parents would benefit too. "How can we love one parent without being made to feel we are disloyal to the other? How can we help our parents? How can we stop rescuing Mom without feeling guilty? How can we trust that a marriage can work when the only model we had was so awful?" I could have added, "How can children be happy if their parents are not?" We said that we do not do magic, that we would see what could be done, and then we suggested they invite the parents in.

The Family Sessions

Early on, the family anxiety was intense and palpable. We spent some time engaging the parents, trying to get to know them, and they us, but it was difficult. Both parents were defensive at first, on guard, fearful of exposing themselves, ready to justify themselves, and responding as if they were on the witness stand. Father said he came only because his children had asked him, and he was also concerned about their multiple divorces. Mother gave short, terse answers and kept looking to each child in a pleading way. The adult children looked uncomfortable and gave the impression that they wished they were somewhere else. The cotherapists were also beginning to wonder whether they were in the wrong business. We cotherapists looked at each other, waiting for the other to come up with an idea on how to break the ice and reduce the tension.

We then conversed with each other, sharing our ideas, repeating some of what the adult children had told us, and we openly expressed our doubts as to whether we could be of help in this situation. I said to my cotherapist something like, "I realize that Mom and Dad have had a lot of misery in their lives, that they had been disappointed and hurt and angry with each other for a long time. They must have really cared deeply for each other at one time for there to have been this much pain over the 17 years since their divorce. What they don't realize, perhaps, is the price their kids have paid for their struggle, need for revenge, and their inability to end their marriage emotionally. My cotherapist then asked me, "Do you think they can put their hurt and hostilities aside for the sake of their kids? I mean sometimes people will do things for their children that they won't do for themselves."

At this point both parents dropped their guard and became less defensive, no longer acting as if this setting was a court of law. We told them that they might have to go through some distressing times if they were willing to listen to some painful things that their children had to say. The parents agreed, and then the children poured forth their feelings about their experiences with their parents, both before and after the divorce. They each told their parents how the parents' marriage and divorce had affected them; how they did not trust relationships; how they would alienate one parent if they were close to the other; how they had felt pressured to take sides; how they were worried about them; their sad feelings about having lost a family; and their anger at both parents for not being able to end their war with each other.

One said, "Because you two failed in your marriage and couldn't get your act together afterwards, we had to suffer." Another said, "When you were still married and fighting, you sent *me* to a psychiatrist. You two were the ones who should have gone to therapy." Another said, "The turmoil never ended; it just took a different form after the divorce, and we got caught in the middle." Still another said, "Dad you've always used money to manipulate Mom, and Mom I feel for you, but I can't respond anymore to your calls in the middle of the night when you're drunk."

The therapists thought that in the face of this onslaught the parents would need considerable support, but although they were surprised by the frankness and the intensity of feeling, they had apparently come to the session because they, too, were prepared for change. The parents said that when they were talking together before the session (the conversation that took place on the park bench that the children had seen), they had decided to ask for help to end their war. Then they each explained to the children the reasons for the divorce, information that the children had never received. Each parent, for the first time, grudgingly, was able to admit his/her contribution to the failed marriage—contributions that anger had prevented them from seeing. We could see the great effort these parents exerted to contain their long-standing resentments and grievances, and we complimented them. The therapists asked the parents about their courtship, and the children were surprised to hear how their parents were once very much in love.

We then engaged the parents separately. Dad told some details of his background and how he seemed to have inherited his father's trait of stinginess. Mom revealed that following the divorce she had cut herself off from her sisters because of shame. We were also able to get her to recognize that clinging to her feelings of betrayal and unfairness had stopped her from living. The house had become a metaphor for what she was owed; her need for reparations for hurt feelings had promoted a strong sense of entitlement which had damaged her and her children.

In the later hours of the family-of-origin sessions, the parents were able to mourn the death of their marriage and to take steps toward forgiving each other. As fault and blame were ending, the emotional divorce could take place. Just bringing their parents together in the same room, seeing that disaster did not occur, watching the bitterness of years drop away, and finding out that the parents once loved each other helped these adult children discover that love *is* possible in this world. We then had the parents tell the children what they liked and admired about each of them, and we had the children tell each parent what they liked and admired about them.

In a follow-up call six months after the family-of-origin sessions, we learned that Mom had moved out of the house, had gotten an apartment, had reconnected with her sisters, and was in a relationship. Dad had sold the house and split the profits with Mom. One son said, "Now that there is fairness and we no longer have to take care of Mom, we can live our own lives."

CASE VIGNETTE: FAMILY-OF-ORIGIN CONSULTATION FOR A SELF-REFERRED, OUT-OF-TOWN SIBLING SUBSYSTEM

Cathy, a 38-year-old social worker, had seen me at a workshop in another city, and she called and requested that she be seen first with her husband for a preparation session.

At the preparation session Cathy told the grim, horrendous story of her family. She said her father had been physically violent to her mother and the children and that all of them had been in a constant state of fear and terror as they were growing up. Her mother at one point divorced Dad because of his drinking and violence, and then married him again. Dad had been in the military and was considered a brilliant genius, but over the years, he had deteriorated. When Cathy was 11 years old, Mother finally left him, took Cathy and her oldest sister, Jean, to live with her, and left the three youngest children with Father.

Over the years her mother started drinking and also became violent in her later years. She died several years ago. Cathy said once when she was in college she looked for her father and found him in an alcoholic ward of a V.A. hospital. Instead of being pleased to see her, he was angry that she and her sister Jean had left him to live with her mother. He was bitter at the world, and Cathy said, "I realized I could get nothing from him." She said her father was now living in squalor in a transient hotel, still drinking, and when she called him to come to the family session, he did not return her calls.

Since the family split up, there were only infrequent contacts between the five siblings. Cathy said her siblings have been "messed up" in different ways. Her role in the family, as the "family success," had been to rescue them when they were in trouble. About the only time they see her is to get help to solve their problems. Her older sister, Jean, was described as being unable to form a stable relationship, her brother Rick has a drug problem, her younger sister Janet is "violent, mean, and crazy," and her youngest brother, George, is a "sociopath." Cathy said crying, "I feel depleted; it's all I can do to hold myself together, and I don't have the resources to deal with their problems. I have myself and my husband to think of. And how do I deal with my memories of the past about my parents? How can I make sense out of those horrible things that happened? How can we all get on with our lives?" Cathy said she managed to survive this family because "I was smart and my teachers took an interest in me, but I have paid a terrible price because I get depressed, and once I made a serious suicide attempt."

Cathy's husband Mickey was very supportive of her, although he was convinced that Cathy should just give up on her family altogether. He said, "I don't like them. They're all crazy, and they take advantage of my wife. I have to hold her during the night when she has nightmares." Mickey wanted children and thought that if his wife could deal with her problems with her family, they would be able to have a family. He was supportive of Cathy having a family-of-origin session, but his agenda was that she should meet with her brothers and sisters so she could give them up. It took some work to get him to see that he would be the beneficiary if Cathy established a different relationship with her siblings, and that a cutoff would likely be detrimental. It was obvious that Mickey really loved Cathy and that he wanted to do what was best for her.

When I asked whom she was able to get to come to the family session, she said she had persuaded three siblings to come. She was afraid to invite Janet; she said that none of the siblings let Janet know where they lived because they were all afraid of her. I suggested she try to get her in anyway and to make another attempt to get her father in. I then asked if she knew any relatives of her parents that she could invite, and she said she might be able to get her father's sister to come in since she had a good relationship with this aunt. It was sadly apparent that Cathy was desperately looking for a family. She could not reconstruct a good family out of the past and felt she could not go on to have a family of her own until she came to terms with that old family.

The family-of-origin sessions were held several months after the preparation session. I had no further contact with Cathy until the family-of-origin session. Cathy was not able to get her father in, but all of the siblings came, and her father's sister, her Aunt Paula, came in as well. We noted that the sister, Janet, sat separately from the rest of the family, and although she hardly spoke during the sessions, it was apparent from her facial expressions and body movements that she was resonating to the transactions and emotions of the sessions.

Usually family-of-origin sessions start slowly and awkwardly as the family and cotherapists get to know each other and settle down. In this case, however, it was if the pent-up feelings that had been dammed up for years finally had a safe outlet for their release. Jean, Rick, George, and Cathy recounted the horror stories of their past family life.

Rick and George told how Dad kept accusing them of having committed "crimes," for which they had to be punished. Rick said, "It was like a Kafka novel. We didn't know what our crime was." He and George told of being brutalized, of being forced to drink water out of the toilet bowl, of severe beatings that drew blood, of being tied to the shower and cold water being turned on. They said their dad regarded these as military punishments for their "crimes."

Aunt Paula, Dad's sister, was shocked to hear those stories, saying she knew her brother drank, but she did not think he was capable of these "sadistic" acts. Rick and George said they knew Mom went out with other men, but that was no reason for Dad to take out his anger on them. None of the siblings could understand why Mom "took it," why she left Dad and remarried him, and they had mixed feelings about Mom leaving him for good the second time. On the one hand, they could understand her leaving, but they did not understand why she did not take all the children with her and left the youngest ones to their fate.

Cathy and Jean spoke of their ambivalence about Mom, saying they felt they had two mothers. One was loving and took care of them, and the other was cruel, explosive, and undependable. Cathy said, "Her mood swings were awful; we never knew from day to day who she was. She could be so nice, and the next day be a monster." Rick and George spoke of having only sporadic contact with Mom after she left and how lost and abandoned they felt. At one point Rick cried, saying he felt he had no parents and no family. I noticed one tear rolling down Janet's cheek. George said that since he was beaten so badly by Dad, he grew up feeling he really must be bad to be treated that way. He said he really felt bad about having hit several women with whom he had been involved.

Cathy sobbed as she spoke of her guilt feelings about her mother's death. She not only felt she should have done more for her mother, but also she was remorseful about not wanting to have a funeral when Mom died. A very interesting thing then happened in the session. The siblings started off weeping about the death of their mother, but as they described the kind of funeral they gave Mom, they all started laughing. Jean said, "We had Mom cremated and we were all sitting around the kitchen table, with Mom's ashes in an urn on the table, between the butter and toast. There we were, eating breakfast, looking at Mom's ashes, and we wondered, "What shall we do with Mom?"

Cathy added, "Well, we knew Mom loved the ocean, so we rented a boat and went out to sea to scatter her ashes. As we moved up the coast, we dropped off part of the ashes at different places since Mom moved around so much. The trouble was, a storm came up suddenly, which we thought was just like Mom. After we scattered all the ashes, the sun came up and everything got calm, just like Mom was after one of her bad moods." Even the therapists were struck by the humor in this account. For a while the pain in the family was lessened as the ritual of disposing of Mom's remains brought all of them closer together.

Apparently there had been much alienation between the siblings in their adult years. Each felt rejected by the other and spoke of how uncomfortable it was for them whenever there were family gatherings. They all acknowledged feelings of envy and competitiveness. Cathy said, "We were all affected by our parents differently; Jean got the fear and withdrawal; I got the guilt and feelings of victimization; Rick got the rage and self-destruction; and George and Janet got the violence."

Cathy then risked being self-disclosing. She told her siblings of her major depression and how she felt "ugly and worthless." She then went on to tell her siblings that she wanted to change her role with them, that she did not have the resources to rescue and save them anymore. She said, "I'm not your parent. I just want to be your sister, and I need something back from you." We suggested to Cathy that in the future she go to them for her problems. Since these disclosures came toward the end of the second two hours, and we did not want to end the sessions on this note, we acceded to their request that we extend the time to several more hours.

The last segment of the family-of-origin sessions was very healing. Cathy's siblings, using her openness as a model, revealed their deeper feelings. George wept about the pain in his life, the loss of his childhood, and how he felt he never had a family. He said, "I fell through the cracks." Both he and Rick spoke of their fear that they would end up like Dad. Jean said she was the only one who would go to Dad's funeral when he died. Rick was confronted by his siblings about his use of drugs, and he stated that he was not ready to stop and needed to stop using drugs on his own. Janet got caught up in the emotions being expressed, and in the few words she ever spoke in the sessions, she said she was scared of herself because she knew she hurt people since she had been so hurt herself. When she cried her sisters joined, and the two brothers got out of their chairs and went over to hug them.

Aunt Paula, Dad's sister, having seen the sorrow and anguish that resulted from her brother's violence, finally opened up to tell them about their father and what he had had to struggle with in his life. She said, "I've never told this to anyone, because I've been ashamed to talk about my family, but my mother never wanted children, especially boys, and she used to beat my brother mercilessly while my father stood by helplessly. She sent my brother off to a very stern military school. If only you could have known your dad when he was a young man. Despite my parents' rejection, he cared about people and was very intelligent and even gifted. Things happened, which made other things happen, and somehow he got warped and full of rage. I want you kids to know, however, that in his own way he loved all of you; I know that because he would come to me and cry and tell me how much he cared for you. I hope God forgives him for his cruelty to you. I'm telling you all this because I figure that if you knew what happened to him, you could find it in your heart to forgive him." The siblings received this information in silence, taking it in. This pause was the only time in the six hours that no one spoke.

The therapists had been touched and moved by these young adults who had experienced so much trauma. We consulted with each other privately and came up with a plan for helping this family to come to terms with their past wretched family life, so they could live less tormented and, hopefully, more satisfying lives. We were, in effect, attempting to bring about an emotional redefinition of memories as well as building on the latent strengths of the sibling bond.

"We will never know," we told them, "all the circumstances that made your parents who they were and why they did what they did. Your aunt gave us some clues about your dad, and we wonder if you all recognize the gift she gave you by making him a bit more understandable. Everybody longs to find some redeeming feature in a seemingly hateful parent, and your aunt helped to provide that. Your parents probably did the best they could with what they had to work with."

We went on to say something like, "Yes, it was true that life dealt you a dirty deal, but you have choices. You could continue to nurse your wounds, or you could accept your losses and go on from there. You might even be able to overcome the generational expectation that you will fail as your parents did. You guys need a family, and you have one right here. Be there for each other, support each other. The world does not have to be a dangerous place. We also think that when Dad dies you should all bury him together, and maybe you'll think of a way of making a statement out of the funeral, as you did with your mom's. Then, maybe, the past will indeed be the past."

We suggested that they listen to the tapes of the sessions and that someone write us in the future about how things were going in their lives. About a year later Cathy wrote the following news: She was pregnant and looking forward to having the baby. Jean had married her live-in partner. Janet and George were still distant from the others, but no one was afraid of them anymore. When all the siblings got together for the holidays, the nameless dread that had pervaded those occasions was no longer present. Rick was in a drug treatment program and was in a meaningful relationship. Cathy, Rick, and Jean were in more frequent telephone contact. Dad had dropped out of sight, but Rick and George were looking for him in the world of the homeless. The eternal search for the father.

Afterword

PROFESSIONAL ASSOCIATIONS

I have given many workshops on the intergenerational approach presented in this book, in nearly every state in the U.S. and in Canada, Mexico, Italy, the Netherlands, Denmark, Ireland, Israel, West Germany, Australia, the Soviet Union, and Central Asia. One of the most satisfying aspects of this work has been the letters I received from therapists around the world who state that this intergenerational orientation has not only been of value in their professional work, but also has helped them personally. Many write that they have been stimulated to reexamine and to do something about their own relationships with parents and siblings. Some therapists have written that they have contacted family members from whom they had been alienated and report how grateful they are that they did so. Sadly, one therapist wrote that after hearing my lecture on this topic, she decided to call her brother from whom she had been estranged for many years; she found out that on that very day he had committed suicide!

Insofar as training is concerned, in addition to the workshops given and the courses I taught at several universities, I have begun to do direct group supervision and consultation on this intergenerational method. Small groups of therapists at various places around the country have invited me to come to their installations for training in this method. I offer week-long training in San Diego from time to time, sometimes in association with Don Williamson. The training consists of didactic material, videotapes of family-of-origin sessions, supervision of the therapists' cases, as well as an experiential component where the group members role play, discuss, or bring in their own families of origin.

In my classes at the university I do not give formal examinations. I have found that writing family biographies is the best way for students to learn firsthand, in the gut, about family dynamics. Some students, feeling disloyal to their family and threatened by the possible exposure of their family's insides, express anxiety-driven anger over this assignment. However, when they complete the task, they report that writing the family biography was the most painful but rewarding assignment they ever had. I also suggest to students *and* clients that they tape record conversations with aged family members (parents, grandparents, aunts, uncles, etc.), get the family histories and stories (Stone, 1989), and find out what it was like in the old days. Older people usually love to reminisce, but they often find it difficult to get anybody to listen. This project is a priceless heritage to leave one's children.

Since moving from the East Coast to the West Coast, I have been doing fewer family-of-origin sessions with clients I see in therapy. About half of the family-of-origin sessions are held with mental health professionals from around the country who request the sessions. It took me a while to figure out why this should be so. I have since realized that people move to California to get away from their families.

PERSONAL ASSOCIATIONS TO FAMILIES

In 1968 I published a very personal paper, "My Family, My Families," concerning how the ghosts of my own family sometimes entered the treatment room when I saw families and couples (reprinted in Framo, 1982). On those occasions when transactions between the family members intersected with my associations about my own family of origin, I experienced flashbacks "at once compelling and fearsome, fascinating and despairing, growth promoting and regressive (Framo, 1982, p. 283)." Most of the time I am able to maintain the boundaries as well as my dual professional stance of being inside and involved with the family while remaining outside as an objective observer.

There are occasions during family-of-origin sessions, however, when

I lose it, when something in the session touches off an emotional reso-nator that is in synchrony with events in my own life, remembered and unremembered. At those times I am glad to have a cotherapist who can carry the ball and give me time to overcome intense feelings aroused by happenings in the sessions—the places where we metaphorically meet and touch. Of all the therapies I do (individual, marital, family, divorce, couples groups, etc.), family-of-origin sessions have the great-est likelihood of eliciting these personal responses. Sometimes things happen in these sessions that gratify, upset, anger, sadden, or deeply move me without my knowing why. At other times events in the sessions summon up remembrances and associations of things past.

What follows is a sampling of events from family-of-origin sessions that have evoked emotional connections and memories: I wept as a mother described her horrific experiences in the Holocaust. . . . I enjoyed that gutsy youth who spoke the truth to his family; he reminded me so much of myself when I was the only one to point out craziness in my family. . . . I get deeply shaken and panicky when I wit-ness fury directed at mothers; how can one allow murderous rage to be expressed toward the one person in this world who gave you life? . . . . I laughed when I heard two daughters confess to their father that they were so angry at him that they plotted his murder by putting gobs of butter on his food so he would die of a cholesterol overdose. . . . I am bewildered by siblings who hate each other, so unlike my own siblings where we can't do enough for each other. . . . I get scared when violence threatens in a family or a couple. . . .

I have trouble understanding the malevolent hatred that some adult children have toward their parents. . . . I get heartened observing fired parents get rehired by their adult children and seeing alienated family members make their peace with each other. . . . I feel helpless when I am unable to stop or divert cruel, massive scapegoating of a family member. . . . I am fulfilled when I receive letters from former clients or therapists or students who say, "Thank you for giving my father (or mother) back to me". . . . I am bothered by parents who won't listen, adult children who won't forgive repentant parents, mothers who dom-inate and vilify their husbands, and rigid, traditional men who deni-grate women. . . . I get anxious when I don't know what to do about a family's pain. . . .

I take pleasure in observing family members become more real, open and authentic. . . . I joined a family's tears recalling memories of their abrasive, irrational mother, now dead. . . . I experience vicariously the joy and guilt over being the favorite child. . . . I tune in to war veterans who describe the horrors and long-term consequences of combat experiences. . . . I resonate with men who cry about their incomplete relationship with distant fathers, and I envy those who get closer to their fathers in the sessions. . . . Having been divorced myself, I empathize with the pain and turmoil of divorcing clients and the effects of the divorce on parents, children, and extended family. . . . I close down inside and leave the field over the unbearable suffering of parents who grieve over the loss of a child. . . .

I reflect on the unique nature of the gut issues of family life: You reserve for your family the best and the worst that is in you; toward these intimates you will show your greatest cruelty, yet for them you will make your greatest sacrifices. Family members, in turn, can frustrate and hurt you the most because you want and expect more from them, and they can also give you the kind of gratification for which no price is too high to pay. . . . Families are where you live, and I am a part of every family I see. We all share the universals of family life: the passions, hates, loves, mysteries, paradoxes, measureless sacrifices, joys, injustices, jealousies, storms, comforts, bonds, and patterns. Family memories persist through space and time, burned into the cauldrons of the mind.

In conclusion, our parents are the first, fundamental relationships on whom our existence and survival depends. Our deepest yearnings and many of our problems in intimate relationships are rooted in our bonds and hidden loyalties to these people who first loved us and shaped our lives. It is necessary to allow forgiveness of old pains and sorrows to occur and to know and be known by these people who, in a way, will always live within us.

Author's Family Biography: One Therapist's Personal Disclosure

Since in this book I have written about other people's families it seems to me that I ought to be somewhat self-disclosing about my own—both my family of origin and my family of procreation. To be sure, I will not and cannot tell all; that can only be done, as O'Neill did in *Long Day's Journey Into Night*, in creative play form that pretends to be fiction. There are hints about my family of origin in my paper, "My Family, My Families" (reprinted in Framo, 1982), and there is a piece about my relationship with my father in Framo, 1990.

Viewed from the perspective of many years that have passed, I now offer a ribbon of random associations, of scattered memories and evocations about both of my families—the joys, the pain and sorrows, the losses, and the deep, rich experiences. For 20 years I have been requiring my students to write family biographies and now, for the first time, I write a short one of my own. I noted as I wrote this brief family biography that I experienced the same kind of anxiety, tearfulness, nostalgic longing, laughter, and excitement that my students have described in writing their family biographies.

I was born and raised in South Philadelphia, a rather unique community that produced pop singers, professional people, working class families, and Mafia-type gangsters. I grew up Italian, and although when I was younger I rejected that culture I now know that it will always be a part of me. For instance, during the 1930's depres-

Editor's Note: At the request of the author, these Autobiographical Notes are presented unedited.
Author's Note: I knew when I wrote this paper I was risking exposing my family's insides and that one of my siblings or my children might object to some statements in this narrative. Therefore, I sent them copies to read and gave them the opportunity to delete or modify. I do appreciate them allowing me to tell my story with honesty.

sion we could no longer afford for me to buy my lunch in the school lunchroom, so I had to bring Italian hoagies to school instead of the white, sliced bread I preferred then since it was what the "Americans" ate. Imagine favoring that white fluff to the best bread in the world! Many of the Italian foods I would not eat then, I eagerly search for now. But back then I wanted to be "American" whereas my parents carried on the traditions of the old country. I wonder whether my having to learn how to balance the conflicting messages and cross the boundaries of the two cultures constituted good training as a family therapist.

I will always remember Sunday mornings in South Philly, when from every house wafted the delicious odor of garlic and onions frying in olive oil, as each family started making their tomato gravy for macaroni. Mom and Dad both cooked (Mom made pizza from scratch before there was a name for it) and one could always get an appetite watching my Dad savor his veal chops and fried peppers. . . . I wonder why I associate to food when I think of my family of origin? Perhaps because the family gatherings around the dining room table on Sundays and holidays, when we were all together, summons up warm, pleasurable memories. However, I never did learn to speak Italian, even when, years later, I went to Berlitz before giving a workshop in Rome. It took me a long while before I figured out why: my parents spoke Italian when they did not want the kids to understand what they were saying.

My family was a traditional one in that my Dad worked and my Mom never had a paying job while she was married, although she worked very hard at home. As a matter of fact, she was a bit of a clean freak, with a rigid schedule of cleaning (downstairs on Thursdays and upstairs on Fridays), and cleaning cracks in the floor with a bobby pin. She complained a lot about how hard she worked, which made all of us kids feel guilty. I used to have to scrub the steps, carry ice in my little wagon for the icebox, take rotten eggs back to the store (which I hated), and clean the cellar every Saturday. My older sister Vi is fond of telling the story that once when I was scrubbing the steps I said to my Mom, "Do you realize you're having a future president of the United States scrub steps." One time, as a youngster, I set some papers on fire in the cellar and another time broke a large box of Christmas tree balls: SOS signals? We saw Mom then as very stingy; she never spent money on frills and I used to resent that I had to read by 20 watt bulbs. Mom made her own clothes and those of my sisters. The only dress she ever bought in her life was still hanging in her closet when she died.

I have one memory about Mom's economizing that I had always planned to write a short story about. When as a boy I needed a new suit she would take me to South Street where there were a series of men and boy stores. I would select a suit I liked but was cautioned by Mom to tell the salesman I did not like it when he showed it to us. He would know we were lying of course but would go along with the predictable routine by claiming that the suit was just the right one for me, and besides, it had very high quality. Then would begin the negotiating on price. Mom would offer much less than she expected to pay and he would counter with an inflated price. Then Mom would walk out of the store in a huff, saying I didn't like the suit anyway, and she would head toward the men's store across the street, "Big-hearted Jim." The salesman would follow her, protesting all the way that if he met her price he would go bankrupt. They would argue back and forth in the street, while I, very embarrassed, observed this performance. Eventually they would agree on a price and then be the best of friends. Mom would be satisfied that she got a bargain and the salesman would feel he had put one over on Mom. This street theater at the time was mortifying for me, but I treasure the memory now. When I buy something today, however, I never bargain.

I realize now that Mom had to watch every penny, especially during the Depression years when everybody was out of work, we had to go on welfare, and there was despair in the land. Still, I used to have the feeling that she would live poor and be a martyr even if she had lots of money. She had a kind of peasant mentality: When we would go for vacations in Atlantic City and pass the big hotels on the boardwalk she would say, "Those hotels are for rich people, not for us." It was many years, even as an adult, before I could allow myself to stay in a classy hotel.

My Mom had an explosive temper which often frightened me; sometimes she would hit or throw things at someone she was angry at, or turn the aggression against herself and bite her own hand. I always felt I had to watch my P's and Q's to pacify her, and I frequently resonated with her pain. As happens with many men, women's anger still panics and disorganizes me. Now that I have raised my own family I appreciate more what she had to struggle with in raising kids, and keeping things together, especially without the stability and cushion of a good marriage. As the years have gone by I have reappraised my feelings about my Mom. For instance, once when I went to see the movie *My Left Foot* I was struck by the scene of the mother putting aside pennies from their meager income in order to buy her crippled son a wheel chair. This scene suddenly reminded me of my mother in the darkest days of the Depression when we were poor, paying for a typewriter for me on the installment plan when I was in high school. Another thing that has helped me value and sympathize with her more is a further understanding of her family of origin.

My Mom came from an immigrant family from Ischia, Italy, an island next to Capri in the Bay of Naples. Her parents were strict with the girls and indulgent with the boys—a circumstance, I am sure, that had something to do with my mother's enduring bitterness, anger outbursts, and gloomy outlook on life. For instance, she and her two sisters had to go to work in paper box and cigar factories at age 13, while the boys were excused from work. Her parents in their will left all their property to the boys. (An unfair distribution from a will leaves a bitter legacy.) Mom used to tell me stories of her being beaten by her parents and locked out of the house all night after going dancing with my Dad when she was about 16. Italian immigrants were most protective of daughters' virtue. Mom was the family rebel and would dare to do things her sisters would not do; this trait stayed with her because my Mom was spunky and would defend her children like a lioness. She felt her mother was cold, unloving, and selfish, whereas she loved her father.

My maternal grandfather was a fascinating character. He was known as "Good-hearted Mike." When my grandparents came to this country and opened up a vegetable and fruit stand and grocery store in the Italian 9th Street Market in South Philly, the story is that he would feel sorry for needy people and give away the fruit and vegetables, much to the consternation of my grandmother. It is interesting that my brother, Mike, named after my grandfather, is always giving to others; when he was a little boy he took change out of my mother's purse and passed it out to people on the street. (The problem with my brother, however, is he cannot allow others to give to him.)

There was a mystery about the circumstances under which my grandfather left Italy: My Mom's family would speak Italian when they discussed this, but I was able to figure out that he needed to leave Italy because he had revenged himself by cutting off the ear of a man who had grievously wronged him. This tale certainly inflamed my imagination, but I couldn't reconcile the story with my experience of my grandfather as a sweet old man who gave me ice cream. Many years later I went to Italy and looked up my mother's relatives who were still in Ischia. I found my grandfather's 88 year old brother, who told me that my grandfather as a young man was an adventurer who, not content to be a farmer, wanted to explore the world. I could identify with that, and that's a piece of my grandfather I think I got. My Mom also told me her father invented a gun powder during World War I, an explosive that would detonate only under certain conditions. She said that President Wilson sent him a letter of commendation for this invention, but that DuPont stole the formula. That story always stimulated my fantasies that we could have been rich like the DuPonts or Rockefellers. My grandfather also mixed herbs and made medicines for people and animals, and apparently these were in such great demand that he was once arrested for dispensing medicine without a license. He also introduced Italian water ice and candied apple taffies into this country. And among his other creative talents, according to my Mom, was the capacity to write with his toes, a feat whose significance is not quite clear to me. Now how many people can claim a grandfather this enchanting?

We four kids were closely involved with my Mom's side of the family, frequently visiting my Aunt Mary, Aunt Alice, Uncle Johnny and Uncle Tony (which Italian kid does not have an Uncle Tony?). My Aunt Mary was the family protector; when I tape recorded her family history, along with her husband, my wonderful Uncle Alec, she told me that when her parents would hit my Mom she (Aunt Mary) would put her body in between and say "hit me instead." Aunt Mary told stories that were entrancing to a young boy, one of which I've always remembered: she said that one night the Devil visited her and sat on her chest and did not leave until she made the sign of the cross.

Subsequently she put bags of salt in each corner of her bedroom, with the rationale that the Devil would have to count every grain of salt before reaching her. I'm still trying to figure out how that worked. My Aunt Alice had flaming red hair, was our fun aunt, went into show business, and was considered the black sheep of the family. I found out later that she was on the outs with her family because she ran off and eloped instead of getting married in church. Following this transgression, her brother, my Uncle Johnny, the moral arbiter of his family, never again spoke to my Aunt Alice, despite my efforts and those of my favorite cousin, Evelyn, Aunt Alice's daughter, to bring them together. How sad that after Uncle Johnny died, my Aunt Alice would visit his grave frequently and cry. My Uncle Tony, the baby of his family, was a truck driver who was loving to me. He would always give me pennies and I would refuse them because my parents had taught me not to accept money from people (which presented me with a problem years later when I had difficulty at first accepting money from clients in therapy). Anyway, Uncle Tony would say to me, "I throw my pennies away, so you might as well take them." Since I didn't want him to throw them away, I took them. A few years ago, when he was dying in the hospital, I told him how much he meant to me, and when he died I put a handful of pennies in his coffin.

We had almost nothing to do with my Dad's side of the family because of some big secret I did not find out about until I grew up. It seems my Mom and my Dad's sister had a big fight (a fist fight) once because this aunt had entertained my Dad and one of his lady friends. Mom always bad-mouthed Dad's sisters. Whenever my Dad took me to one of his sisters' houses I always felt uncomfortable, like I shouldn't be there. I refused all offers of candy. It is not accidental that I did not get in touch with my cousins from my Dad's side of the family until after Mom died. I knew about family loyalty before I knew there was a concept for it. As an adult, since one side of my genogram was blank, I took a page out of Murray Bowen's book, searched out as many of my father's family as I could find, and invited them to a family reunion. At this gathering I learned that my father's parents had both been married twice, their previous spouses having died, so there were numerous siblings and half-siblings of my Dad. Both of my father's parents had died before I was born. The only information about my Dad's background that I got directly from him was that his grandfather had been a "pirate" on a ship, that his father was "a good man," and that he was close to his sisters. I really regret that I did not systematically collect family histories from my parents while they were still alive—something I now advise students and clients to do. At this family gathering where I was meeting first and second cousins for the first time, I learned nothing about my paternal grandmother, but I did find out something about my paternal grandfather John. I discovered that he escaped political oppression by moving from Albania to Calabria in Southern Italy, and then to the U.S. These cousins also told stories about my Dad and how everyone loved him and "couldn't get enough of him." I have since become closer to my cousin Joe, who was the son of my Dad's sister with whom my Mom had the fight. In many ways my cousins gave my Dad back to me. It is one of my lifelong sorrows that I did not get to know my father better. When I was in analysis I had finally built up the courage to ask my Dad if we could have a heart-to-heart talk, but although he readily agreed and we set up a time, he died suddenly before we could meet.

All the power in my family emanated from my Mom; it seemed my Dad had little or no influence, certainly in major decisions. My mother and her two sisters clearly dominated their husbands. (Many decades later, when feminists claimed that women were powerless and oppressed by men I had great difficulty understanding what they were talking about.) My parents fought a great deal, and at times they would become physically violent toward one another. We kids were terrorized by these fights and had the fear that they would kill each other. The fights were usually about my Dad's gambling and running around with other women but included disputes over Mom's nagging, humiliating, and shaming of Dad. They knew how to hurt each other. As we kids got older we would be pulled into their arguments, but my own attempts at marriage counseling, as expected, were conspicuously unsuccessful. It took a while for us to pick up on the game-like or ritualistic quality of some of their fights. For instance: Dad would borrow money from loan sharks in order to bet on the numbers, and when he couldn't pay up they would threaten to break his legs. He would then go to Mom for the money (he always turned his pay checks over to her). If he could find her hiding place he would steal the money; once he replaced the money with confederate bills. If he could not find her hiding places he would cry and charm her and after she yelled and carried on, she would give in and they would make up behind closed doors. Even as a youngster I figured out the script of this dramatic opera, so once I made a brilliant intervention: I suggested to Mom that instead of hiding the money at home, she put it in the bank where Dad couldn't get at it. This advice was ignored, of course, and I got my first lesson on how systems worked and how hard it is to change them. Often after the biggest rows they would go to the movies together, a sequence that provided the basis for our feeling that they would never divorce. It is interesting that movies have always been an escape for me as well.

Mom told us the story of the time she went to the loan sharks (Mafia) to pay them off, and she said, "Don't lend my husband any more money or I'm likely to shoot him." She quoted them as replying, "We sell guns, too, lady." After Dad died my Mom told me to go to my father's old neighborhood and tell an old friend of his about my Dad's death. I tried to do that but when I asked people in the neighborhood where I could find him no one would admit to having heard of him. Getting the hint, I asked them to get word to him about my Dad's death and told them where and when the viewing would be held. This guy did come to the funeral; I found out later he was the hit man for the mob; he was a burly guy who had a knife scar from his ear to his mouth. He took me aside and said "Your Dad was an o.k. guy and if you ever need my help you let me know." This was an offer I never took advantage of until years later when I treated a bonafide Mafia family. I casually mentioned his name and the family then looked at me with new respect.

My Dad was a charming and engaging but irresponsible kid in some ways. Yet we knew he really cared for us and his sacrifices for his kids were not as visible as those of Mom. He worked very hard to support us. He brought fun and laughter into the household, even though his gambling and running around with other women did create turmoil in the family, particularly between my parents. Still, I used to have the feeling that without Dad there would be no enjoyment of life because Mom regarded life as a travail to be endured and suffered.

Dad was a glamour figure for us kids because he was a singer who had been in vaudeville and minstrel shows. During the 1920's he was a singing waiter in nightclubs and speakeasies in Philadelphia and Atlantic City. A Damon Runyon character, he sang by the name of "Jimmie Slicks." We were the only kids on the block whose Dad went to work in a tuxedo. As much as Mom was a saver, Dad was a big spender; he even once owned a racing dog. I think my love of movies and show business came from Dad. During the summers we would go to Atlantic City where Dad worked, and sometimes we would stay with our Aunt Marie, a relative who was the real aunt of Clark Gable. I remember as a child one New Year's Eve my Dad coming home from work putting $100 on the table that he had made in tips—a fortune in those days.

Within the family my Dad's role was very different from his position in the outside world. Outside, he was liked by everyone who met or knew him; in the home he had little status. He would say from time to time, "Nobody respects me in this family," and we kids would say, "But we love you, Dad." From time to time, embarrassed by his gambling and cheating on Mom, he would try to explain his behavior to us kids by saying, "It's the business I'm in." Dad looked forward every day to see what number would come out that day, and when he "hit" the numbers, there would be a celebration and a scrambling for the proceeds. Somehow this ritual—losing mostly and winning on rare occasions—seemed built into the family culture. It is curious that although I do not gamble as an adult, when I go to Las Vegas I can see how tempting and addictive it can be.

For me personally, Dad was, in Fairbairn's terms, "the exciting but disappointing object." It was not until I was in analysis that I got in touch with my hurt over his distance from me and my longing for closeness with him. I felt he was closer to my sisters and brother than to me. He also had a tight relationship with my younger brother. For instance, when he needed to borrow money he went to my brother, but he never asked me. My brother and he were the same kind of guys—street smart. Even though, as an adult, I knew that if I loaned him money I would never see it again, I wished he would ask me. I think my Dad regarded me as the different one and he really didn't know what to make of this kid who read books and excelled in school. I remember him once saying to my mother, "What kind of a kid do *you* have?" There is no question that I was Mom's favorite, really *her* kid, and I suspect that his jealousy of this relationship could account for his distance from me, especially since my mother frequently said, "When the children come, your love goes from your husband to the children." Because of the hurts he had done to her, Mom would humble and debase him. I remember that when I volunteered for the army during World War II I heard Mom say to Dad, "You didn't have the guts to go in the army in World War I, like James is doing now." I will always be haunted by the look on Dad's face by that remark. How could he relate to a son who was set up as superior to him? Although I knew he had wounded her many times, he did not deserve that humiliation. So there I was, left with the guilt of being the oedipal winner.

Dad did get closer to me as I got older. When I was in combat in Italy during World War II he painstakingly put together many packages of food to mail to me—fruit cake and other goodies. These packages came regularly and were put together with love. I heard the story that someone told Dad I was on the newsreels when we captured Rome, on June 4, 1944, and Dad prevailed upon the theater management to show the film to him over and over again until he thought he saw me. When I was shipped home to Valley Forge Army Hospital and my parents rushed to see me there, Dad hugged me as he never had before. My parents gave the biggest party, celebrating that I had survived.

Toward the end of his life Dad began to admire my accomplishments, which felt so damn good. I remember watching Kirk Douglas, the movie actor, being interviewed on TV about his relationship with his father; it is noteworthy that despite worldwide acclaim, Kirk Douglas still longed for some recognition from his long-deceased father. My Dad came to Penn State for my graduation, but was not alive when my first book came out (Mom showed it to all her friends). Until the day he died, however, Dad never understood my work. He would say, "You mean you get paid for talking to people?" and he marveled that I did not have to "work" for a living.

Dad, who had always been happy-go-lucky, got depressed toward the end of his life, worried about his health and advancing age. I feel guilty about not trying hard enough to help him more then. In April, 1959, I got a call at work to come to the hospital, that my Dad had had some sort of attack. When I got there I found out he was dead of his first heart attack. I was selected to identify his body, and afterwards I leaned against the wall and cried. I cried over the loss. I cried over the lost opportunities. I cried that I did not know my father well. I cried over the incompleteness of our relationship. I cried when I realized it was too late.

At Dad's funeral hundreds of his friends came, the many people who liked and loved him. Mom was astonished at the number of people who came. She said, "I guess I'm the only one who knew his faults." Mom cried inconsolably at Dad's viewing, saying over and over again, "All my life you hurt me, and now this is the biggest hurt of all."

I have often wondered what that heart-to-heart talk with my Dad would have been like had we ever had it. I suspect, based on the family-of-origin work that I do, that my Dad would have told me that he loved me but that he felt intimidated by and inferior to *me*. It's odd that while we men worry about whether our fathers loved us, we do not stop to wonder about our impact on them.

It is not possible, of course, for me to be objective about my own role in my family. From my perspective, and those of my siblings as well, I was unlike anyone else in my family—so much so that there was the shared family fantasy that my parents brought the wrong baby home from the hospital. This quality of differentness had both advantages and disadvantages. I was the "good" kid who never got in obvious troubles and in some ways I was the conscience of the family. When unrealities, myths, and shams made their appearance, I would comment on them, sometimes critically. Looking back on it now, I think I was a bit of a prig. I read a lot of books as a youngster, using those fantasies as an escape from the occasional family turmoil. Although I was studious, as a youngster I did love to go out and play with my friends. How joyous it was to come home from school, throw down the books, and go out to play (half ball, buck buck, one foot off, sides, and orange crate scooters with skates as wheels). I do remember that when I was a boy I desperately wanted a two-wheel bicycle, but I never asked for one because I did not want to add more problems to the family. We always went to Mom for money because she controlled the output, but since she complained so much about not being able to pay bills, I kept quiet about my wish for a bicycle. Since Dad spent so much money gambling, I do wonder why I never asked him.

Growing up and learning through school and books I discovered that there was a whole world out there that I wanted to know about. Although my sisters and brother dropped out of high school, I was an academic achiever and always knew that I was going to college. (I also intuited that one day I would go to war). I worked for two years in Stouffers restaurant as a dishwasher and busboy after high school, saving money for college. Despite being studious, I was also the risk-taker and adventurer of the family and knew that I had to get out of South Philly. It was necessary for me to go to college away from home, so I went to Penn State, 200 miles away, a school I have always loved. During my first semester there, Pearl Harbor occurred.

I joined the army because I honestly thought that if Hitler won the war life on this planet would be unthinkable. Sent overseas right out of basic training, I was shipped to North Africa and then spent two years in combat in the Italian Campaign, from Cassino to Bologna. World War II had a powerful effect on me, which persists to this day (e.g., when I hear certain sounds that are similar to those made by incoming shells, my body flinches and is ready to hit the ground). My Mom had been in agony while I was overseas, perhaps not believing my lies in letters that I had a safe typing job in the rear echelon. Dad's worries were not as obvious, but I have heard how heavy hearted he was about me. My sister, Vi, incredibly, wrote me a letter every single day. . . . How to describe the indescribable experience of war—the suffusing fear that erodes and that is just as present on the last day of combat as on the first, the mud and mountains, the lonely terror, the thunderous sounds of war, the homesickness, living in the earth like an animal, watching the mutilation of bodies in horrible fascination, seeing young men die in great numbers, and not know-ing if one will be alive from one day to the next. It's enough to make a guy get foxhole religion—which was easy in Italy since there were crucifixes at every crossroad. I did learn the number one rule of war: *survive*! After being taken out of the front lines following an explo-sion of a German 88 shell next to my foxhole north of Florence, I later came to realize I paid a high price for remaining alive. When I was returned to the states, and was carried off a hospital ship in a stretcher, one of the GI's carrying me said, "We owe you so much," and I responded with, "You don't owe me a goddamn thing." Even though I had gone through 450 days of combat, had directed artillery fire that killed many Nazis, I still felt terribly guilty about abandoning my outfit on that mountain in Italy. The guilt persists somewhat to this day, underneath and over other guilts. Along with the guilt came the realization as to how it is that, through the centuries, wars could be fought: soldiers do not fight for their country, for patriotism, or any of the other reasons given. Soldiers stay in combat and don't run away because they don't want to let their buddies down. Perhaps that is why I am so cynical when I hear Memorial Day speeches that say, "We dedicate this day to those who gladly gave their lives for their country." I say to myself, "Bullshit. Those guys did not gladly lay down their lives. When they got killed they were trying like hell to stay alive."

When I got home from the war I felt so strange, like I'd been away for a hundred years. Everyone in my family was most understanding and supportive of me. For a long while I could not take a walk or a drive through the countryside without viewing the terrain as places to put gun positions or ditches to jump into when the shelling started. After some time the countryside became scenery again as I gradually adjusted to civilian life. . . . When I came back from the war I felt like the son in the play, "The Subject was Roses".* In that play the son, Timmy, returns from the war and tries to heal his parent's marriage. I, too, wanted to marry my parents, bring them together, lessen the tensions between them. Following the euphoria of my returning home alive, my parents renewed their relentless battle, however, and I sometimes got caught in the crossfire. I had always been torn in my loyalties to my parents. As a youngster my Dad was the bad guy because I saw my mother cry. In later years I felt more sympathetic to Dad and I thought that if I had a wife like that I would have done what he did. That is why I felt the impact of the son in the play who said to his parents, "When I left this house three years ago I blamed *him* (Dad) for everything that was wrong here. When I came home I blamed *you* (Mom). Now I suspect no one's to blame, not even me." Like the parents in the play, however, my parents, as an act of love, let me go and made it possible for me to leave. I returned to Penn State and in 1946 got married.

Returning to the narrative of my family of origin, I need to

---

*Gilroy, F. (1964) *The subject was roses.* Columbia Pictures, based on Broadway Play.

describe my siblings. Despite my parent's conflicts (or maybe because of them), we have always had a strong sibling sub-system. Through the various crises of our lives (deaths, divorce, illnesses) we have always been there for each other. When we hear about brothers and sisters who hate each other, we find that incomprehensible because we can't do enough for each other. Even though I am quite unlike my brother and sisters in terms of interests, values, taste and lifestyle, we are close and loving toward one another. I trust my brother and sisters with my life. When we do get together we share old family stories, talk about what is going on in our lives, discuss movies (our Dad's show business background), and in recent years we talk about our aches and pains. A great fear, however, hovers over us that something awful is going to happen to one of us. More about this fear later. First a few words about each of my sibs.

My sister Viola, known as "Vi," is four years older than I and she was like a second mother to me. As teen-agers we teased each other and fought over doing the dishes, but even then there was always an infrastructure of caring. Even though our parents were not religious and neither discouraged nor encouraged us, Vi and I went to Mass every Sunday for years. I'm not sure what that was all about. Religion is still very important to Vi. When I got scarlet fever at age 8 and they put me in a hospital for contagious diseases, Vi cried. And when they found a spot on her lung when she was 18 and had to go to a sanitarium, I cried. When my two sons died she was the one I wanted with me. . . . Mom was pregnant with Vi when my parents' first child died at 18 months of age. The death of that first child has had long term consequences, one of which was that my Mom, in her grief, probably had difficulty bonding to Vi. Despite my Mom doing many things for Vi (e.g., sewing clothes for her), Vi always felt Mom was against her. Vi and I (who are closer in age) are more free to criticize Mom than are my brother Mike and my sister Eleanor (closer in age); the younger ones are very protective of our parents and will not brook criticism of them. . . . Vi has not done badly with her life, having raised two children and having lots of grandchildren and even great grandchildren. However, watching two husbands die slowly from cancer has taken its toll on her.

My brother Michael is six years younger than I. He is generous, and would take the shirt off his back for you. As I said previously, however, he is unable to accept gifts and has to be on the giving end. When we go to a restaurant we struggle over paying the bill since he insists on paying it. Although he is not as educated as I, he has more common sense than I do. Intensely loyal to our parents, he believes that no one (including a spouse) can ever take the place of a mother and father. Mike got involved in some minor difficulties as an adolescent, and I always felt bad when he was unfavorably compared to me by teachers. I've often wondered whether he felt like he had fallen short of a standard of achievement I had set. He went into the army just after the war and was part of the occupation army in Japan. For years I have tried to improve him, give him advice on what he should do with his life (go to therapy, take courses), but he has wisely resisted my best efforts by doing what he wants to do anyway. My wife Felise suggested I stop trying to change him, that he's o.k. with the way he lives his life. . . . Mike married and divorced the same woman twice, and his son died when the boy was 21 years old. Another loss. . . . I consider my brother my best male friend. I confide in him and we talk on the phone nearly every week.

My sister Eleanor is 11 years younger than I, and since I was away at college and in the army as she was growing up, she is the sibling I knew the least. Eleanor has a heart of gold, is tenderhearted, and tends to put others' wishes before her own. She is always doing for others and is most like Mom in terms of being self-sacrificing for her children. (An interpretation has been made to me that I have been distant from her because she is most like Mom. It seems to me she is like Mom only in being self-sacrificing.) Eleanor always had an inflated view of me, seeing me as the family hero. She chose the only spouse who was acceptable to my Mom; it is interesting that her husband was most like my Dad, and brought some grief to Eleanor. I always urged Eleanor, as I did my other siblings, to take courses, join organizations, and go to therapy, because it seemed that they lived such constricted lives. For instance, Eleanor has never been on an airplane in her life and has never travelled farther from South Philly than New York City. Since her husband died I renewed these efforts to get Eleanor involved with something other than her children, but she says yes to me and goes about her business as usual. As the years have gone by Eleanor and I have become much closer. She has been there for me and I for her.

After Dad died in 1959, unbelievably, Mom started gambling at the race track—she who had pinched pennies all her life! This behavior makes sense to the professional in me—that this was her unconscious way of holding on to Dad, the formula being, "If I can't have him, I will *be* him." Another interpretation you could get for half-price is that perhaps my Dad had acted out a dissociated aspect of Mom. In any event, as her children we were becoming alarmed at the amount of money she was losing at the track. A year before she died she had a stroke, but recovered. The gambling continued and so did the criticism and bitterness of Dad even though he was dead. We kids did not want to hear the criticism of Dad. Once my brother created our all-time family joke when he became angry at Mom for putting Dad down. He said to Mom in a fury, "Your mother was a whore!" and Mom answered, "Well, your mother was a whore too!". . . . In some ways, now, we are glad Mom decided to have some fun toward the end of her life. In a way it was fitting that she died of her second stroke in 1965 at the race track in Camden, New Jersey. I will never forget how we found out our mother had died. The hospital called us, and when we were sitting all together in a room, an intern stuck his head in the door and said, "Is your name Framo? Your mother is dead," and he left. Since my role had changed to that of the second father of the family, it became my responsibility to identify my mother's body. I remember my throat constricting. . . . Family systems are more open at funerals, and at Mom's funeral I found out from Mom's sister that my mother and father had once been very much in love, until their first child died at 18 months of age. Apparently my parents' alienation from each other began then, as did my Mom's over-attachment to her children. Her unresolved grief, I am sure, had much to do with her obsessive worries about terrible things happening to us. Mom frequently talked of a fear of cancer; she would say, "I should get cancer if that's not true." (In actual fact, cancer does not run in my family; it's always been heart trouble.) That first loss is also possibly the genesis of the sense of foreboding and dread that has pervaded my family; subsequent deaths in the family have reinforced this feeling of imminent catastrophe. . . . When Dad died he had been buried in a certain cemetery. Subsequent to Dad's death they opened up a new cemetery, where my mother was going to be buried. Nonetheless, we arranged for my Dad's body to be moved to the new cemetery so our parents could be buried together. Married at last.

When I moved to California in 1983 I'm sure my siblings felt I abandoned the family. My brother is the man on the scene and looks after my sisters since their husbands have died. They all live within a block of each other in South Philly. I was always the most out of the enmeshment, and I have mixed feelings about that. The old fears still hover over that threesome. All of them have an illness of one sort or another, and if one phones the other and that person does not answer the phone, the caller immediately worries that that person is seriously ill, been in an accident, or has died. Mom's old fears, and the real losses in the family have left their heritage. My siblings are sometimes afraid to travel because something terrible could happen while they are away. Sometimes I get caught up in these fears when I am there, and it is only when I am away from the family that I can be more objective (as Bowen earlier discovered with his family).

From time to time I go back to South Philly; it feels like a foreign country, yet in some ways familiar and comfortable. I know, however, that I could never live in that world again. But I will go to Pat's for a steak sandwich, will get Italian water ice, will take a ride in Fairmount Park, and my sisters will make a great dinner and we'll sit around and tell family stories, and all of that still feels so good.

When I started writing this family biography I had only planned to write a couple of pages. As I started, however, one memory would trigger off another and a chain of associations exploded in my head. In truth, I could have gone on and on, but this book had been delayed long enough. Writing down these memories, I have discovered, is a very different and more powerful psychological experience than talking about one's family. This project took on a greater emotional significance than I originally intended. It became for me a kind of reminiscence therapy, a life review, a therapeutic experience. I wrote this paper for me, not for family therapy students to study for theory or technique. They are my experiences. If others get something from it, that's fine. The reader will note that I have not organized this biography with neat headings, and I have tried to avoid use of any technical language or concepts.

Looking back at my family of origin from my present vantage point, I see things differently and understand more. My family was a colorful, richly variegated, interesting family that had much turmoil and perhaps too much love. I think my family lacked integration. I have not written about the happy, joyous times and there were plenty of those. We used to have great vacations in Atlantic City where as a child I loved the Steeplechase and the Steel Pier. We went on picnics. We had wonderful family dinners and many life-affirming rituals on holidays. We were involved a lot with a large extended family on my Mom's side, and, as I have mentioned before, we were the only kids on the block whose Dad went to work at night in a tuxedo. . . . During the time I was with my family I thought at times it was crazy, albeit caring. Yet I knew, bottom line, that my Mom and Dad were concerned parents who did the best they could with what they had to work with. When I compare my family of origin to families I see professionally, I can see that my family was not all that dysfunctional. There was no mental illness, criminality, suicides, alcoholism or drugs. When I conduct family-of-origin sessions, at the end of the sessions I tell despairing, guilty parents, "You must have done something right—your kids turned out pretty good." That's the way I feel about myself and my brother and sisters.

One part of the assignment I give my students relative to their family biography is that they write a short piece at the end on how their family of origin experiences have affected their intimate relationships. Those parts of the family biographies are always more guarded. Understandably, this final section, on my own family of procreation, will also be more circumspect because the people and events are more proximate and recent, at close emotional range, and some of the pains are more accessible. I realize now why some people publish personal papers posthumously. In my case, brevity and limited disclosure will help preserve the privacy of those who are mentioned.

Mary D. Framo and I were married a long time and, like most marriages, we had our good times and bad. How does one condense in a few words what happened in a long term marriage—the stages it went through, and the hundreds of thousands of events and feelings that are involved in any marriage? In actual fact I don't believe anyone can do it. No one can ever know the whole truth about anyone else's marriage (including marital therapists)—least of all the partners themselves. I want to avoid the usual trap of blaming a former spouse and I also need to acknowledge my own contributions to our marital difficulties. I can make a couple of speculations, from my own perspective. I think that in some ways, in my marriage to Mary, I felt similar to my father in his marriage to my mother. On a deeper level, I suspect that our hostility to each of our opposite sex parents got displaced onto each other. We became skilled at hurting each other, but the wounds I inflicted were probably more publicly apparent. I do not know to what extent the deaths of our sons were related to or accelerated our estrangement, although serious difficulties preceded these events. . . . Mary and I were divorced in 1986. The divorce was extremely painful, I am sure for both of us, complicated particularly by mutual bitterness, legal proceedings, depositions, etc. that were very stressful. That was the time I developed the auto-immune disease of lupus, which was superimposed on my arrhythmia heart condition. My second marriage, to Felise Levine, has worked much better. Another partner can bring out different aspects of a person, which in turn can affect one's behavior. It took me years to rework the image of being a man that I got from my father, and this change may have something to do with why, in my second marriage, I am more free to give and get love.

Mary and I were better parents than we were spouses. We had four children in all and lost two sons—Jimmie in 1961 and Michael in 1972. Both died suddenly at age nine of the congenital heart defect that I have. Those were the greatest tragedies of my life, and for years I wanted to die and join them. At one point, because of a deep depression, I had to return to analysis. A well-timed interpretation (that I identified with my dead sons and felt dead inside) helped lift the depression. But despite the comfort of my family and friends I felt very alone in my grief. A complicating factor was that I had had difficulty relating to my first son Jimmie, and found out later in therapy that I had unwittingly repeated with him the distance that had existed between me and my father. I am not a very religious person but when my second son was born I got down on my knees and thanked God. Michael gave me a second chance to be unambivalently loving to a son.

For years I had been wanting to move to California, but I could not bear to leave my boys, whose grave I frequently visited. I got a good therapist, a real Mensch (a great Jewish word that I use to describe as the primary qualification of a good psychotherapist). He helped me to go to California with the recognition that no matter where I was the boys would always be with me, in my heart. Jimmie and Michael were both so bright and creative and delightful and how sad it is that I will never know what they would have been like as adults. Although I do not so often cry buckets of tears, the pain of the loss of my sons will never leave me.

I have two wonderful daughters, Joan and Patty, and I am so proud of the kind of people they turned out to be. I feel I have an excellent relationship with my daughters and grandchildren. Joan and Patty are warm, caring persons, each with a good sense of self. Even if they were not my daughters I would want to be their friends. Again, Mary and I did something right. Joan is an oncological social work supervisor on the east coast, and she and her husband Dan have three children—Matthew, and twin boys, Jonathan and David. Patty, who has a social work background and who markets mental health services, and her husband Treacy have a daughter Kalin. To be sure, I happen to think my children and grandchildren are special and the greatest. . . . I have been more emotionally open and available to my daughters and my second son than my father was to me. Besides, having two daughters has given me a more balanced perspective about gender issues that were carried over from my family of origin.

Despite some of the sorrows of my life and concerns about health problems that advancing age brings, when I take stock of the traditions of my family of origin, my relationship with my siblings, my children and grandchildren, my many friends, my professional accomplishments, and a second chance at a happy, fulfilling marriage, in many ways I feel very blessed.

References

Ackerman, N.W. (1966). *Treating the troubled family.* New York: Basic Books.

Anderson, C.M., & Stewart, S. (1983). *Mastering resistance.* New York: Guilford.

Anthony, E.J. (1971). An introduction to family group therapy. In H. I. Kaplan & B. J. Sadock (Eds.), *Comprehensive group psychotherapy.* Baltimore: Williams & Wilkins.

Baker, F. (1982). *Framo's method of integration of family of origin with couples therapy: A follow-up study of an intergenerational approach.* Doctoral Dissertation, Counseling Psychology Dept., Temple University, Philadelphia, PA.

Bank, S.P., & Kahn, M.D. (1982). *The sibling bond.* New York: Basic Books.

Beck, R.L. (1982). Process and content in the family of origin group. *International Journal of Group Psychotherapy, 32,* 233–244.

Bengston, V.L., & Robertson, J.F. (Eds.) (1985). *Grandparenthood.* Beverly Hills: Sage.

Bloomfield, H.H. (1983). *Making peace with your parents.* New York: Ballantine Books.

Bly, R. (1990). *A gathering of men.* Interview of R. Bly by Bill Moyers. PBS. January, 1990.

Boszormenyi-Nagy, I., & Framo, J.L. (Eds.) (1965). *Intensive family therapy.* New York: Harper & Row Medical Dept. (Reprinted by Brunner/Mazel, New York, 1985).

Boszormenyi-Nagy, I., & Krasner, B.R. (1986). *Between give and take.* New York: Brunner/Mazel.

Boszormenyi-Nagy, I., & Spark, G.M. (1973). *Invisible loyalties.* New York: Harper & Row Medical Department. (Reprinted by Brunner/Mazel, New York, 1984).

Bowen, M. (1974). Toward the differentiation of self in one's family of origin. In F. O. Andres & J. P. Lorio (Eds.), *Georgetown family symposia, Vol. 1 (1971–1972).* Washington, DC: Georgetown University Medical Center, Department of Psychiatry, Family Section.

Bowen, M. (1978). *Family therapy in clinical practice.* New York: Aronson.

Bowlby, J. (1969). *Attachment and loss: Attachment (Vol. 1).* New York: Basic Books.

Bray, J.H., Harvey, D.M. & Williamson, D.S. (1987a) Intergenerational family relationships: An evaluation of theory and measurement. *Psychotherapy, 24,* 516–528.

Bray, J.H. & Williamson, D.S. (1987b) Assessment of intergenerational family relationships. In A.J. Hovestadt & M. Fine (Eds.) *Family of Origin Therapy,* Rockville, MD: Aspen Publications.

Bray, J.H., Williamson, D.S., & Malone, P.E. (1984). Personal authority in the family system: Development of a questionnaire to measure personal authority in intergenerational family processes. *Journal of Marital and Family Therapy, 10,* 167–178.

Brubaker, T. (Ed.) (1983). *Family relationships in later life.* Beverly Hills: Sage.

Byng-Hall, J. (1973). Family myth used as a defense in conjoint family therapy. *British Journal of Medical Psychology, 46,* 239–250.

Byng-Hall, J. (1988). Scripts and legends in families and family therapy. *Family Process, 27*, 167–179.

Chasin R., Grunebaum, H., & Herzog, M. (Eds). (1990). *One couple: Four realities: Multiple perspectives on couple therapy.* New York: Guilford Press.

Cicirelli, V.G. (1981). *Helping elderly parents: The role of adult children.* Boston: Auburn House.

Dicks, H.V. (1964). Concepts of marital diagnosis and therapy as developed at the Tavistock Family Psychiatric Units, London, England. In E.M. Nash, L. Jessner, & D.W. Apse (Eds.), *Marriage counseling in medical practice.* Chapel Hill: University, North Carolina Press, Chapter 15.

Dicks, H.V. (1967). *Marital tensions.* New York: Basic Books.

Engel, B. (1990). *Divorcing a parent.* Chicago: Contemporary Books.

Erikson, E.H. (1964). *Childhood and society.* New York: Norton.

Everstine, L., Everstine, D.S., Heymann, G.M., True, R.H., Frey, D.H., Johnson, H.G., & Seiden, R.H. (1980). Privacy and confidentiality in psychotherapy. *American Psychologist, 35,* 828–840.

Fairbairn, W.R.D. (1952). *An object-relations theory of the personality.* New York: Basic Books.

Ferreira, A.J. (1963). Family myth and homeostasis. *Archives of General Psychiatry, 9,* 457–463.

Fine, M. & Norris, J.E. (1989) Intergenerational relations and family therapy research; What we can learn from other disciplines, *Family Process, 28,* 301–315.

Flomenhaft, K., & Kaplan, D. (1968). Clinical significance of current kinship relationships. *Social Work, 13,* 68–75.

Forward, S. (1989). *Toxic parents.* New York: Bantam Books.

Framo, J.L. (1962) The theory of the technique of family treatment of schizophrenia, *Family Process, 1,* 119–131.

Framo, J.L. (1965a). Rationale and techniques of intensive family therapy. In I. Boszormenyi-Nagy & J.L. Framo (Eds.), *Intensive family therapy.* New York: Harper & Row Medical Dept. (Reprinted by Brunner/Mazel, New York, 1985.)

Framo, J.L. (1965b). Systemic research on family dynamics. In I. Boszormenyi-Nagy & J.L. Framo (Eds.), *Intensive family therapy.* New York: Harper & Row Medical Dept. (Reprinted by Brunner/Mazel, New York, 1985).

Framo, J.L. (1968). My families, my family. *Voices: Art and Science of Psychotherapy, 4,* 18–27.

Framo, J.L. (1970). Symptoms from a family transactional viewpoint. In N.W. Ackerman, J. Leib, & J.K. Pearce (Eds.), *Family therapy in transition.* Boston: Little, Brown. (Also reprinted in H.S. Kaplan & C.J. Sager (1972). *Progress in group and family therapy.* New York: Brunner/Mazel.)

Framo, J.L. (1972). *Family interaction: A dialogue between family researchers and family therapists.* New York: Springer.

Framo, J.L. (1973). Marriage therapy in a couples group. In D.A. Bloch (Ed.), *Techniques of family psychotherapy: A primer.* New York: Grune & Stratton.

Framo, J.L. (1975). Personal reflections of a family therapist. *Journal of Marriage and Family Counseling, 1,* 15–28.

Framo, J.L. (1976). Family of origin as a therapeutic resource for adults in marital and family therapy: You can and should go home again. *Family Process, 15,* 193–210.

Framo, J.L. (1978a). The friendly divorce. *Psychology Today,* February.

Framo, J.L. (1978b). In-laws and out-laws: A marital case of kinship confusion. In P. Papp (Ed.), *Family therapy: Full length case studies*. New York: Gardner.

Framo, J.L. (1980). Marriage and marital therapy: Issues and initial interview techniques. In M. Andolfi & I. Zwerling (Eds.), *Dimensions of family therapy*. New York: Guilford.

Framo, J.L. (1981). The integration of marital therapy with sessions with family of origin. In A.S. Gurman & D.P. Kniskern (Eds.), *Handbook of family therapy*. New York: Brunner/Mazel.

Framo, J.L. (1982). *Explorations in marital and family therapy: Selected papers of James L. Framo*. New York: Springer.

Framo, J.L. (1989) How AFTA got started. *Newsletter, American Family Therapy Association*, No. 37, Winter.

Framo, J.L. (1990) The question never asked: Dad, who are we to each other?, *Contemporary Family Therapy*, 12 (3), 219–221.

Framo, J.L. (1991). Memories of Murray Bowen. *Family Therapy News*: Newspaper of the American Association for Marriage and Family Therapy, 22, No. 1, Feb. 1991.

Framo, J.L., Weber, T.T., & Levine, F.B. (in press). *Coming home again: A full-length family-of-origin consultation*. New York: Basic Books.

Friday, N. (1987). *My mother, myself*. New York: Dell.

Goldberg, A. (1987). The place of apology in psychoanalysis and psychotherapy. *International Review of Psychoanalysis*, 14, 409–417.

Gordon, R.M. (1982). Systems-object relations view of marital therapy: Revenge and reraising. In L. Wolberg & M. Aronson (Eds.), *Group and family therapy, 1982*, New York: Brunner/Mazel.

Greenson, R.R. (1954). The struggle against identification. *Journal of the American Psychoanalytic Association*, 2, 200–217.

Guntrip, H. (1969). *Schizoid phenomena, object relations and the self*. New York: International Universities Press.

Gurman, A.S., & Kniskern, D.P. (1978). Deterioration in marital and family therapy: Empirical, clinical, and conceptual issues. *Family Process*, 17, 3–20.

Haas, W. (1968). The intergenerational encounter: A method in treatment. *Social Work*, 13, 91–101.

Halpern, H.M. (1978). *Cutting loose: An adult guide to coming to terms with your parents*. New York: Bantam Books.

Headley, L. (1977). *Adults and their parents in family therapy*. New York: Plenum Press.

Herr, J.J., & Weakland, J.H. (1979). *Counseling elders and their families*. New York: Springer.

Hoffman, H.M. (1979). *No one is to blame: Getting a loving divorce from Mom and Dad*. Palo Alto: Science and Behavior Books.

Hovestadt, A.J., Anderson, W.T., Piercy, F.P., Cochran, S.W., & Fine, M. (1985). A family of origin scale. *Journal of Marital and Family Therapy*, II (3), 287–297.

Hovestadt, A.J., & Fine, M. (1987). *Family of origin therapy*. Rockville, MD: Aspen.

Jaffe, D.S. (1968). The mechanism of projection: Its dual role in object relations. *International Journal of Psychoanalysis*, 49, 662–677.

Johnson, E.S., & Bursk, B.J. (1979). Relationships between the elderly and their adult children. In G.S. Phelan (Ed.), *Family relationships*. Minneapolis: Burgess.

Kahn, M.D., & Lewis, K.G. (1988). *Siblings in therapy*. New York: Norton.

Kerr, M.E., & Bowen, M. (1988). *Family evaluation: An approach based on Bowen Theory*. New York: Norton.

Klein, M. (1946). Notes on some schizoid mechanisms. In J. Riviere (Ed.), *Developments in psychoanalysis*. London: Hogarth Press, 1952, pp. 292–320.

Klein, R.S. (1990). *Objects relations and the family process*. New York: Praeger.

Kornhaber, A. (1986). *Between parents and grandparents*. New York: St. Martins Press.

Kramer, J.R. (1985). *Family interfaces: Transgenerational patterns*. New York: Brunner/Mazel.

Kramer, S.Z. (1988). *Psychosynthesis and integrative marital and family therapy*. In J. Weiser & T. Yeomans (Eds.) *Readings in psychosynthesis*. Dept. of Applied Psychology, Ontario Institute for Studies in Education.

Kuhn, T. (1962). *The structure of scientific revolutions*. Chicago: Univ. of Chicago Press.

Laham, J.W. (1990) Family-of-origin intervention: An intergenerational approach to enhancing marital adjustment. *Journal of Contemporary Psychotherapy, 20,* 211–222.

Laing, R.D. (1965). Mystification, confusion, and conflict. In I. Boszormenyi-Nagy & J.L. Framo (Eds.), *Intensive family therapy*. New York: Harper & Row Medical Dept. (Reprinted by Brunner/Mazel, New York, 1985.)

Lansky, M.R. (1981). Treatment of the narcissistically vulnerable marriage. In M.R. Lansky (Ed.) *Family therapy and major psychopathology*. New York: Grune & Stratton.

Leader, A.I. (1979). The place of in-laws in marital relationships. In G.S. Phelan (Ed.), *Family relationships*. Minneapolis: Burgess.

Lieberman, S. (1979). *Transgenerational family therapy*. London: Croom Helm.

Lindsey, K. (1982). *Friends as family*. Boston: Beacon Press.

Lynch, J.J. (1977). *The broken Heart: The medical consequences of loneliness*. New York: Basic Books.

Mancini, J.A. (1990) *Aging parents and adult children*. Lexington, MA: Lexington Books.

Mandelbaum, H. (1979). *Personal communication*, March 21.

Mandelbaum, H. (1990). Beyond the ordinary: Personal reflections on spirituality in family therapy. *Newsletter of American Family Therapy Association.* Spring, No. 39.

Margolin, G. (1982). Ethical and legal considerations in marital and family therapy. *American Psychologist, 37,* 788–801.

Mazer, G.E., Mangrum, O.L., Hovestadt, A.J. & Brashear, R.L. (1990). Further validation of the family of origin scale: A factor analysis. *Journal of Marital and Family Therapy, 16,* 423–426.

McGoldrick, M., Pearce, J.K. & Giordano, J. (Eds.) (1982). *Ethnicity and family therapy*. New York: Guilford.

Menninger, K. (1958). *The theory of psychoanalytic technique*. New York: Basic Books.

Meth, R.L. and Pasick, R.S. (1990) *Men in therapy*. New York: Guilford.

Nerin, W.F. (1985). *Family reconstruction: Long day's journey into light*. New York: Norton.

O'Neill, E. (1955). *Long day's journey into night*. New Haven: Yale Univ. Press.

Osherson, S. (1986) *Finding our fathers*. New York: Fawcett Columbine.

Papero, D.V. (1990) *Bowen family system theory*. Boston: Allyn & Bacon.

Papp, P. (1977). *Family therapy: Full-length case studies*. New York: Gardner Press.

Paul, N.L. (1976). Cross-confrontation. In P.J. Guerin (Ed.), *Family therapy*. New York: Gardner Press.

Paul, N.L. (1980). Now and the past: Transgenerational analysis. *International Journal of Family Psychiatry, 1*, 235–248.

Paul, N.L., & Grosser, G.H. (1965). Operational mourning and its role in conjoint family therapy. *Community Mental Health Journal, 1*, 339–345.

Paul, N.L., & Paul, B.B. (1975). *A marital puzzle*. New York: Norton.

Paul, N.L., & Paul, B.B. (1982). Death and changes in sexual behavior. In F. Walsh (Ed.), *Normal family processes*. New York: Guilford Press.

Pincus, L., & Dare, C. (1978). *Secrets in the family*. New York: Pantheon.

Robertson, J.F. (1979). Significance of grandparents: Perceptions of young adult children. In G.K. Phelan (Ed.), *Family relationships*. Minneapolis: Burgess.

Rubinstein, D., & Weiner, O. (1972). Co-therapy teamwork relationships in family psychotherapy. In G.H. Zuk & I. Boszormenyi-Nagy (Eds.), *Family therapy and disturbed families*. Palo Alto: Science and Behavior Books (pp. 206–220).

Satir, V., & Baldwin, M. (1983). *Satir step by step*. Palo Alto: Science and Behavior Books.

Scharff, D.E., & Scharff, J.S. (1987). *Object relations family therapy*. Northvale, NJ: Aronson.

Schenck, Q.F. & Schenck, E.L. (1978). *Pulling up roots: For young adults and their parents. Letting go and getting free*. Englewood Cliffs, NJ: Prentice-Hall.

Schwartz, R., & Perrotta, P. (1985). Let us sell no intervention before its time. *The Family Therapy Networker*. July-August, *9*(4), 18–25.

Scott, J.P. (1983). Siblings and other kin. In T.H. Brubaker (Ed.), *Family relationships in later life*. Beverly Hills: Sage.

Seinfeld, J. (1990) *The bad object*. Northvale, NJ: Aronson.

Sheloff, L. (1981). *Generations apart: Adult hostility to youth*. New York: McGraw-Hill.

Silberschatz, G., Fretter, P.B., & Curtis, J.T. (1986). How do interpretations influence the process of psychotherapy? *Journal of Consulting and Clinical Psychology, 54*(5), 646–652.

Slipp, S. (1984). *Object relations: A dynamic bridge between individual and family treatment*. Northvale, NJ: Aronson.

Slipp, S. (1988). *The technique and practice of object relations family therapy*. Northvale, NJ: Aronson.

Sonne, J.C., & Lincoln, G. (1965). Heterosexual co-therapy team experiences during family therapy. *Family Process, 4*, 177–197.

Sonne, J.C., Speck, R.V., & Jungreis, J.E. (1962). The absent-member maneuver as a resistance in family therapy of schizophrenia. *Family Process, 1*, 44–62.

Stierlin, H. (1988). Systemic optimism–systemic pessimism: Two perspectives on change. *Family Process, 27*, 121–126.

Stone, E. (1989). *Black sheep and kissing cousins: How our family stories shape us*. New York: Penguin.

Sullivan, H.S. (1947). *Conceptions of modern psychiatry*. Washington, D.C.: The William Alanson White Psychiatric Foundation.

Sussman, M.B. (1960). Intergenerational family relationships and social role changes in middle age. *Journal of Gerontology, 15*, 71–75.

Titelman, P. (Ed.) (1987). *The therapist's own family: Toward a differentiation of self*. Northvale, NJ: Aronson.

Troll, L., Miller, S.J., & Atchley, R.C. (1979). *Families in later life*. Belmont, CA: Wadsworth.

Troll, L.E. (1983). Grandparents: The family watchdogs. In T.H. Brubaker (Ed.), *Family relationships in later life*. Beverly Hills: Sage.

Uzoka, A.F. (1979). The myth of the nuclear family. *American Psychologist, 34*, 1095–1106.

Vaillant, G. (1977). *Adaptation to life.* Boston: Little, Brown.

Van Heusden, A., & Van Der Eerenbeemt, E. (1987). *Balance in Motion: Ivan Boszormenyi-Nagy and his vision of individual and family therapy.* New York: Brunner/Mazel.

Wallerstein, J.S., & Blakeslee, S. (1989). *Second chances: Men, women and children a decade after divorce—who wins, who loses—and why.* New York: Ticknor & Fields.

Walters, M., Carter, B., Papp, P & Silverstein, O. (1988) *The invisible web: Gender patterns in family relationships.* New York: Guilford.

Wechsler, J.A. (1972). *In a darkness.* New York: Norton.

Whitaker, C.A. (1976a). The hindrance of theory in clinical work. In P.J. Guerin (Ed.), *Family therapy.* New York: Gardner Press.

Whitaker, C.A. (1976b). A family is a four dimensional relationship. In P.J. Guerin (Ed.), *Family therapy.* New York: Gardner Press.

Whitaker, C.A. (1989). (Edited by Margaret A. Ryan) *Midnight musings of a family therapist.* New York: Norton.

Widiger, T.A., & Rorer, L.G. (1984). The responsible psychotherapist. *American Psychologist, 39*, 503–515.

Wilcoxon, S.A. & Hovestadt, A.J. (1983) Perceived health and similarity of family of origin experiences as predictors of dyadic adjustment for married couples. *Journal of Marital and Family Therapy, 9*, 431–434.

Wilde, O. (1893). *A woman of no importance.* Act ii.

Williamson, D.S. (1978) New life at the graveyard: A method of therapy for individuation from a dead parent. *Journal of Marriage and Family Counseling, 4*, 93–101.

Williamson, D.S. (1981). Personal authority via termination of the intergenerational hierarchical boundary: A "new" stage in the family life cycle. *Journal of Marital and Family Therapy, 1*, 441–452.

Williamson, D.S. (1982a). Personal authority via termination of the intergenerational hierarchical boundary: Part II–The consultation process and the therapeutic method. *Journal of Marital and Family Therapy, 8*, 13–37.

Williamson, D.S. (1982b) Personal authority in family experience via termination of the intergenerational hierarchical boundary: Part III. Personal authority defined, and the power of play in the change process. *Journal of Marital and Family Therapy, 8*, 309–323.

Winnicott, D.W. (1960). The theory of the parent-infant relationship. *International Journal of Psychoanalysis, 41*, 585–595.

Wynne, L.C. (1965). Some indications and contraindications for exploratory family therapy. In I. Boszormenyi-Nagy & J.L. Framo (Eds.), *Intensive family therapy.* New York: Harper & Row Medical Dept. (Reprinted by Brunner/Mazel, New York, 1985.)

Zinner, J. (1976). The implications of projective identification for marital interaction. In H. Grunebaum & J. Christ (Eds.), *Contemporary marriage: Structure, dynamics, and therapy.* Boston: Little, Brown.

Zinner, J. & Shapiro, R. (1972). Projective identification as a mode of perception and behavior in families of adolescents. *International Journal of Psychoanalysis, 53*, 523–530.

Name Index

Subject Index